# Munsell's Historical Series.
# No. 19.

# THE
# GERMAN ALLIED TROOPS

IN THE

## North American War of Independence,

### 1776-1783.

TRANSLATED AND ABRIDGED FROM THE GERMAN OF

MAX VON EELKING,

*Captain Saxon-Meiningen Army; Member of the Historical Society of New York.*

BY

## J. G. ROSENGARTEN.

ALBANY, N. Y.:
JOEL MUNSELL'S SONS, PUBLISHERS,
1893.

# Notice

In many older books, foxing (or discoloration) occurs and, in some instances, print lightens with wear and age. Reprinted books, such as this, often duplicate these flaws, notwithstanding efforts to reduce or eliminate them. The pages of this reprint have been digitally enhanced and, where possible, the flaws eliminated in order to provide clarity of content and a pleasant reading experience.

Originally published:
Albany, New York: 1893

Reprinted:
Janaway Publishing, Inc.
2011

Janaway Publishing, Inc.
732 Kelsey Ct.
Santa Maria, California 93454
(805) 925-1038
www.janawaygenealogy.com

ISBN: 978-1-59641-253-8

*Made in the United States of America*

# THE GERMAN ALLIES IN THE AMERICAN REVOLUTION, 1776-1783.

### By MAX VON EELKING,

Captain in the Saxon-Meiningen Army, and Corresponding Member of the Historical Society of New York.

*"SUUM CUIQUE."*

TRANSLATED (AND ABRIDGED) FROM THE GERMAN.

NOTE.—Published in Hanover, in 1863, in two volumes, of pp. 379 and pp. 271, this book still remains full of interesting details as to the German troops serving in America. Leaving out all that relates to the general history of the Revolution, there is much that is likely to have value for special students of American history, and to them these pages are submitted as a contribution that cannot but serve to give a better idea of the actual facts of the part taken by the German soldiers in the British army, in the struggle for American independence, than can easily be gathered from other sources.

# PREFACE.

It is now just eighty years* since the German troops returned home from the seven years' war beyond the Atlantic, in which they had fought as allies of England against the great American rising. They are known as the German Allied or Subsidiary Troops. Since that long and hard-fought war, the Union, with passing exceptions, has enjoyed the blessings of a long peace. Now a new war is raging; this time the sword is not drawn against a foreign power, but between hitherto sister states — their own flesh and blood. Again Germans are fighting, just as before throwing their weight in the balance, now not for a foreign interest, but for their own. Even if nearly a century has elapsed between the first great war and that now being waged, the careful observer will find much resemblance between the war of that day and the present war. Let us look, however, at the subject we have in hand. While we find in other campaigns in which German soldiers

---

* The original was published in Hanover in 1863.

have taken part the results gained by them more or less fully described, there is wanting, in the most marked way, the history of the share they took in the war of the American Revolution. There has been plenty of time to fill this void, but hitherto it has not been attempted in any complete form. In the literature of Germany it has appeared only in separate accounts in historical works and periodicals. Even this proportionately brief material is not only small in bulk, but is, for the most part, either of particular portions of the forces engaged, or from ignorance, or by accident, it is erroneous. The absence of any complete or impartial story is noteworthy in the present wealth of German history. Hitherto the archives in which the original documents were preserved have been jealously closed to the world. There is, however, abundance of other material in the journals and correspondence of the principal leaders, of officers and private soldiers, who shared in the war. Most of them wrote with no expectation that their pages would ever be made public, and plainly put down what was seen and what was heard. The value to be ascribed to such material is to be seen in its use in modern works on the history of recent wars. To gather such material has been no light labor. Much was lost, much in family papers not willingly given to strangers. The reader will see in the following pages what has been obtained in various parts of Germany and from various sources. It has been the aim of the author to give a general view, avoiding repetition, and emphasizing the part— a subordinate one, of course—taken by the German troops, but allowing the German writers to tell their own story, even when it differed from the recognized English and American authorities. He has sought to protect and restore the good name and credit of German soldiers, ruthlessly attacked on all sides for their share in the American Revolutionary War. Hard indeed was their situation—denied the privilege of fighting for any national cause at home, they were reproached for taking part in a foreign war, although they did so in strict obedience to the orders of their military and civil superiors, at risk of losing health, discipline, and even honor, and it is only right that their deeds should speak for them and give the true version, even at this late day, of their share in the events here described.

# MANUSCRIPT AUTHORITIES.

*A. Hessian :* (1) Journal of Captain v. Münchhausen, from the time of his appointment as Howe's Adjutant, 18 November, 1776, to 22 May, 1778.
(2) Correspondence of Col. v. Heeringen, Capt. Burmeister, and other Hessian officers.
(3) Journal of an expedition under General Clinton to the Southern Colonies, from 18 December, 1779, to 8 August, 1780.
(4) Diary of Captain Friedrich v. d. Malsburg, of the v. Ditfurth Regiment, from February, 1776, to 16 November, 1780.
(5) Diary of Captain v. Dinklage, of the Guard Regiment, from 14 January, 1776, to 29 May, 1784.
(6) Journal of the most noteworthy incidents of the Hereditary Prince Regiment, begun in February, 1776, when it went to America, ended May, 1784, on its return to Marburg, by Regimental Quartermaster Lotheisen.
(7) History of the Fusilier Regiment v. Lossberg, in a diary, begun 1776, down to 1783, kept by the Hessian Lieutenant Biel (Rall's Adjutant).
(8) Diary of Lieutenant Wiederhold (of Rall's Regiment), afterwards Captain of v. Knyphausen's Regiment, from 7 October, 1776, to 7 December, 1780.

(9) Diary of the voyage of the 8th Hessian Recruit Transport to America, from 10 April to 28 October, 1782.
(10) Journal from the arrival of the French Fleet in Rhode Island, 1779, to 22 May, 1784, by a Hessian officer.
(11) Journal of Lieutenant Rüffer, from 1 March, 1776, to 28 December, 1777.
(12) Species facti of the surprise and capture of three Hessian Regiments, v. Knyphausen, v. Lossburg and Rall (now Wöllwarth), 26 December, 1776. Philadelphia, 19 March, 1778. Schäffer.
(13) Species facti of the surprise and capture of Rall's Brigade at Trenton, 26 December, 1776, especially Rall's (now Wöllwarth's) Regiment; by J. Matthaüs (Major).
(14) Report of the capture of Rall's Brigade in Trenton, 26 December, 1776. Phila., 20 March, 1778. Baum, Staff Captain, Knyphausen's Regiment.
(15) Reports of Captains of Engineers Pauli and Martin and Lieutenant Biel, on the events at Newport.
(16) Report of a Hessian officer of the surprise at Trenton.
(17) Letters of Lieut. Henkelmann, of Seitz's Regiment, to relatives at home, and some extracts from his diary.
(18) Letters of Adjutant Henel.
(19) Letters of Captain Ries, of Lossberg's Regiment.
(20) Letters of Sergeant Flockshaar.

## Manuscript Authorities.

(21) Part of a diary of non-commissioned officer Casper Recknagel.
(22) Diary of non-commissioned officer Reüber, of Rall's Regiment, from 1 January, 1776, to 29 December, 1783.
(23) History of the Yäger Battalion, by Capt. Mahlburger. [A few copies only lithographed.]

*B. Brunswick:* (1) Papers left by Lt.-Gen. v. Riedesel at Eisenbach.
(2) Journal of the Brunswick Troops, from 22 February, 1776, to 15 January, 1779, kept by Quartermaster-General Gebhardt.
(3) Journal of Col. v. Specht, from the voyage to the capitulation at Saratoga.
(4) Correspondence of Major Cleve, Riedesel's first Adjutant, and Captain Tùnderfeld.
(5) Journal of Captain Ranzaù, from 8 April, 1777, to 29 August, 1778.
(6) Journal of Schuler, from 15 May to 20 June, 1776.
(7) Journal of the voyage from Portsmouth to Quebec, and from there to the Southern Colonies, and thence of the return to Europe, by C. v. Schuler, known as v. Senden. [The journal begins 23 June, 1776, and ends April, 1781. An extract was printed in 1839, in the "Journal for Art, Science and History of War," vol. 47. Schuler v. Senden died a Prussian General of Division.]
(8) Journal of the Field Chaplain Melzheimer.

(9) Journal of Major Cleve of his imprisonment, 1779.

(10) Journal of the Voyage to America and of Three Campaigns there, from 15 May, 1776, to 10 October, 1783, including the return to Wolffenbüttel, by Frederick Julius v. Papet, First Lieutenant of the v. Rhetz Regiment, and, since 20 November, 1777, Brigade Major of the German Troops in Canada. [Two stout volumes.]

(11) Journal of Corporal Scheither.

*C. Waldeck:* (1) Short Description of the Journey and Campaign of the Third Regiment to America, from 20 May, 1776, until its return in 1783, by Carl Philipp Steùernagel, Quartermaster of the Regiment, of Captain Teùtzel's Company.

(2) Diary of the Third Waldeck Regiment, by Ph. Waldeck, Chaplain.

*D. Ansbach-Bayreŭth:* March, route and description of the most remarkable events in America, by John Conral Döhla, of Zell—described to a former companion in arms. [Döhla was a school teacher.]

*E. Anhalt-Zerbst:* History of the Zerbst Regiment in the English service during the American War. [This Ms. gives the history of the Regiment from 1776 to 1793. The part relating to the war in America is from the diary of a member of the regiment who took part in the events it describes.]

## THE TREATIES.

The American armies were recruited by the help of liberal promises. Twenty dollars and one hundred acres of land were guaranteed every private and non-commissioned officer. Recruits could be got only by bounties and pay. The Germans were used to being sent outside their own country to serve under foreign flags, but the money paid for their services went to their sovereigns. Those sent to America brought home much useful knowledge of actual war, and the Hessians and Brunswickers, who had fought in America, were among the best soldiers in the German army during the wars of the French Revolution. Their operations in America were closely followed at home; newspapers and journals were filled with their letters.

A Hessian officer who had served as adjutant with Donop and Knyphausen, wrote afterwards: "No one found fault with our going into the British service for pay," and none of the officers or men complained. There were many volunteers, especially in Hesse, among them v. Ochs, later General, and in the letters home, from soldiers and officers, there was no complaint, but all showed a thoroughly German spirit of discipline wherever they were ordered.

When England found its need of allies, it naturally turned to its old comrades of the Seven Years' War. Hesse Cassel and Brunswick were first approached. George the III. wrote to their princes — the wives were both English princesses — and offered not only a subsidy for their troops, but treaties of alliance and protection, for it was easily to be anticipated that France would side with the rebels and threaten Germany. The troops from Hanover were sent, five battalions, to Gibraltar, relieving English soldiers sent to America. Hesse Hanau and Waldeck joined the other German allies.

Toward the end of 1775, Col. William Faucit, of the Guards, came to Germany to make the Treaties for the allied forces. On January 9, 1776, that with Brunswick was signed, on the 15th that with the Hessian government, and on the 5th of February that with Hanau; that with Waldeck had been made in London on April 25, 1775. Hesse Cassel agreed to supply fifteen Regiments, each of five Companies, four Grenadier Battalions, two Yäger Companies, and some artillery, in all 12,500 men. Brunswick promised a corps of 4,000 men, four Infantry, one Dragoon, Regiments, one Grenadier, and one Light Infantry Battalion. Hesse Hanau promised one Infantry Regiment and some artillery, in all 900 men; Waldeck, one Regiment 750 strong.

The three treaties were printed at Frankfort and

## The Treaties.

Leipsic in 1776, and in the Parliamentary Transactions, Nos. 17 and 18. For each man England agreed to pay thirty marks hand money, one-third one month after the execution of the Treaties, the balance within two months. For every man killed, wounded or captured, or made unserviceable by wounds or sickness, a like sum was to be paid, and like provision was made for those lost in sieges or by infectious disease or on shipboard, but for deserters no compensation was to be made.

To meet the heavy expenses of so quickly equipping so large a force, England paid in advance for two months, besides all the transportation from the first day's march. The Brunswick Treaty provides that the subsidy should begin to run from the date of its execution at the rate of 64,500 German thalers, as long as the soldiers received pay, and when that ended, it was to be doubled, and this 129,000 thalers should be paid for two years after the return home of the troops. They were to take an oath of service to the King of England, thus putting them under double allegiance to their own sovereign and to that of Great Britain. Their own princes were to supply equipments and keep up the standard by new recruits, and were to maintain their legal control over their subjects. Food and clothing were to be supplied just as to the British army. The forage money paid to the officers was a handsome addition to their regular pay. Gen. v. Riedesel, who was of an economical turn of mind, was said to have saved 15,000 thalers from this source on his return to Brunswick.

This was the tenth treaty of the kind that Hesse had made since the seventeenth century. The King of England pledged himself, in case of great loss in any regiment, to equalize its strength as best he could with the others. With Brunswick and Hesse Cassel he specially agreed to employ their soldiers only in the North American Continent, and not in the unwholesome West Indies. It is not easy to ascertain the exact amounts paid by England to Germany under these treaties, for the details were kept secret, although the public approval by Parliament annually shows that the following were about the amounts thus voted, viz.:

| | |
|---|---|
| Hesse Cassel, eight years, | £2,959,800. |
| Brunswick, " " | 750,000. |
| Hesse Hanau, " " | 343,130. |
| Waldeck, " " | 140,000. |
| Ansbach-Bayreuth, seven years, | 282,400. |
| Anhalt-Zerbst, six years, | 109,120. |

As these subsidies were to continue for two years after the close of the war, that would be £1,150,000. The bounty for 20,000 men at £6, would be £120,000. The Artillery received an additional £28,000, and the annual subsistence cost £70,000. Altogether, with additional allowances, £850,000 annually must have been paid to the German princes for their soldiers, out of which, of course, they paid the expense of equipping, keeping their arms, etc.

## The Treaties. 19

The Treaty with Hesse Cassel was even better for that prince than that with Brunswick or Hanau, and Cassel received yearly £50,000 more than it ever got before for the same number of its soldiers.

Baron v. Schlieffen made a special visit to London on behalf of Cassel—he was an old soldier, had served in the Seven Years' War in command of Hessian troops, and was Adjutant of the Duke of Brunswick, and was as good in using his pen as with his sword; his Memoirs have been highly commended by later historians. When he went to London, the only man in the English Ministry he knew was Lord George Germain, who, as Lord Sackville, had been discredited by his conduct in the Seven Years' War. Schlieffen, however, gained such a foothold with the Secretary of State, Lord Suffolk, that he was able to recover for Cassel £40,000, an old claim for hospital moneys spent in the Seven Years' War.

An offer of an additional sum, as compensation to Cassel for Schlieffen's services in rescuing the great magazine at Osnabruch, and thus helping to win the victory at Minden, was refused, but he secured for himself the honor of maintaining his independence and personal honesty, and for his native country a welcome increase of the growing reserve in its well-stocked treasury.

The later debates in the British Parliament often turned on the avarice of the German princes in thus securing the payment of old claims, in addition to the liberal amounts paid for the subsidies given by treaty; but it must be borne in mind that England was in the position of asking for help, and the Germans were not offering it, so that of course the latter were justified in making the best terms they could.

# CHAPTER I.

The German Princes, who had promised their help to the King of England, after the execution of the Treaties providing for subsidies, completed the military organizations and prepared them for their long journey. The Elector of Hesse, Frederic II.,* whose arsenals were well filled, and whose troops were always ready, was the most active, and by the end of February his Regiments were in Cassel, prepared to start.

As the departure of the troops depended on the arrival of the transport ships, the time of waiting was used in exercising the soldiers, in reorganization, and in preparing the recruits and the men who had joined after a long leave of absence. In spite of the weather, the men were drilled daily, often in deep snow. Every effort was made to adopt the English system; the Grenadier companies, which had been distributed among the Musketeer and

---

*[NOTE I.—The Elector Frederic II., then fifty-six years old, was not unpopular in his country, which he had enriched by many benevolent institutions and by others for art and science. He is unjustly reproached with avarice—a charge which belongs to his son and successor. As he gave the largest contingent for the allied army sent across the Atlantic, and derived the greatest pecuniary benefit, he drew down on himself the most reproaches, which often exceeded his deserts. He was better than his reputation. He died soon after the War, in 1785.]

Fusilier battalions, were formed in four independent bodies. A Grenadier Regiment was organized of men picked from the different infantry regiments, and as good riflemen were in demand by the English authorities, the Yäger battalions were increased. The Regiments, according to the English system, were very weak—each with an average of 633—and in the reports, etc., the same force is sometimes described as a regiment, sometimes as a battalion; the proportion of officers was unusually large.

Each Infantry Regiment had
    21 Commissioned Officers,
    60 Non-Commissioned Officers,
    5 Non-Combatant Officers,
    22 Musicians,
  525 Men.

Each Grenadier Battalion had
    16 Commissioned Officers,
    44 Non-Commissioned Officers,
    1 Non-Combatant Officer,
    20 Musicians,
  420 Men.

Each Yäger Company had
    4 Commissioned Officers,
    12 Non-Commissioned Officers,
    1 Non-Combatant Officer,
    3 Musicians,
  105 Men.

Each Artillery Company had
    5 Commissioned Officers,

14 Non-Commissioned Officers,
1 Non-Combatant Officer,
3 Musicians,
129 Men.

The Hessian Corps, at the outset of the War, had a strength of 12,054 men, besides staff, engineer, supply train and servant men. It consisted of

15 Infantry Regiments,
4 Grenadier Battalions,
2 Yäger Companies,
2 Field Artillery Companies,

and was organized in two Divisions and four Brigades.

Gen. v. Schlieffen, the Commander-in-Chief, was very earnest in his entreaties to be assigned the command, but the Elector chose Lt.-Gen. Philipp v. Heister, an old officer who had served with distinction in the Seven Years' War.

Owing to want of transportation, only the First Division, under Gen. v. Heister, was sent forward—it consisted of the Guard Regiment, the Prince Charles Regiment, the Hereditary Prince's, Knyphausen's, Lossberg's, Ditfurth's, Donop's, Trümbach's, Mirbach's, the Grenadier Battalions of Rall, Bloch, Minnigerode, and Linsingen, a Yäger Company, 138 strong, and a Field Battery, 242 strong.

The Elector inspected the Regiments and reviewed them as they marched out in the presence of a large crowd, which cheered them heartily. It was not until February 29th that they finally left, and Rall's Regiment not until March 6th. On the 10th of March the First Division marched through Bremen past great numbers of spectators. On March 21st and 22d, the troops were mustered into the English service by Col. William Faucit, and on the 23d the loading of the transports began, lasting until April 15th. The quarters were very crowded, and each man had a small mattress, a pillow and a woolen coverlet, and every six a wooden spoon and a tin cup. The food consisted of peas and bacon on Sundays, four pounds for six men; soup, butter and cheese on Mondays; four pounds meat, three pounds meal, one-half pound raisins, one-half pound suet, for pudding. This was repeated on Wednesdays and the rest of the week. Every six men received daily four cans of small beer and a cupful of rum, often increased by an exchange for bread and cheese.

On the 16th, Gen. v. Heister went on board the Commodore's ship "Elizabeth," and owing to the lack of transportation, he was obliged to leave Rall's and Mirbach's regiments, and 154 men of Knyphausen's, behind. On the 17th the fleet set sail — forty-four vessels under Commodore Parker. On the 26th it reached Portsmouth, where the English troops already on other vessels, gave them a hearty welcome. On the 28th divine service was held — in accordance with the German piety of the time, every soldier had a prayer book in his knapsack, and men and officers were in the habit of daily pious exercises.

The English authorities urged the instant departure of the German division, but Heister tried hard to secure delay until all his troops were in hand, but he was obliged to yield. On May 6th, the fleet, under Admiral Hotham, consisting of 150 sail, finally got under way; the convoy consisted of six men-of-war and two cruisers. There were 12,500 troops on board, of which 7,400 were Hessians.

The voyage was long, tedious, stormy and uncomfortable. There was a duel between Lieut. Kleinschmidt and Capt. v. d. Lippe, in which the latter fell.

On August 17th, the fleet reached Sandy Hook, and found there the rest of the German division, just arrived. Twelve men only were lost on the passage, but many were sick with scorbutic diseases. The Germans were heartily welcomed, and gave glowing descriptions of the harbor of New York and the adjacent country.

The first order was to remove all silver from the uniforms, just as the British had already done, to lessen the risk of the American riflemen, whose unerring aim was greatly feared.

At the time of the arrival of the German troops, affairs stood about in this position. On the 18th of April, 1775, the first blood had been spilled at Lexington, followed by armed rising everywhere. In the North, Gen. Carleton, with a small force, formed the right wing; he had resisted an attack on Quebec during the winter, and was preparing to drive the Americans back. In the South, in Carolina, the left wing was under Clinton, sent to co-operate with Parker's fleet, but did nothing effectual there. Howe, who had received the general command in place of Gage, recalled, was in command of the center, and by orders from England, evacuated Boston, up to that time the only place on the northern coast held by the British.

He left March 17th, 1776, and sailed to Halifax, but on receipt of the news of the arrival of fresh forces from Europe, he left Halifax, on June 11th, and on the 29th reached Sandy Hook. His plan was to establish himself in or near New York, and to unite all his forces. He went to Staten Island, with about 9,000 men, and there waited the return of Clinton from the South and the arrival of the force coming from England.

The line of operations, stretching from Canada to South Carolina, was out of all proportion to the strength at hand, and there was no possibility of any united plan of action or mutual support. The two commanders were brothers. Richard, Lord Howe, the admiral and viscount, the elder, was active, energetic and able, and had gained credit and experience in his service; he looked with undisguised contempt on the rebels now in arms. Sir William Howe had fought with credit in the old French War, and was one of the ablest and most experienced general officers in the British army; he was very unlike his brother in manner — much gentler and kinder—but was not as energetic and active; indeed, showed a carelessness and negligence, even in weighty matters, that were inexcusable.

The elder brother was sober and self-contained; the

younger social and pleasure-loving — forgetting his military duty in the excesses of the table and other dissipation. He had his mistress at his side and his table was open to all. He encouraged others to the same sort of life, and was easily influenced by his boon companions. These qualities made him popular — were looked on as chivalric — and even a Hessian officer said that Gen. Howe was worth more than an army.

The British government thought that the two brothers would work in perfect harmony, and took credit for their selection.

Gen. Howe, on the arrival of his new forces, set on foot his plan for driving the enemy from Long Island and New York. The Hessians were assigned their part. The Brigade of v. Stirn was ordered to relieve the Thirty-fifth and part of the Fifth English regiments, and take position well forward on the shores of Staaten Island, separated from the enemy's advance posts by a narrow strip of water. The Brigade was posted along the shore in small detachments, the Guard Regiment at Amboy Ferry; the camp was placed in two lines, but it had to be moved to the rear, to escape the American riflemen, and the Artillery under Lieut. Grenke threw a few shot into Amboy to quiet the enemy.

The width of the water was a little over three hundred paces, and the Americans gathered on their side to watch the German soldiers, who were now for the first time in sight. One of the Hessians said that few of the rebels were in uniform; most of them looked like a mob, hastily gathered together.

The arrival of the German allies had spread no little alarm among the Americans. The Germans were greatly feared, and many of the inhabitants had abandoned their homes, flying to New York and leaving in their houses many articles of value. The soldiers were quartered in these houses and were very coolly received. Orders were given to behave with great propriety, for the hope of reconciliation was still cherished. When the inhabitants found that they were kindly treated, the soldiers were well treated and many sick and wounded were well cared for. The general comfort and prosperity of the country, little the worse for the war that had been waged, was a constant subject of praise among the German troops.

Gen. Howe, with 35,000 soldiers, well in hand, out of a total force of 55,000 soldiers, including 16,968 Germans, and 28,000 sailors, decided to drive the enemy from Long Island, where they were entrenched at Brooklyn. Separated by the Narrows from Staaten Island, a mile's width, well occupied by the English Fleet, and from New York by the East River, of about the same width, the Brooklyn Heights commanded three roads — that on the left to Bedford, that in the center to Flatbush, that on the right to Gowan's Bay. The Heights were strongly held by Washington's best troops, under Gen. Greene, one of his best generals.

On the 21st August, the Hessian Grenadiers were transhipped, and brigaded with the Yägers, under Gen. Donop, as an advance. The Americans abandoned the shore, after setting fire to some barns.

Lord Cornwallis was detached with the reserve and the advance under Donop and six guns to Flatbush, with orders not to attack if that place was held firmly. Cornwallis took position at Gravesend and sent Donop forward, and as he moved up, the 300 Riflemen withdrew, followed by a few cannon balls.

On the 23d, in the morning, the right wing of the advance was attacked, but when a battery was brought up, the Americans fell back. Another attack was attempted in the afternoon, some of the soldiers pushing into the village and setting fire to some houses; but a battery soon drove them back. On the 25th, a strong force, with guns, renewed the attack, but were again repulsed by the Artillery.

The Hessian Yägers had a little rest on the 24th and 25th, but were again attacked on the morning of the next day—and after resisting it, when Cornwallis wanted to withdraw them, Donop begged to be allowed to stay and to entrench his position.

On the 25th August, Gen. v. Heister and his Hessians were moved from Staaten to Long Island. Only Lossberg's Brigade, consisting of the Guard Regiment, that of Prince Charles, Ditfurth's and Trumbach's, with the Fourteenth British Regiment, and the convalescents and recruits, remained.

Gen. v. Stirn was assigned the First Brigade—the

Hereditary Prince's, Donop's and Mirbach's Regiments. The troops had moved forward on the middle road to Flatbush, Cornwallis took his position on the right wing, and the line extended from the Narrows to Utrecht and Gravesend.

The Americans held the Heights strongly, their right flank stretching from Brooklyn to the mouth of the Hudson, in front Gowan's Bay, with the left flank on Wallabout Bay.

On the 26th, Heister detached Col. v. Heeringen, with 306 men and a battery, as an advanced post for the left wing; the American riflemen made an attack, but were driven back by the artillery. In the evening, Clinton led his troops on the road to Bedford, to seize a pass which he thought strongly held. He learned by his own advance—from a captured American picket—that the road was clear, and sent a battalion of light infantry to hold it. Behind him was the main body of the British force, under Lord Percy; the Second, Third and Fourth Brigades, the Forty-second Regiment, and sixteen batteries, and Gen. Howe himself.

At dawn the troops moved forward, to turn the American left. A small body of American militia abandoned the heights, to avoid being cut off, and it was with difficulty that the British force was prevented from attacking the entrenchments, and withdrawn to a hollow under the American works. Heister, with the center, engaged the enemy on the Flatbush road, so as to make a demónstration, while the main attack on the American left was being made. Donop asked and received permission to lead his Yägers and Grenadiers in the first assault on the Heights at Guiana. Heister, at the first report of guns on his right, moved forward. The Grenadiers were placed in three sections, well forward, with the Yäger company of Wreden in advance. Mirbach's brigade had to cover the left flank.

The troops moved up the Heights in good order, flags flying, bands playing, the men pulling the guns through the woods. When the troops reached the Heights, in spite of a fire that did little harm, they were put in position. The Americans were driven out, while the German soldiers pursued them. Col. v. Heeringen reported that the enemy had strong defences of all kinds, but their riflemen took a quarter of an hour to load, and the Germans overwhelmed them by rapid firing and drove them with the bayonet. The Yägers of the left wing pushed into the American camp and captured the Americans in bands of 50 and 60 men. Col. Hand was in command, but Gen. Sullivan hurried forward, only in time to be struck by the British Dragoons, followed by Clinton's Light Infantry of the right wing.

The Americans were cut off and under fire on both flanks, but fought obstinately, at great disadvantage and with heavy loss. It was believed by them that the Hessians gave no quarter, while the Hessians, angered at the useless resistance, after firing only once, used the bayonet, drove the enemy into the woods and swamp, and only a few were able to get through to their own lines.

Mirbach's Brigade, on the left, took part in the action. Rall's Regiment wheeled from the center, through a narrow road, only to be attacked by a little body of 50 Americans; their flag was captured and, throwing down their arms, they surrendered; a subaltern seized the flag and was about to hand it to Col. Rall, when Gen. v. Mirbach came up and seized it. Rall cried out, " My Grenadiers took it and they shall have it," and after a sharp exchange of words, it was left with the Regiment, and on a report at head-quarters, Rall was made Brigade Inspector.

On the left, Gen. Grant was directed not to make a serious attack, but to engage the American forces. He had the Fourth and Sixth Brigades, the Forty-second Regiment, two companies of New York Provincials, and ten guns. He seized the outposts at midnight, and when he heard the heavy fire on his right, made an attack in earnest, driving Lord Stirling, the American commander, between two fires — that of Cornwallis on his left, moving forward with the reserves, and cutting off the retreat to Gowan's Bay — so that Stirling, surrounded on all sides, was forced to surrender; giving his sword to Gen. v. Heister, to avoid the British commanders.

Admiral Parker, under orders from Howe to attack the American shore batteries, with six men-of-war, succeeded, in spite of wind and tide, in bringing one ship within range.

Howe reports the American loss at 3,500 killed, wounded and captured, and among the last, three Generals — Stirling, Sullivan and Udell, or Woodhull; three Colonels, four Lieutenant-Colonels, three Majors, eighteen Captains, forty-three Lieutenants, one Adjutant, eleven Ensigns, and 1,011 men, besides fifteen guns—of which the Hessians took seven—and ten found in the works; the Hessians alone took one flag and five guns and 520 prisoners, among them Gen. Sullivan and 35 officers. Sullivan was captured by three Fusileers, in a field of corn, trying to escape by hiding there.

Heeringen said: "Sullivan is a lawyer, who has served in a very humble capacity, but he is a man of genius. Among the so-called Colonels and other officers, many were tailors, shoemakers, barbers and base mechanics. My men would not let them pass as officers. On searching Sullivan, I found Washington's orders, showing that there were 8,000 of his best troops there, ordered to hold the Heights at all hazards.

"The British loss of 150 killed and wounded was due rather to their disorderly attack than to the bravery of the enemy. I have not found one of the captured officers who ever served abroad. They are mere rebels. Lord Stirling is no lord at all, although the perfect counterpart of Lord Granby. Gen. Putnam is a butcher.

"The rebels desert in great numbers — Colonel, Lieutenant-Colonel and Major leaving, with all their men. The captured standard was brought by 60 men, who begged for their lives. Hardly one regiment was uniformed or armed — every man has his own fowling-piece. Stirling's Regiment was in blue, with red facings, and consisted of three battalions, mostly Pennsylvania Germans. They were fine, tall fellows, with good English guns and bayonets. This regiment met an English regiment, but the latter, taking them for Hessians, did not fire, and this cost the life of Col. Grant, some of his officers, and 80 men. The English then completely destroyed the American Regiment. The Artillery consists of wretched iron guns, badly served, and mounted on ship's carriages."

The Hessians lost Capt. v. Donop, Major Pauly, and a Lieutenant, with 23 men. The Germans complained that, as no horses were brought over, the field and staff officers were at a disadvantage, and were obliged to carry guns to protect themselves from the American riflemen. The men had to give up their heavy uniforms, and soon learned to adjust themselves to the trying hot weather.

The English forces engaged numbered about 15,000, the other half being left on ship-board and on Staaten Island, while the Americans had 8,000 men in their works, under Sullivan, and 5,000 in the lines around Brooklyn.

Greene was to have commanded, but owing to his sickness Sullivan succeeded him, knowing little or nothing of the plan and ignorant of the necessity of holding the pass at Bedford, or of the condition of the works on the Heights.

Here, for the first time, the European and the American tactics were sharply contested. The American lines were too long, not properly supported, and covered by heavy detachments of sharpshooters, to no great advantage in the end.

The British and Hessian troops developed their strength in heavy columns and drove the thin lines back with the bayonet. When the left wing of the rebels was driven from the Heights, it broke in the swampy ground below, and was turned by Clinton with great disorder.

Hessian blood was here first spilled on American soil. The Germans learned that they had met a new method of fighting, quite unlike the old prescribed fashion in vogue in Europe. The Americans cried out against the bloody pursuit of the Hessians and their refusal to accept a surrender. The dread of the Germans grew from a belief that they would give no quarter. It was reported that over two thousand rebels had been slaughtered in cold blood. The Hessians retorted that a hostile band, after surrender, had fired on their captors, and by this violation of German usage had brought on their own heads an angry return.

Col. v. Heeringen, in his report to Col. v. Lossberg, said: "The English gave little quarter to the enemy and encouraged our men to do the same thing." He complained that Col. John (?) with a Pennsylvania regiment, cut off from the main body, fired on the Hessian Grenadiers when resistance was hopeless.

The fact that Rall's Regiment captured a body of the enemy and did them no harm, showed rather the fear the rebels felt, while the Germans expressed the greatest contempt for an enemy which had shown, in this first conflict, so little genius for war.

Lieut. Rüffer, in his diary, says many of the rebels refused to surrender when it was offered them, for their officers had told them that they would be hanged.

The captured rebels were employed in dragging guns to the ships, but this was rather from want of horses, than as a mark of contempt. Howe treated the captured officers with great politeness, and Stirling and Sullivan were his daily guests at his table.

The Americans anxiously waited for daybreak, fearing an attack on their lines, which, with their reduced force and the shattered confidence of their men, they could not hope to resist. Howe opened a cannonade on the morning of August 27th and began to fortify his camp, but the rain interfered. He had neglected to put men-of-war in the East River, to cut off the retreat of the Americans. When at last, on the 29th, he ordered this to be done, a thick fog covered land and water, and the retreat, ordered by Washington, after a Council of War, was successfully effected, and on the morning of the 30th Donop's and Lossberg's Regiments occupied the abandoned lines.

Heeriugen had, on the night between the 29th and 30th, through Lieut. Zoll, reported to Howe the retreat, and the two Howes, the General and the Admiral, came to his quarters to decide what next to do. Men-of-war were ordered to the other side of Manhattan Island, and lay so near New York that the people in the streets could be seen and even the color of their clothing distinguished.

Eleven guns, much ammunition and food were found; the Hessians seized over a hundred horses and three hundred head of cattle. They found, too, an order stating that against such an enemy as the Hessians, resistance was impossible, and nothing was left but retreat.

The English regretted not having accepted Heister's offer to attack the American lines on the 27th, when he reported an opening on the left of their fortified camp.

Gen. v. Heister, with two Hessian brigades, occupied the abandoned Heights of Brooklyn, and Donop, with the Grenadiers and Yägers, seized Bushwick.

Howe moved his head-quarters to Newtown, while Hellgate and Flushing were occupied. The English made every arrangement to secure New York, and the Americans were loath to yield it. So near were the lines that one day, when Washington was inspecting his outposts, a Hessian Captain of Artillery opened fire, and with the third shot, the little band soon disappeared.

Howe erected batteries in the rear, and put the

men-of-war in front of New York, and on the evening of September 13th, five large English men-of-war moved past the forts, under fire from the batteries, to the point chosen for a landing. Commodore Hotham brought flat-boats and gallies to the same place, and six transports brought troops, under a heavy fire. To distract attention, on the morning of the 15th, three frigates and a schooner went up the Hudson as far as Bloomingdale, drawing the fire of all the guns within range. Under the fire of five men-of-war and of the English and American batteries, the first division was landed, including the Hessian Grenadiers and Yägers, in the reserve, led by Donop.

The point selected was at Kip's Bay, although preparation had been made at Stuyvesant's Cove and Harlem; so that there was little resistance, and the Americans hurriedly retreated to Kingsbridge, abandoning bag and baggage in their flight.

The Hessians pushed on to New York. Donop went with the advance into a wood where the American sharpshooters were posted; as these fell back, five were taken. Donop wanted to drive the enemy, but Howe ordered him to occupy the high ground on his right, just when Col. von Block discovered the enemy on his left. Not to have his left turned, he kept his position and advised Col. v. Minnigerode of it. When Donop received this report, he left von Block's battalion and moved with the rest of his force to the right, on the road from Kingsbridge to New

York, to seize the high ground. Although fortified, he found the position abandoned, and the force that had left it was in the ditches in front of the wood. When they found themselves cut off, they offered to surrender, but just then Block's battalion opened fire on them from the other side, and as it was returned, the rebels escaped, leaving only one Colonel, six other officers and 50 men as prisoners, while the Grenadier battalion lost two killed and sixteen wounded. About 3 P. M., Donop was relieved by British troops, and after moving forward four miles, bivouacked. The Americans had made so little resistance that Washington was enraged by his vain efforts to rally them.

The second division, under Grant, with Mirbach's brigade, landed at Turtle Bay, and drove the enemy, who made one stand, through Gowan's Pass to Morris's Heights. Washington at once gave orders to evacuate the city.

On the 15th of September, the invading force was posted, with its right on Horen's Hook, on the East River, its left at Bloomingdale, on the Hudson, where Donop was drawn up.

The Americans held the heights on both sides of Kingsbridge, and on the west side of the Hudson. New York was in the rear of the British-German army, and horses were obtained on requisition, especially for the Hessian officers.

The Americans lost 20 officers, 300 men and 74 guns, with ammunition and many supplies. On the retreat, a company of Hessian Yägers led the pursuit, capturing a battery of five guns, and taking post at John's House.

On the 15th, Admiral Lord Howe received a deputation of three Congressmen—Franklin and Adams were of the number—at the Hessian Camp at Amboy Ferry, and Col. von Wurmb gave his quarters for the meeting.

Howe was reproached for allowing Putnam to escape, and for not capturing the city and Washington's army at one blow.

On the 16th of September there was a sharp fight, the Americans sending a strong detachment from their lines to attack the British left, and then falling back, in order to draw the enemy into the woods, where a reserve of 3,000 men was posted, to attack. Col. v. Donop, with the Yägers and v. Linsingen's Grenadier battalion, pushed forward, sending Block's and Minnigerode's battalions around to seize the road to Kingsbridge.

The Americans fell back, before the advancing Germans, who lost eight men wounded, among them Lieut. Hinrichs; and Donop pitched his camp at Bloomingdale.

Col. Donop, in his report to Gen. Heister, said that his two regiments had saved Gen. Leslie from the results of a serious blunder in pushing his men into the woods, without any support. Captains Wreden and Lorey were particularly distinguished.

The enemy lost 300, the English 14 dead and 78

wounded. Lieut. Hinrichs wrote many descriptions of the scenes he witnessed, and these were published in the principal German newspapers.

Stirn's brigade, consisting of the Knyphausen, Lossberg and Rall regiments, remained on Long Island, under command of Col. v. Heeringen, a brave old officer, who died and was buried in a Brooklyn church-yard.

The troops left on Staaten Island suffered for want of supplies, and were in daily fear of an attack, reported to them by loyalists and deserters. Frequent efforts were made by the rebels to land, and although successfully resisted by constant vigilance, the inhabitants were continually sending news to the rebels, while living under the protection of the Hessians. Congress issued proclamations making tempting offers to officers and soldiers to abandon the British flag and become American land-owners and citizens, but these met with little response.

On the 17th September, the Hessians had a sharp contest with the Americans at Amboy Ferry. A two-masted American vessel was driven from its anchorage and went ashore; the Americans tried to get it off with boats, but Col. v. Wurmb brought up his guns and opened fire, driving the Americans off, and the vessel was taken by the Hessians.

The Americans brought down some twelve-pounders to the shore, but they were soon silenced by the Hessian artillery. Howe thanked them in general orders.

On the 20th and 21st, the inhabitants of New York and the garrison were alarmed by the outbreak of fire in wooden houses in different parts of the town, and a third of the houses were burned before the troops could put out the fire. Disorderly mobs had started the fires, and their preparations were found in various places, while the crowd hooted the soldiers as they worked to put out the flames, and cheered as the tower of St. Paul's fell into the burning church. The mob charged the sailors of the fleet with having started the conflagration. Donop says, in his diary, that it was planned by Col. Scott, of the American forces, once a lawyer, who had forty desperate men employed in putting incendiary material in the houses of fugitive royalists, and that the whole plan was found when Scott was arrested.

As soon as Gen. Howe was established in New York, he authorized the publication of *The Royal American Gazette.*

On the 14th October, orders were issued to the troops to be ready to move, and the next day, at 5 A. M., Lossberg's brigade, the Guards, Prince Charles' and Ditfurth's regiments, left Staaten Island, to join the rest of the army. In the evening, the advance, under Donop, went on board the transports; v. Trumbach's regiment was left on the island, with orders to join an English detachment of 200 men posted at Fort Dalrymple. Captain Parker had command of the four vessels on which the troops were embarked, and was kept by head winds at anchor off Bushwick.

The officers were warmly welcomed at the houses of the loyalists living in the neighborhood. The vessels moved up to the northern end of the island, and were so near the shore that Capt. Parker ordered the officers to keep the curtains drawn before the cabin windows, lest the Americans should fire on them. The hostile camp was in plain sight. Two frigates guarded the fleet; the other vessels were protected by pickets, and all were kept ready.

The secret of the object of the expedition was at first kept even from the officers, but finally it was found out — to leave two British brigades and Stirn's Hessians in the garrison at New York, and the lines before Harlem, under Lord Percy, while the rest of the army was to be landed in Westchester county, to cut the Americans off from Connecticut—their only line of retreat and source of supplies—or oblige them to abandon their strong position.

On the 15th October, at 6 A. M., the vessels sailed on, passing undisturbed by fire from the American lines, although they were so near that the officers could be distinctly seen on both sides. After touching at Frog's Neck, and finding that the Americans had cut the only bridge leading to the main land, the troops from Staaten Island, including Mirbach's brigade, the Hessian Grenadiers and Yägers, were brought in boats, a landing was made at Pell's Neck, under cover of the men-of-war and gunboats, engaged with the Americans; Stirn's brigade was brought up and the Americans retreated, the British taking up their position with the left on East Chester and the right on New Rochelle.

The Americans lost one lieutenant-colonel killed, a major wounded, and 50 dead and wounded. Tents and baggage being left on the vessels, the troops were obliged to camp in the open air on a sharp autumn night.

On the morning of October 19th, the Guard regiment was posted on a hill near New Rochelle, on the high road from New York to Boston, and the line of retreat to Connecticut and Boston was cut off by the British army. Washington, fearful that his forces would be entirely surrounded, led them off the island, leaving only a garrison at Fort Washington, and took up a new position, with his right on Valentine's Hill, his left on White Plains, his front on Bronx River. His long line forced him to divide his army into four corps, connected by outposts and patrols.

On the morning of the 20th, the English light infantry, the Hessian Yägers, Rall's brigade and the English Grenadiers moved forward and drove a small American force back into their entrenchments.

On the 21st, Capt. v. Malsburg, of Ditfurth's regiment, was ordered to guard head-quarters. Gen. v. Heister, with his two Hessian brigades and one English, took up a position vacated by advancing the right wing to White Plains. The Rangers, a body of loyal Americans, under Lieut.-Col. Rogers, seized Mamaroneck, on the right, and successfully resisted an attack of the American forces, losing 17 killed and wounded, 36 prisoners and one flag, but inflicting much heavier loss on the rebels.

On the 22d, fresh forces were brought up, the Second Hessian Division under Knyphausen, and the Waldeck regiment, just arrived, after leaving Cassel early in May, and reaching New York October 18th. They included Wutgenan's, Mirbach's, Rall's Grenadier, Stein's, Wissenbach's, Huyne's and Bünau's regiments, the Fourth Grenadier battalion, and the Second Yäger company, under an able officer, Capt. Ewald. Among the English reinforcements were the Sixteenth Light Dragoons, but so badly were the cavalry organized that Washington offered a reward of $200 for every dragoon captured with his horse.

## CHAPTER II.

The British government had not transports enough to carry all its forces, native and foreign, across at once, and this had to be done piecemeal, and for this purpose Dutch and other ships were hastily hired at high rates, but in very bad condition. The second fleet of transports carried to America, Hessian and Waldeck troops. Little Waldeck had a prince with love and experience of war—he had served in Austria and was a lieutenant-general in the Dutch army, and had three regiments ready to serve for pay on any foreign service. His third regiment was soon ready, and inspected by the prince and his court; his mother gave the soldiers a handsome present for a farewell entertainment, but the native workmen had a sharp fight with the soldiers and the recruiting officers. The regiment marched away on the 20th of March, 1776, and the last farewell was a promise that all who returned should be taken to their homes in carriages. It consisted of a Grenadier company, 134 strong, and four musketry companies, each 130 strong, two three-pound guns and 14 artillerymen, and with a staff of 16, counted in all 684 strong.

The Colonel was v. Hanxleden, the Adjutant Lieutenant Stierlein, the Captains Hacken, von Horn Alberti, Pentzel. On its march, it was escorted by the Waldeck sharpshooters, in their green uniforms, to prevent desertion and keep order, but some of the old soldiers took offense at this precaution and succeeded in evading it. After a tedious march to Bremen, the men went on board the transports, which finally set sail on June 3d, and on the 20th were in Portsmouth, where the Brunswick, Hesse Hanau and Hessian divisions were all gathered.

The Waldeckers received from their prince each a hymn book, in addition to the prayer book given him as part of his regular outfit.

It was not until July 20th that the fleet of 64 sail finally started from Portsmouth, where the vessels had been forced to wait for a favorable wind. A fire on one of the ships was the principal incident of the voyage, but fortunately there was no loss of life and no serious harm done.

On the 18th October, the fleet reached New York, and on the 24th the troops joined the force under Gen. v. Heister, at New Rochelle. On the 25th, Howe ordered a reconnoisance, and Captain Ewald here gave the first proof of his efficiency and received Howe's praise, with a caution not to be so rash and venturesome, for his daring advance caused a sharp loss. Washington was reported to be falling back, and Howe, anxious to force a battle, sent, on the 25th, two columns, leaving Knyphausen to protect the rear and keep open communication with the garrison in

New York. The Hessians, under Heister, were the left column, while the Hessian Grenadiers and Yägers were in the right, under Clinton.

A sharp attack was handsomely repelled by Knyphausen's division. Rall's regiment had a skirmish and drove back the Americans, and a Hessian Grenadier captured by them was taken to Washington, who, according to Capt. v. Malsburg's diary, urged him to join them, and when the man refused, gave him a guinea and sent him back to rejoin his regiment.

Washington took up a strong position, and Howe sent Donop in advance, while Rall was on the left, and had the lines of the enemy felt, in the effort to turn them.

The two armies faced each other; Rall and Donop moved their troops and made great fires, and in various ways tried to exaggerate their apparent strength, on the night before the battle of White Plains.

The Hessians and the Waldeckers lost heavily in the operations between October 9th and 28th — 13 killed, 63 wounded and 23 missing. The Hessian artillery was especially commended, and Lossberg's regiment lost in the action 50 in killed and wounded. At the most trying time, two of its officers especially distinguished themselves, and Baumeister, Heister's adjutant, mentioned them, as well as others, as particularly notable for their bravery.

Both armies strengthened their lines, and Howe made frequent plans for attack, but one after the other was given up. Tired of the long delay, the soldiers often committed excesses, and the Waldeck regiment was especially embittered by the loss of some wine and spirits belonging to the American General Lee, captured by them, but, by Howe's order, emptied on the roadside; this, at a time when the cold weather was very trying, naturally made the men angry.

Warned by a deserter, Washington withdrew still further northward into the mountains, leaving many houses of the royalists in ashes, to mark his line of retreat. Donop, supported by Rall and Stirn, was ordered to seize the American works, but was forced back until the evacuation was completed. The Hessian officers praised the skill shown in the abandoned defenses, and were surprised that they were so easily given up.

Howe determined to take Forts Washington and Lee, on the Hudson, and Knyphausen was sent in the advance in that direction. Much adverse criticism was expressed by the Germans as to Howe's want of ability in this operation, and still more that he had given up his plan of advance to Albany.

Howe made the Hessian Captain v. Munchhausen his adjutant, as a mark of respect for the Germans. Ditfurth's regiment had the honor of drawing the first fire from the guns of Fort Washington. The Waldeckers took possession of Fort Independence, abandoned by the Americans in their retreat, with its 12 heavy guns, and 62 guns were left in other works. In Fort Washington there was a garrison of 3,000 men, under Col. Magraw, who rejected Howe's summons to surrender. Howe ordered an attack in four columns; Knyphausen, on the left of the Americans, having the hardest task, while the frigate Pearl was to support him with its fire.

Knyphausen, on November 17th, issued his orders for the attack; the Yägers and 40 Grenadiers, under Captain Bornin, to lead, followed by 160 men under Col. v. Borbeck, and then the Grenadier battalion of Köhler, and those of Wutgenau, Lossberg, Rall, Knyphausen, Huyne, Bünau and Waldeck. Preparations for assault were ordered in great detail. In the morning, at half-past five, Knyphausen advanced, his right under Rall, his left under Schmidt, Donop in the advance of the former, v. Medern of the latter. At seven o'clock the firing began, and the advance was well on its way, when Howe ordered Knyphausen to wait the movement of his other wing. At 11 A. M., the order to attack was finally carried into operation, and the outworks were gallantly seized, while the Americans were crowded into the fort itself.

Captain v. Hohenstein, who spoke both English and French, was sent by Rall to summon the fort to surrender, and at once moved forward with a white flag, presented his terms, and gave half an hour for their acceptance, and at the end of that time, Knyphausen received the flags, and the garrison, 2,870 strong, 44 guns, and large supplies of all kinds, were the result.

When Captain v. Malsburg was looking around,

after taking possession of the works, he was welcomed by a rebel soldier, who claimed acquaintance in Germany, and pointed out a number of Germans serving in the American army. The four regiments surrendered to the regiments of Rall and Lossberg. The Hessians lost, in the attack, more heavily than any other of the English troops—killed 53, wounded 273 —while the total American loss was 53 killed and 15 wounded.

Knyphausen was congratulated by Howe and Heister, and Fort Washington became Fort Knyphausen, as a special compliment to its captor. The Hessians themselves were not at all satisfied with Howe's delays, which cost them a large part of their loss. The wounded were sent to Harlem, where Captain v. Griesheim was in command; the Hessian brigade of Schmidt garrisoned Fort Washington, and the Waldeck regiment Fort Independence.

With the fall of Fort Washington, Fort Lee became useless, as alone it could no longer bar the passage of the Hudson. Washington had already given orders to evacuate it, when, on the 20th, he received news that the allied forces had made a landing two miles up the river—Donop led the three battalions of Hessian Grenadiers and the Yägers. Cornwallis commanded the force and handled it so skilfully that it made good its hold on the Jersey shore, seizing the road from Bergen Point to Orange, before the rebels had any guess at their plan. The two Yäger companies were in the advance, one on the left, the other, on the right, led by Captain Ewald, who found the rebels retreating from the fort; instantly notifying Cornwallis, he was greatly surprised on receiving orders to fall back, and while Cornwallis waited to order the advance in force towards the fort, the rebels completed their retreat, and not a man was left to be taken with the fort.

The Americans saved only two guns, leaving even their tents, and their kettles hanging on the fire; 32 guns, 7 mortars, 400,000 rounds of ammunition, 432 tents, and provisions for 5,000 men for three months, were all left, along with 73 sick, out of a garrison of 2,000 men.

Cornwallis pursued the Americans through Elizabeth to Brunswick, Donop often under fire, as he led the advance, or covered the flanks. Rall's brigade, consisting of his own regiment, Knyphausen's and Lossberg's, started under orders to go to the Delaware, and on the way were heartily welcomed by the inhabitants, mostly Holland settlers and good loyalists. The Hessian Grenadiers and Yägers were in the right column, which Cornwallis led to Princeton. Howe was with Donop, in the advance. Rall's brigade left Lossberg's regiment at Brunswick, to be relieved by the Waldeck regiment. The advance suffered from the fire of the American sharpshooters.

Howe, on arriving at Trenton, was urged by some of its loyalist citizens to hurry up his troops and capture the retreating Americans before they could cross the Delaware, but Howe went with the Yägers to reconnoiter the open ground, and soon drew the fire from 37 guns, mounted on the other shore, losing 13 men. Münchhausen especially commends Howe's coolness under this heavy fire, and his own good fortune in receiving, in place of an old horse, disabled as he rode by Howe's side, a fine English horse, which Howe gave him.

Münchhausen made vain efforts to find a passage for the troops, for while Washington held the front, Lee threatened the rear and captured 700 head of cattle and 1,000 sheep.

On the 11th, Donop, with his Grenadiers and Yägers, was sent on the left bank of the Delaware, to go as far as Philadelphia, collecting boats, but without result, while his movement was sharply watched by the Americans, who had sent 13 gallies, with 36-pounders, up the river, which was completely commanded on both shores. Rall's brigade had a rough march from Brunswick to Princeton, bivouacking in the snow, without shelter, and the regiments were ordered to find winter quarters in Trenton, while Donop went to Bordentown and Burlington.

Münchhausen declares that the Germans were anxious to cross the Delaware and capture Philadelphia. Howe, however, had gone to New York and formed his lines, with the left on the Hudson and the right on the East river, about a mile in front of the city. The mob had again set fire to many of the best houses and churches, while the garrison was quartered in other churches, and in Fort St. George and in wooden barracks. The party feeling ran high in the city; its civil government was in loyal hands, and the Germans found evidences of luxury and hospitality in the well-furnished houses on Queen street and Water street, where the rich merchants then lived; but their hope of being quartered there was disappointed by Howe's orders to them to move in another direction. Many of the churches were used as prisons for the captured rebels. The city was divided into seven sections, and a mayor, with seven councillors and seven aldermen—loyalists, of course—had charge of the civil government. Many of the citizens were supplied with arms and employed as militia, to guard the city.

## CHAPTER III.

While Gen. Cornwallis was driving the enemy before him through New Jersey, Howe suddenly ordered him to halt. Instead of pursuing his advantage, he decided to go in the other direction, and an important part of his force was sent to Rhode Island, where for three years it was practically useless. The harbor of Newport had some value, but it could have been taken just as well after Cornwallis had completed his successful campaign.

In the expedition to Rhode Island, the Hessians were about one-half the force — including Huyne's brigade, the Guard regiment and a part of Lossberg's. Sixty transport vessels, mostly supplied by the East India Company, were divided in three portions, each convoyed by three men-of-war. They left New York November 27th, and on the 7th December anchored off Prudence Island. No vessels were in Newport harbor, but the red flag flying from all the defenses gave notice of an obstinate resistance.

On landing, the troops were surprised to learn that the Americans had gone, the night before, to Bristol and Providence, carefully carrying off 30 guns, and leaving only a few cattle, captured by Prescot. The

Prince Charles and Ditfurth regiments occupied the town just in time to prevent its being set on fire. Two Yäger companies were organized in each of the Hessian regiments, to serve as light infantry.

Newport then had 1,100 houses, and in those of the rich and well-to-do families, there was great luxury. Soldiers were quartered in the houses of those who had gone away, and few of those who stayed behind gave the soldiers a very hearty reception. The great want was wood, and the Hessian soldiers were sent to Shelter Island to secure a supply. There the fear of the Hessians was found to be exaggerated, but the negroes and Indians were soon reconciled to the soldiers.

Six Hessian regiments were sent to join Cornwallis, and the Lossberg regiment was left in Newport. Huyne's brigade was sent out on the island, and on January 22d drove off a landing party of Americans, and with its battery nearly sunk the galley which brought them over. Another attempt, on March 15th, was equally ineffectual.

On April 2d, Lord Percy gave up the command and returned to England. A Hessian officer wrote home that he was an active soldier and a great friend of the poor and distressed, but that his hope of reconciling the rebel colonies to the mother country had been rudely disappointed.

The spring clothed the island with a beauty of vegetation that charmed the German soldiers, who appreciated the kindly welcome of the Quakers and Baptists, and of the women of all sects. The Guard regiment was sent off on May 6th, and one of its officers said that almost all the women shed tears, good rebels as they were. This was part of the reinforcements sent to New Jersey, to help atone for the wretched close of the campaign, in the surprise and defeat of the Hessian regiments at Trenton, through the unpardonable neglect of their commander. It was not only the only disaster of the kind during the whole war, but another complexion would have been given to the struggle if this unfortunate affair had not strengthened the rebels and disheartened the loyalists.

When Lord Cornwallis was in New Brunswick, Gen. Howe, turning the command in New York over to Gen. Heister, came to Cornwallis' head-quarters and ordered him to push his force to the Delaware. Cornwallis turned the command over to Gen. Grant, and returned with Howe to New York, to prepare for a visit to England, on leave.

On December 8th, Donop reached the Delaware, just as the last American soldiers had crossed the river, and they saluted him with a few shots. Gen. Grant assigned the winter quarters of the Guard regiment in New Brunswick, and of Donop's brigade in Bordentown. Rall came with his brigade, and 50 Hessian Yägers under Lieut. v. Grothausen, 20 light dragoons and six field pieces, to Trenton, on the 14th December. He had asked for this post and it was given him for the bravery he had shown at

White Plains and Fort Washington. Howe had promised his and the other Hessian regiments which had distinguished themselves, the best of winter quarters.

The American forces were dispirited and discouraged; and discontent, mutiny and desertion would have distressed a man of less decision than Washington, and led to an early failure of their efforts to secure independence.

The English troops, on the other hand, were eager to move, and Howe neglected to make use of his opportunity. His fancied security led to carelessness, and men and officers had no fear of an attack from the American army.

Trenton was then a village of 130 houses, surrounded by woods, divided by the Assanpink, a branch of the Delaware, into an upper and lower town, connected by a stone bridge.

On the road to Princeton, there was a woody height, commanding the place. It was so near the river, that the Americans, from the other side, could fire on it. Another creek, Draw-Creek, also crossed by a stone bridge, was on the road to Burlington and Bordentown, where Donop lay with his Hessians. At the bridge, there was an outpost of 12 men, with a non-commissioned officer, detached from the main guard of 70 men and one officer in the town. Northward, on Pennington Hill, was another outpost of 20 men, strengthened at night by a Yäger picket of 15 men. The regiments were so quartered that Rall's and Lossberg's were in the northern part of the town, Knyphausen's in the southern, with some of the men in the houses scattered on the other side of the bridges. At night the companies must occupy certain houses, two or three men together, as outposts, from which to give the alarm, in case of attack; their arms, in good weather, were piled outside the houses, guarded by two or three sentries.

These were the only precautions which Rall took in such a dangerous situation and so near the enemy. Neither his flanks nor his rear were protected, nor did he attempt to connect with Donop, and a sentry was rarely posted. He himself was very negligent, rarely visiting his posts or his sentries, and this negligence soon spread throughout his force.

Every where there were rumors of an attack by the Americans, and the negroe servants especially seemed to know of such a plan; it was first hinted and then told warningly to Rall, but all in vain, and his conduct was such a riddle to his more watchful officers, that some of them spoke to him on the subject.

Major v. Dechow, an old and experienced soldier, suggested that an outwork be thrown up to guard against a sudden attack, and offered to build it, with the help of Lieut. Wiederhold. Rall's refusal was very rude — ending with "Let them come. What, outworks! We'll meet them with the bayonet." Major v. Dechow answered calmly, "It won't cost any thing, and if it does no good, it can do no harm." Rall, however, repeated his refusal, and turned away, laughing.

Later on, Dechow spoke to him of the supplies, and of fixing on a place to which they could be brought in case of an attack; but Rall answered, "Don't talk to me of supplies; the rebels are not coming, and if they do and take me, they may take my last wagon; let every wagon go where it suits." Old and experienced Major Matthäus inquired if it would not be well to place a detachment at Pennington, to protect the right flank, and to send a patrol to Johnson's Ferry, on the river; but Rall would not listen to them, and to other officers who agreed in these suggestions — asking if they wanted the detachments to be taken.

The Americans at times crossed the river, and pushed on so as to cut the communication with Princeton. When Rall sent a despatch to Leslie, in command at the latter place, the two dragoons carrying it were attacked and one of them killed, in a wood, by a party of American sharpshooters. When the survivor returned with the news, Rall sent a command of three officers and one hundred men, with a gun, in the worst weather, to carry the despatch, which could have been easily sent by fifteen men.

The English laughed at the Hessians when they found that all this force was used to carry a despatch. Rall, instead of making better use of this occasion for a reconnoisance, ordered the command to return at once, and during the trying night march, many of the men fell out on the way.

Donop had begged Rall to entrench himself, and to send strong patrols between Trenton and Bordentown; but Rall answered the Captain of Engineers Martin, who came for the purpose, that "It was unnecessary; the rebels were a bad set;" and later he said, "The enemy had landed several times on this side, below the bridge, and had been quietly allowed to withdraw, but now he was ready for them; he hoped that Washington himself would come over, that he might be taken prisoner." Martin reported this when he was captured at Horen's Hook, August 29, 1778.

The measures taken by Rall consisted of sending every morning, after December 23d, two hours before daybreak, a detachment with two guns, under a staff officer, to the south end of the town, and standing guard for two hours at the office of the surgeon, and then returning. For this the pickets were taken from the right wing, where the Pennington Hills were situated, thus leaving the north side entirely unprotected. Rall insisted that there was no danger, and thus walked into the pitfall which Washington had dug for him.

After much pressure, Rall sent out a patrol, on the 24th December, of 200 men, under Major Matthäus, to Pennington; the latter divided his force, one-half, under Captain Steding, going to Johnson's Ferry, on the Delaware; the other, Matthäus took towards Pennington. He was soon followed by Rall himself, with the British dragoons. In a couple of hours Steding rejoined Matthäus and the return was then quietly made. Nothing was seen of the enemy. There had been a few shots from the other side of the river, and Matthäus thought he heard a drum in a wood.

The officers looked on their situation and Rall's conduct as very serious. The staff officers of Lossberg's regiment determined to write to Gen. v. Heister, but their letter was too late. Lieut.-Col. Scheffer worried himself sick in his anxiety.

Gen. Grant was as negligent as Rall; for when the latter wrote to him of sending a detachment to Maidenhead, to ensure better communication between Trenton and Princeton, Grant made a rude reply and spoke contemptuously of the rebels, declaring that he could hold the Jerseys with a corporal's guard. However, he ordered Leslie to send a patrol from Princeton, and Rall one from Trenton, of twenty or thirty men, every two or three days. The first patrol from Leslie came to Trenton on the 24th, with a message from Leslie to Rall, that he must be on the lookout, for Washington was preparing to cross the Delaware, and would attack one or the other.*

Rall received other warning, too. Shortly before the 26th, two American deserters came in and reported that Washington had issued four days' rations to his

---

* Reuber says, in his diary, that Leslie sent three English regiments, which halted in front of Rall's quarters; but he at once sent them back.

## In the American Revolution. 65

men, and that it was reported that he was about crossing the Delaware, to attack Trenton.

On the morning of the 24th, a citizen of Trenton named Wahl [*sic*] called on Rall and warned him that he would be attacked and ought to be on his guard. Rall replied, laughing, "Let them come," but sent out neither a patrol nor a spy—made no preparation; not even choosing a point for assembling or a line of retreat. His six guns, instead of being distributed, were in front of his quarters on the market square, as if for show.

On the evening of the 24th, the two pickets on the north side were suddenly attacked, and in the fight six men were wounded. The Americans withdrew. In the town, the force was under arms, but when Rall heard the result, he simply ordered the outer picket to be strengthened by an officer with ten men, and thirty men with an ensign were sent to the point where the enemy had retreated. Hardly had they gone two miles, when they were ordered back. Rall allowed the regiments to disperse, ordering only his own, which was on duty that day, to remain in their barracks. He himself went to an evening entertainment, thinking the attack was that which Leslie had warned him of, and that it was all at an end.

It was Christmas eve, dark and stormy—and the Hessians were to receive an awful Christmas present. When the officer with his ten men reached his post, he put seven on picket and ordered them to march carefully over the prescribed line.

The morning of the 25th was half an hour begun, the last sentry had returned and reported all quiet, and as the Yägers had withdrawn their night guard, the officer in advance did the same thing. It was a wretched, stormy night—raining and snowing—and the driving storm forced the men to seek shelter wherever they could find it.

No one expected an attack—the officer himself had just come out of a little house, when the enemy came in sight, and all were taken prisoners; for the men had just left their guns on the rack, and the sentries were looking for shelter. The officer took the Americans, at first, for his own patrol, but suddenly discovering the truth, cried out, "The enemy!" The attacking force fired three times before the picket could seize their arms and fire, and on all sides, as if out of the earth, the enemy came in force, surrounding the picket; which, however, succeeded in retiring, firing.

In Trenton the alarm was sounded with bugles and drums. Lossberg's regiment was the quickest to gather, and the company of Capt. v. Altenbockum, which lay in the outer row of houses, took position across the street in front of its quarters, and as the retreating pickets fell back, gathered them up on its right; the captain, however, to prevent being cut off —for he heard firing on the other side—drew nearer to the rest of the regiment.

Meanwhile, part of Rall's regiment, which was on duty that night, came up. After a while, Col. Rall arrived, on horseback and in great excitement. The officer of the post first attacked went up and gave his report. Rall asked how strong was the enemy. The officer replied that he could not say positively, but three battalions came against him and he saw two more come out of the woods.

By this time they were surrounded. Rall rode up to the front of his regiment and halting there, cried out, "Forward, march! advance! advance!" But it was impossible to resist the strong attack of the Americans, with his disorganized little band.

The Americans pushed forward with their guns and attacked the colonel's quarters. The battery posted there opened fire, but was soon captured. The Grenadiers threw themselves wildly on the enemy and recovered their guns, but Rall moved off to the right, in an apple orchard, to attack the enemy on the road to Princeton, and was met with a hot fire.

Lieut.-Col. Scheffer, in command of the Lossberg regiment, ordered an advance, to try to break through and join Rall.

The Americans had come in increasing force into the city and fired from houses and gardens. Rall hit upon the idea (some said in order to recover the baggage left in the town) of returning and retaking the place. He pressed on with his two regiments, crying out, "All who are my Grenadiers, forward!" but was met by a destructive fire.

The Hessians could do nothing with the bayonet, for there was no enemy in mass or line in sight—the deadly bullets came from the riflemen behind walls and trees, out of windows and doors, under cover. It literally rained balls and cartridges. The guns of the Hessians were made useless by the wet weather, and their fire became steadily weaker, while that of the Americans became stronger. The artillery, too, was unlucky; the guns with Rall's regiment fired only six times, when men or horses were disabled; those of the Lossberg regiment were left in a marsh.

Order was soon lost, men left their ranks, and the two regiments were all confused; many officers were killed or wounded; Rall himself fell from his horse with two wounds and Lieut.-Col. Scheffer took command. Of Lossberg's regiment only five, of Rall's only four officers, were left; Lieut.-Col. Brethauer was wounded.

Lieut.-Col. Scheffer advised with Majors v. Hanstein and Matthäus and they agreed that the only thing left was to cut a way out. Under continuous fire, they drew the two regiments out of the town, on the road to Maidenhead; but the bridge was cut off by the Americans in two lines, with their artillery, forming a half circle around the town, so that it was impossible to break through. To avoid a further useless loss of blood, the rest of these regiments surrendered.

Very much the same was the course of affairs in the southern part of the town. Here Knyphausen's regiment lay; on the alarm, it rallied and formed in front of the quarters of Major v. Dechow, on the

Princeton road. The major waited for orders, and as the fire increased, detached a company to ensure the communication between the town and the bridge, and another to hold the entrance from Princeton.

With the three remaining companies he moved off toward the upper town, to support the regiments attacked there. As he got part way, Rall rode up and ordered him to move to the left, to the church, and hardly had he moved in that direction before Rall's regiment came back, driven by the heavy fire of the enemy. Here Rall tried to draw off into an orchard, to protect his men from the destructive fire; the Knyphausen regiment followed and was joined again by its two detached companies.

When Rall went forward to attack with his two regiments, Major v. Dechow, who saw there was no hope, again fell back, in order to get to the bridge, and hold it, or, if it was taken by the enemy, to recapture it and, if possible, maintain communication with Donop.

Just at this important point, Dechow was severely wounded. At the same time, the two regimental guns stuck fast in a marsh, and valuable time was lost in halting to drag them out. When the regiment at last moved forward, it came out on unknown ground, through a deep hollow, and finally on a hill covered with trees, behind which the creek flowed. Here the regiment halted. Staff-Captain Baum went in advance to consult the major, but as he came in front of the regiment, instead of the major he met

Captain v. Biesenroth, who told him that the major had ridden over the hill to make a favorable surrender with the enemy, as the two other regiments had already been captured and the bridge taken. Both officers disapproved the major's conduct, and consulted as to some way of breaking through. To force a passage over the bridge was impossible, and they tried to get across the creek. Capt. v. Biesenroth, as senior, took the responsibility. The staff-captain was the first to spring into the water, followed by the non-commissioned officers, so that when they got over, they could carry over the colors and thus save them. The water was up to their necks and the opposite bank was so steep that it was hard to get up. Others crossed at better points. Some succeeded; more, however, fell on the way. At the same time, those who had crossed found that the enemy's guns were posted on the opposite hill, in front of the regiment, so that it was cut off and captured. The part that had crossed reached Princeton. The English cavalry and the Yägers were also there. They had escaped by fighting their way through, but Lieut. v. Grothausen was reproached with having retreated too soon.

In two hours, all was over. Col. Rall had paid with his life the penalty of his carelessness, and left a dark shadow on his hitherto glorious career. Death had saved him from answering for his neglect, for Münchhausen says that if he had not lost his life, he would have lost his head. He died as a brave soldier; when he fell from his horse, two old non-commissioned officers raised and supported him; just then Washington came up and the two regiments presented arms. Pale and covered with blood, Rall surrendered his sword. In a few broken words, he begged Washington to be kind to his men, and Washington promised that he would, and in a friendly and sympathetic way tried to console him. He had the dying man carried to the house of a well-to-do Quaker family and commended him to their care.

Before Washington left Trenton, in company with Gen. Greene, he visited the dying man, and both generals expressed their respect and regret. Rall again asked that his captured men be kindly treated and their effects returned to them, and this was sacredly promised.

Rall died the same evening and was buried with due ceremony in the Presbyterian church-yard. One of the officers of Lossberg's regiment said that he died gladly, rather than outlive his honor.

Little can be said in defense of Rall. The night before the attack he had been carousing, and he was still in bed when the first shots were fired. Lieut. Biel, his regimental adjutant, had been up since five o'clock, and on hearing the firing, hurried to the colonel, but could hardly waken him, much less get him to act. Biel hastened to the main guard, where Lieut. Sternickel was posted with 40 men, and sent him, with all the force he could spare, to support the picket. Hurrying back to the colonel's quarters, he found him in his night-shirt, lying on the window; to the question, " What's the matter ? " the adjutant asked if the colonel had not heard the firing, and Rall answered that he would come at once, and was soon at the door, in uniform.

Biel said later, at the investigation, that Rall paid no attention to his duties, and only cared for his pleasure. The adjutant had to attend to the correspondence. One post the colonel had never visited, and he never advised with his officers. He worried officers and men by all sorts of annoyances and kept 300 men always on duty. The men were worn out, and he neglected to give them time to clean their arms.

When Major v. Dechow called his attention to the want of shoes and asked him to order them from New York, Rall replied, " That was nonsense; he would lead the brigade in bare feet over the ice to Philadelphia, and if Major Dechow did not want to share the honor, he might stay behind."

When Major v. Hanstein asked if there were to be good winter quarters in Trenton, Rall answered, " Oh ! we'll get those in Philadelphia."

On the other hand, Rall was a warm friend and good comrade. Biel wrote home that he " mourned his death; that his bravery at Fort Washington had secured the command at Trenton from Howe. He was more a friend than a commander." Another officer wrote in his diary, " Rall was a good soldier, but not a good general. He had courage to execute the boldest things, under orders, but wanted cool presence of mind to take the necessary measures at such a time as the attack at Trenton."

Gen. v. Schlieffen says that Rall showed the greatest courage in his early campaign, under Orloff, as volunteer in the Russian war with the Turks, but paid with his life the penalty of underestimating the enemy at Trenton.

He fancied that his name alone would keep him safe. There is a report that Rall was betrayed by his host, a Dutchman named van Dassel, who brought four strangers to a supper given by Rall on Christmas eve. When Rall woke up, van Dassel fired at him, but missing him, hit the servant who held Rall's horse. The four strangers were said to have been American officers. Van Dassel was seized by Emmerich, the leader of the Hanau volunteers, and sent to New York.

A few days before the attack Rall was visited by some men who said they had property near Trenton and wanted his protection. They, too, were officers from Washington's camp, who were gathering information for him.

Tradition says that Rall surrendered to his own uncle, who had emigrated many years before, from the Pfaltz, and was then a colonel in the American army.

The Hessians showed in this critical affair all their old courage and fought as well as possible. If they had been better led, no such bad fortune would have followed. Rall either lost his head, or would not retreat before the enemy he despised. As his well-disciplined troops rallied promptly, he had time to pass the bridge, to get into the open country, and to fall back to Donop's quarters. Instead, he pressed forward to attack the Americans and failed, and while he was thus engaged, leaving the place, it was occupied from the other side. When he changed his plan and tried to regain the town, he was between two fires, and lost a regiment entirely.

There was no good leadership; no combination. The Hessians fought as long as they could — not to save themselves, but as a duty, which they fulfilled to the last minute. The enemy recognized and acknowledged their bravery.

Washington, in his report of December 27th, to Congress, said: "The advance guard made a slight resistance, and, considering their number, held their position as long as was possible, and in retreating kept up fire from the cover of the houses. We saw the troops form promptly, but from their movements it was clear that they were uncertain what to do."

Another American officer commends the bold resistance of the Hessians, and says they were in a position where the bravest soldiers had to yield.

But for the detachment posted on the north, not a man could have escaped—and this was left there by accident; for the order was to relieve it every morning and double the force on the south. Major v. Dechow, who was officer of the day on the 25th, failed to give the necessary orders; when it was reported to him that the two guns assigned his command were ready to move, he said he did not need them, and the horses were unharnessed, and the ruin was all the more complete.

At Burlington, where Donop stood, Cadwalder made a demonstration, not intending to attack, but only to prevent help being sent to Trenton. Donop, generally so cautious, allowed himself to be led on and followed the Americans to Mount Holly. He pursued with the greater part of his force—the Forty-second regiment, the Grenadier battalions of Linsingen and Block, and a Hessian Yäger company under Captain Ewald. The last-named officer had already turned the left flank of the enemy, taken two light guns, and cut off a hostile force which had crossed the stream that divides Mount Holly in two parts.

When Donop heard the cannon at Trenton, he recalled Ewald, and so the latter was obliged to lose his captures.

Donop drew his detached forces together at once, and tried to reach Crosswicks, so as to keep open the road to Princeton, where Gen. Grant had a force. To cover his retreat, he left Ewald with a rear guard of 90 men—Scots, Grenadiers and Yägers—and with positive orders to hold the place until the last man had fallen, and at all hazard until midnight. The task was a difficult one; the inhabitants were bitter enemies of the royal cause, and Ewald knew that arms and ammunition were hidden in the village—

the native population could use them at any minute on his little band.

There were two bridges which made the approach of the enemy easy. Ewald showed his energy and readiness by the way he acted. He covered the bridges and the nearest houses with straw, and then summoning the leading people, told them that the moment there was any outbreak he would set fire to the place. As Mount Holly was a well-to-do village, and the shops were full of valuable goods, his precaution was effective, and he remained undisturbed until midnight, then withdrew and joined Donop at Crosswicks. Ewald had no intention to burn the village, but his threat enabled him to hold it quietly.

The loss of the Hessians at Trenton was 17 killed, 78 wounded, 84 officers, 25 musicians and 759 enlisted men prisoners—in all, 963; besides the Yäger battalion, 398 men escaped. Major v. Dechow died in Trenton, soon after, of his wounds. Lossberg's regiment suffered most; it lost 27 killed and wounded— Captains v. Benning and Riese, as well as Lieutenant Kimm, were killed; Captain v. Altenbockum, Lieutenants Zoll and Schwabe wounded. Many of its officers were left sick or wounded in New York, and it brought to Philadelphia only 199.

The Americans lost only two killed, two frozen, and four or five wounded.

If Washington's plan of a surprise had been carried out, it would have cut off those who did escape, and might have ensured the capture of Donop, although he was more watchful than Rall. Washington had divided his force into four bodies; one, of 2,500 men and 20 guns, he led on the evening of the 25th, across the river nine miles above Trenton. Once over, he detached Gen. Sullivan, with a strong force, to go around and to attack Trenton on the south. Gen. Ewing was ordered to cross the Delaware a mile below Trenton, to seize the bridge over the Assanpink, and to cut off the retreat of the garrison to Bordentown. Gen. Putnam was to cross, with Gen. Cadwalader, at Burlington, and make a feint attack on the lower posts of Donop's command, so as to prevent help being sent to Rall. The two, however, were prevented by the heavy ice from crossing all their force.

Gen. Putnam could only send Col. Griffin, with 500 militia, across—much too small a body to meet Donop's 2,000 men—so he was ordered only to hold them and prevent their going to Trenton. The plan succeeded, and Donop followed the retreating enemy to Mount Holly, twelve miles from his own position and eighteen from Trenton.

The misfortune that befell the Hessians is not due to Rall alone, but to the British generals, who separated their forces at such distances. The outposts had neither the necessary communication with one another, nor sufficient supports. Howe acknowledged this in his report of December 20th, to Lord Germain, in which he said " The troops are scattered too much, but the loyal inhabitants of Burlington and Monmouth county want protection." Others reproached him with sending the Hessians so far into the country, when, through their strange language and the rumor of their cruelties, they were so much hated. The fact was, that they were more feared than hated —and this was shown by the greater kindness shown to the captured Germans by the natives.

The Hessians who were so hardly treated by the fortunes of war at Trenton, had a bitter experience in the sudden change from victory to defeat and imprisonment.

In Cassel it was reported that of 8,000 men, only 800 had escaped, and the whole of Germany was stirred up by the news.

The bitter feeling of the Americans against England and her allied troops might well cause harsh treatment of the prisoners, and this was sometimes the case, but there were many instances of kindness.

During the fighting, a body of soldiers moved forward and formed with their flag; Washington, who thought it was to make further resistance, ordered his men to prepare to fire, when one of his adjutants called attention to the fact that the flag was reversed, in sign of surrender. Washington rode up and received the salute, and, after saying a few kind words, ordered an escort to take the prisoners safely across the river. The officers, twenty-four in all, were left in a little ferry house, while the men, with little food or clothing, were taken to the other side. In the morning, they were all taken to Newtown, where the other prisoners filled the churches, prison and other buildings. Col. Weedon was in command, and showed much kindness. The officers were paroled and quartered in private houses. They paid their respects to Lord Stirling, who had been taken by the Hessians at Long Island and exchanged. They had treated him very kindly, and he tried to return it. He said, " Your Gen. Heister treated me like a brother, when I was his prisoner, and I will do what I can for you." He took them to Gen. Washington, who invited many of them to dine with him. He was a very gracious host, and at table told one of the Hessian officers that the American force was 6,000 men, with 14 guns and two howitzers. He received the Hessian officers with great courtesy. A Hessian officer says in his diary: "His countenance is not that of a great hero; his eyes have no fire, but a friendly smile when he speaks inspires love and affection. He is a courtly man of fine aspect, polished and somewhat restrained; says little, has a shrewd look, is of middle height and a good figure." Among the officers there, was the one who had been at the first outpost attacked and gave the order to fire on the Americans. Washington was particularly attentive to him, praising his conduct, but spoke of the unfortunate Rall with the greatest consideration and sympathy, and took no notice of the somewhat harsh criticism by the young officer of his commander. In Lieut. Widerhold's diary he says: " On the 28th we dined with Gen. Washington. He did me the honor of talking with me about the battle at Trenton, and when I said frankly that we had managed things badly, and that we ought not to have been captured there, he asked what I would have done. I pointed out the mistakes on our side, and how we could have escaped, and he praised me for this and for my watchfulness, and for my stout resistance with my handful of men. He also gave me leave to go on parole to Trenton to collect my effects left there in the retreat."

The prisoners did not stay long in Newtown, but were sent on the 29th and 30th to the southern provinces—the officers being separated from their men. The prisoners were sent to Virginia, as yet not the scene of any hostilities, their journey being through Philadelphia, and five wagons being given to the officers. Great crowds gathered at every place to see the dreaded Hessians, whose reputation had spread far and wide. Many expected to see wild robbers and murderers, with terrible angry faces—devils in human form—and beheld only neat soldiers, preserving, even in their misfortune, cleanliness, order and discipline. They were looked upon with astonishment, and sometimes with real or affected anger, and then they were abused and even stones were thrown at them.

In Philadelphia, many of the officers paid their respects to old Gen. Putnam on New Year's day, and were received in a very friendly way. One of them says: "He gave each of us his hand and we must drink a glass of Madeira with him. He may be an honorable man, but only the rebels would have made him a general."

The officers were escorted to Baltimore and were assigned to the village of Dumfries. They began their march on January 18th, escorted by Lieut. Lindenberger, a German, a cabinet-maker by trade. The Potomac was frozen so that wagons could cross it. The country was wild and woody, the journey very severe, owing to rain and bad roads.

On the 24th, they reached Dumfries. The inhabitants are described in the letters of a German officer printed in Schlözer's Correspondence, as very hospitable. The German officers were involved in the quarrel over the exchange of Gen. Lee. Washington thought Lee was hardly treated in having a sentry posted before his door. As Howe would not accept Washington's terms of exchange, nor yield to the threat of reprisal, in March, 1777, the six staff officers of the Hessian prisoners at Dumfries were put under sentries, too. This lasted until August, when the British Gen. Prescot was captured in Rhode Island. As he was of equal rank with Lee, their treatment was improved, and on the 27th August they were released from close confinement.

When the British fleet appeared in the Chesapeake, the imprisoned Hessians were sent from Dumfries and Lancaster, where the enlisted men were quartered, some 80 miles further inland, to Winchester, a place of 150 houses, mostly wooden, where the officers were quartered in hotels. At the end of September, Congress decided to send the officers to Staunton, a hundred miles south of Winchester, and to send 300 of the men to the latter place; but as it was reputed to be a very poor place, the officers petitioned Congress to be sent to Fredericksburg, and on the 30th September, they were ordered to Millerstown, to wait the answer. There they found it impossible to get quarters for twenty-eight officers, and some were sent to Stowentown[?].

On December 8th, Congress granted the request to go to Fredericksburg. The Hessian officers had gained the confidence of the Americans, so that each was allowed to choose his own time to go there. Some went by way of Dumfries and renewed acquaintance with old friends there. On the 13th, they were all in Fredericksburg, and as quarters could not be found there for the whole number, some went to Falmouth, an attractive village on the other side of the Rappahannock, and found the stream and its shores very romantic and attractive.

At the end of February, the Hessian and British officers were allowed to go on parole to Philadelphia, to be exchanged by Gen. Howe.

The enlisted men left New Frankfort on the 1st of January, 1777, and on their way were frequently threatened with violence by the mob.

Corporal Reuber says, in his diary: "Big and little, young and old, looked at us sharply. The old women cried out that we ought to be hanged for coming to America to rob them of their freedom; others brought us bread and wine. Washington had ordered our American guard to march us through the whole city [of Philadelphia?], but the mob was so rough and threatening that the commander said, 'Dear Hessians, we'll go to the barracks,' and then drove the mob off."

Washington quieted the people by posting a notice in which he said the Hessians had not come voluntarily, but under orders, and they should be treated as friends, not as enemies. This had the best result, and the prisoners were loaded with food and every kindness shown them. Each man received a pound of meat, with bread and vegetables, daily.

On the 8th of January, the men were taken to Lancaster, where they worked during the summer on the farms. Congress paid them in money the value of their rations, and the farmers gave them their meals and pay besides; but any one who allowed a Hessian prisoner to escape was fined two hundred paper dollars. The non-commissioned officers remained in Philadelphia.

On the king's birthday, June the 4th, the British troops imprisoned in the barracks at Lancaster celebrated the day with great excesses, finally driving off the guard of fifteen men, and were only subdued when a regiment and some guns were brought up and, opening fire, killed and wounded some of the prisoners.

The Hessians kept quietly out of the fracas, and

were all the more kindly treated by the Americans, but greatly abused by the English.

On the 25th of August, an English fleet landed men on the Elk river, and the prisoners were ordered further into the interior, but as there was no time to collect the men scattered on the farms, many of them escaped altogether—there were 300 Hessians. The prisoners reached Baltimore September 30th, where they were as badly received as in Philadelphia, but the commander of the escort gave the signal to rally to their defense and marched the prisoners out of the town, and at a safe distance had food and camp equippage brought to them. When the Virginia border was reached, the Pennsylvania escort refused to go any further, fired off their guns and went home. The escort from Winchester had not arrived, and the American commander was left with his prisoners in a wild country; but he had won their confidence, and he went on alone to Winchester to hasten the escort, leaving them for three days to follow on the prescribed route, and when the American captain finally joined them again, with the Virginia escort, there were all the Hessians, and only a few of the British prisoners had gone. The American was so pleased that he treated every Hessian to brandy, while the British looked on. The fugitives were nearly all captured and surrendered to the authorities. At Winchester, the American commended the Hessians so warmly that they were quartered in private houses, while the British were put in prison, and the Hessians had six hours of freedom daily, while the British could not go out without a guard.

On August 26th, 1778, the prisoners marched back to Philadelphia, reaching there on October 14th, then on the 22d going through Trenton, reaching Princeton and Brunswick on the 28th, where they were exchanged and received by a British commissary and sent to the Hessian camp on Long Island.

"At last," writes Reuber, " we were once more with our fellow Hessians. What pleasure and joy thus to be free from slavery!"

## CHAPTER IV.

The Brunswick troops marched, like the Hessians, in two divisions. The first left Wolfenbüttel on the morning of February 22, 1776, consisting of

| | |
|---|---|
| The Dragoon regiment under Lieut.-Col. Baum, . . . . . . . . . . . . . . . | 336 men. |
| The Grenadier battalion, under Lieut.-Col. Breymann, . . . . . . . . . . | 564 " |
| The Infantry regiment, "Prince Frederick," Lt.-Col. Prätorius, . . . . . . | 680 " |
| The Infantry regiment of Col. v. Riedesel, Lt.-Col. v. Speth, . . . . . . . | 680 " |
| The general staff, . . . . . . . . . . . | 22 " |
| Total, . . . . . . . . . . . . . | 2,282 " |

The command was given to Col. Frederick Adolph von Riedesel, Freiherr of Eisenbach, a good and experienced soldier, who had fought as officer of Hussars and adjutant of the Duke of Brunswick in the allied army in the Seven Years' War, and won a name for himself. He enjoyed the well-earned confidence of his sovereign, the confidence of his superiors and the love and obedience of his men. He belonged to a wealthy old family, which is still respected.

In addition to the detail given in Eelking's Life of Riedesel, many facts of interest are found in the diary of Brigade-Major v. Papet, in two volumes, coming down to the return to Germany.

The troops marched through the city of Brunswick with a great display, reviewed by the reigning duke and by his brother Ferdinand, the hero of the Seven Years' War. With an army of 12,000 men, Brunswick found in the English money paid for its troops the only way to avoid bankruptcy, and yet the duke hesitated to agree to the English terms. He died in 1780. The Hannoverian Gen. Braun welcomed the Brunswick force on its arrival in Hannover, and Col. Faucit, of the British army, mustered it into that service. Riedesel received his commission as major-general.

During the whole march, there was not a single desertion. For the numerous recruits, there were two daily drills. With the general staff and 77 soldiers' wives, there were in all 2,367 Brunswickers on board the ten vessels anchored in the Elbe. Two hundred and fifty Hannoverian volunteers, for different British regiments, went along, under Lieut.-Col. Scheiter.

Gen. v. Riedesel went on the "Pallas," and on the 26th March the fleet set sail, anchored on the 28th at Portsmouth, where on the 30th four vessels joined with the Hesse Hanau regiment, 760 men, under Col. v. Gall. It was the Crown-Prince's regiment, for the crown prince of Hesse was also the count of Hesse Hanau, and carried on a law-suit for twenty-eight years with his father, as to their claims. The father, born in 1743, was a lover of art and science, owned a fine library, and needed the English money to help support his two extravagances—building and military. The son succeeded his father in 1783 and died in 1821, leaving an evil reputation on account of his avarice and his severity.

The English fleet welcomed the troops with every honor.. Gen. Phillips, with part of the English artillery, and Gen. Burgoyne, also embarked for Canada, thus making a large fleet. Gen. v. Riedesel received £5,000 from the English commissariat.

The fleet consisted of 30 sail, including the two frigates, Juno and Blonde, as convoys, each carrying 36 guns. On April 3d it sailed, and was joined at Plymouth by six transports, with the Twenty-first Scotch Fusilier regiment. On the 20th it met the English fleet of 40 sail, with the Irish regiments on board, going to Canada.

On May 12th, land was seen, and on the first of June Quebec was reached. Gen. Riedesel went ashore and returned with orders from Gen. Burgoyne—who was in command during the absence of Gen. Carleton—to leave the Dragoons and Prince Charles' regiment to strengthen the Quebec garrison, while the rest of the troops went on to Three Rivers. There

Gen. Riedesel paid his respects to Governor Carleton —one of the ablest and most popular of the British officers. He had entered the service in 1742, and was now about fifty years old. In 1759 he was quartermaster-general of Wolf's army. He had been wounded at the battle of Quebec, was brigadier-general in the expedition to Havannah, and after the war was made lieutenant-governor of Quebec. He was a man of great honesty and unselfish, winning the love and confidence alike of his men and of the Canadians.

Riedesel noted and reported to his sovereign the strained relations between Carleton and Howe—the former cold, calm and stoical, the latter proud and intoxicated by the favor and confidence of the king and his ministers, claiming all the credit for himself.

On June 6, Lieut.-Col. Baum disembarked, with the troops to be stationed at Quebec—then a place of 1,500 wooden houses, for it had suffered greatly in the late war, and Carleton had demolished 500 houses in the suburbs, to protect the town from a surprise. The north side was covered by fortifications of earth and wood, in great decay. They were renewed and armed with some eighty iron guns and some mortars, mostly taken from old men-of-war.

The year before, Carleton had been hard pressed to resist the American attack under Montgomery and Arnold—the former had fallen, and Arnold withdrew on receiving the news of the arrival of more British troops.

Carleton, on arrival of the Germans, determined to send them to the relief of Montreal, still besieged by the Americans, and Gen. v. Riedesel received command of a corps, consisting of the Riedesel and Hesse Hanau regiments, the Brunswick Grenadier battalion, the British regiment of McLean, a division of Canadian troops, and a band of Indians. He was to move up the south shore from Three Rivers, while Burgoyne went, with an English force, up the north shore.

The German general was not a little astonished at the Indian force, for he knew nothing of their customs or way of fighting, and had heard only bad reports of both. They were Abenakis, Iroquois, Utawas and Hurons, and to show their fiery temper they had painted their eyelids red, and smeared their new uniforms with red as a mark that they were to fight for life, or to the death. They were armed with long shot-guns and sharp knives, to use in taking scalps.

On the 7th of June the expedition started, reaching Trois Rivieres on the 11th. Here they learned of two skirmishes, on the 8th and 9th, in which Lieut.-Col. v. Speth, with part of Riedesel's regiment, had taken part. The Americans, with a force of 1,500 men, had made an attack on Frazer's corps of 300, and were making preparations to surround it. Their guide was a royalist, who led them so far out into the forest, that Frazer had time to bring reinforcements from the fleet and turn the American position.

The Germans now formed the left wing of the army and the whole force advanced to Montreal, which the Americans abandoned, and on the 15th the Twenty-ninth (British) regiment took possession of the city and island. The German troops marched to Vergeres (or Verchés), where Carleton had his headquarters, until he moved to Montreal, and Riedesel then put his force in cantonments.

On June 26th, Carleton established himself at Chambly, where the Americans, on their retreat, had burned a well-built fort. Fort St. John had also been abandoned by the Americans, and both were now rebuilt.

The English plan was to move the northern army, under Carleton, to Lake Champlain, drive the Americans out of the forts, and push on to the Hudson. A southern corps, under Lord Howe, should move up the Hudson from New York and join the other at Albany. Col. St. Leger was to make a diversion, by going to the right from Oswego to the Mohawk valley and so to Albany, to rejoin the main body. He was to engage Schuyler's force of Americans, take Fort Stanwix, and destroy the other forts on the Mohawk—thus, if successful, cutting off the northern from the southern provinces, and ending the war.

The British worked hard at getting ready boats for transportation across Lake Champlain, and the Americans, under Gen. Gates and Gen. Arnold, increased their fleet and strengthened their defenses, Crown Point and Ticonderoga. News from Europe and the southern provinces came slowly to Canada, letters from Germany were often eight or ten months on the way, and of the Second Brunswick division nothing was known.

The troops under Riedesel suffered greatly from sickness, due to the trying climate, in spite of his efforts to secure them fresh vegetables and good food. He lost a few by desertion, but the officers amused themselves and exchanged civilities. Burgoyne was a guest at a great dinner on the birthday of the Duke of Brunswick.

The German soldiers were trained in the American method of target practice and fighting in loose order. Riedesel was slow to give up his old preference for the methods he had seen at home, but finally saw the advantage of the new system.

Col. v. Speth, on August 12th, took a detachment of 200 men to St. Johns, where a depot of supplies was established. On August 31st, Captain v. Pausch came with the Hesse Hanau artillery, to La Prairie— six light guns, four officers and 126 artillerymen. In the night, between the 4th and 5th of September, Riedesel received word that 5,000 Americans in 400 boats had landed above Isle aux Noix, and at once returned from Montreal, but the Americans had withdrawn, and Col. Breymann was sent, with his Grenadiers, to establish a camp near Fort St. John, while a camp at Savanna was fortified, and in addition to the Hanau artillery, six English guns were served by the German artillerists.

The German corps under Riedesel consisted of the Grenadier battalion and the Riedesel and Hanau regiments, 1,300 strong.

The English corps consisted of over 6,000, including 1,000 Indians and Canadians, while Col. St. Leger was to form a separate corps.

The Second Brunswick division having reached Quebec on the 17th of September, the Dragoon regiment was, at Riedesel's request, added to his force, and 390 boats were assigned to him to transport his command.

---

The Second Brunswick division, under Col. v. Specht, consisting of the regiments of v. Specht and v. Rhetz, the Light battalion of v. Barner and a Yäger company, had embarked at Stode on May 30th.

Specht, in his journal, says that the men came very gladly. With the division, came Quartermaster Bär and Chaplain Kohli — the latter volunteering, and giving up a comfortable position in the church.

At Plymouth, it joined the Second Hessian division and the Waldeck regiment. The transport fleet consisted of 19 sail, convoyed by two men-of-war, the Amazon and the Garland. Sailing on May 26th, it reached Quebec September 14th. The supply of provisions was so small and so bad that 19 men died and 131 were sick of scorbutic diseases.

Gen. Carleton pushed forward the advance, so as to escape the early winter. On September 23d, Brigadier Fraser received orders to move, with the force assigned him, from Isle aux Noix to Riviere la Colle and there establish a post. The head of his column, consisting of Indians, Canadian and English volunteers, went to Point au Fer.

On the 28th, the German brigade were ordered to Isle aux Noix, and 103 boats were assigned for their transportation. Gen. Burgoyne established his headquarters there, by order of Gen. Carleton.

Riedesel had not yet gathered together all his German troops, and only on October 13th did the second division reach Fort Chambly, and earlier in the month the Dragoon regiment got to Sorel. Many loyal Canadians joined this column, most of them in their ordinary costume — a long, white oversuit, a long shotgun, a powder-horn and a knife at the side, and a pocket-full of ammunition; their little baggage in two-wheeled carts.

Gen. Burgoyne led the First English brigade, consisting of the Ninth, Twenty-first, Thirty-first and Forty-seventh regiments, with the German brigade as its left wing, the Grenadier battalion and the regiments of v. Riedesel and Hesse Hanau.

On the night of the 4th of October, Gen. Carleton sailed with his little fleet to Point au Fer. His nephew, Captain Carleton, moved up the left bank with his Indians, and Captain Fraser led another corps of Indians and Canadian volunteers.

Gen. v. Riedesel received orders to remain at Isle aux Noix until the arrival of the Second English brigade under Powell. New works and magazines were erected, and supplies brought from St. John.

Gen. Carleton burned with impatience to meet the enemy on the water, and on October 10th received news that the Americans were at Great Island, and at once started to capture them. The dark and foggy night favored their escape, but of 16 vessels with 100 guns only five small boats reached Crown Point—some were taken, others beached and burned; the men escaping to the woods. Gen. Arnold was in command and showed great courage, but v. Riedesel, in his journal, reports that he set fire to his boats in such haste that he did not remove the wounded, and they were burned to death—their cries being heard above the crackling of the flames and the noise of the guns.

On the 12th, a boat reached Isle aux Noix with eight wounded men, a British naval lieutenant and a drummer of the Hanau artillery, which had taken part in the fight. Lieut. Foy, of that force, had saved a twelve-pound battery and put it on Captain Pausch's boat, with a loss of two killed, two drowned and a number wounded.

On that day, Gen. v. Riedesel received orders to move, with his five regiments, to Riviere la Colle, relieving the English brigade, taking ten days' provisions, and sending a Brunswick Yäger company by land on the west side.

On the 15th, Burgoyne ordered the Brunswick force to Point au Fer, leaving a staff officer and 300

## In the American Revolution. 97

men at Riviere la Colle to forward provisions, while Burgoyne advanced with his first division.

On Carleton's advance, the Americans had retreated from Crown Point, after setting fire to the works, and they were still smoking when the allied troops entered, on the 14th. Carleton established his headquarters there, and on the 20th Gen. Burgoyne came on the "Washington," one of the vessels captured from the Americans, with orders to go into winter quarters.

The Germans were posted from Trois Rivieres to Chambly, on the west bank of Lake St. Peter, between the St. Lawrence and Richelieu rivers. The Hanau artillery was ordered to Montreal, and the other forces distributed in different villages. The ground covered by them was necessarily very extended—the Brunswick troops over thirty-three German miles. German head-quarters were established at Trois Rivieres, the smallest of the three Canadian cities, with 250 houses, 1,200 inhabitants, an Augustinian convent and an English barracks for 500 men.

On October 22d, Carleton moved his troops to the assigned posts for the winter, abandoning the fort at Crown Point, for want of material to provide quarters for the garrison. The Americans had established a permanent camp at Ticonderoga—their force had diminished from 10,000 to 7,000, so weak that Brigadier Fraser, with a small force, drove 150 oxen from under the entrenchments without a shot. The troops were quartered in the houses of the inhabitants, with as much regard as possible to their comfort and that of the owners. All seigneurs, curés, captains of militia, and post houses, were exempt. The soldiers received every thing free, and had no right to ask for any thing more without paying for it. The men were obliged to cut wood in the forest, but the landlord had to bring it to the house. Each man received daily one-half pound of meat, half fresh, half salt, bread and necessary vegetables for soup, etc. The troops were kept in strict discipline, and on leaving the officers were obliged to give a strict account of their conduct.

On December 7th, orders were issued from headquarters at Montreal, assigning points where the troops could rally, and giving them orders to be constantly ready to move. The loss during the winter was a small one, three officers and 83 men covering that of the Brunswick division up to the middle of November. The winter opened mildly, and was long spoken of as the German winter; not a shot was fired and the men fished and hunted for amusement. At the end of February and beginning of March the German force was inspected by Captain Foy, and Gen. Carleton expressed his satisfaction with their good condition and exemplary conduct. By the end of December, eight feet of snow lay on the ground, and warm clothing had to be supplied to protect the men, who showed great endurance.

1777.

## CHAPTER V.

With the new year, Great Britain looked for more help to break the revolt of its colonies. A New York newspaper reported that more troops were to be got, and that the following negotiations had been completed, with

| | | |
|---|---:|---|
| Wurtemberg for | 3,000 | men, |
| Hesse Cassel | 2,500 | " |
| Mecklenburg | 3,000 | " |
| Ansbach Bayreuth | 1,000 | " |
| Sachse-Gotha | 2,000 | " |

while Russia had refused very tempting offers. Of the German courts only Hesse Cassel, Hesse Hanau and Ansbach Bayreuth would come to terms, and the following were fixed on, viz.:

| | | |
|---|---:|---|
| Hesse Cassel | 13,467 | men, |
| Hesse Hanau | 1,080 | " |
| Brunswick | 4,300 | " |
| Ansbach Bayreuth | 1,285 | " |
| Waldeck | 670 | " |
| A total of | 20,802 | " |

Hesse Cassel and Hanau were to lend their Yägers as light troops.

Parliament voted for this year further subsidies of five million pounds, of which

| | |
|---|---|
| Hesse Cassel was to get | £336,932 |
| Brunswick | 149,720 |
| Hesse Hanau | 18,181 |
| Ansbach Bayreuth | 39,588 |
| Waldeck | 17,370 |
| The Artillery | 26,053 |
| For Provisions, etc. | 41,427 |

Hesse Cassel was also to receive £6,617 for extra subsidies, and Hesse Hanau £1,013 — and the artillery was also to get an additional payment for the past year. For the Yägers sent the year before,

| | |
|---|---|
| Hesse Cassel got | £36,728 |
| And for the Artillery | 13,973 |
| Hesse Hanau, for its Artillery | 3,383 |
| And for an additional Yäger regiment | 16,326 |

Lord Howe offered to every American volunteering for two years in the British army, as an officer, 200 acres, as an enlisted man, 50.

The recruiting for the Hessian Yäger corps went on well during the winter of 1776–7. Only experts were taken, and they were to be well paid and cared for. After giving each man a Louis d'or, as the volunteers grew less, the premium grew higher — for foreigners, four Louis d'or; for natives three, and for each recruit, one. A recruiting office was opened in Waldau, near Cassel, under Captain Romstädt. The men were not forced; all enlistments were voluntary. The Yägers received better pay, were free from work on the forts, etc., and were well armed and well clothed.

Hesse Hanau sent a Yäger corps, 500 strong, in four companies, under Col. v. Kreutzberg; Hesse Cassel two new Yäger companies, under Major v. Prüschenk.

Once embarked — after nine of the Hessians had been formally betrothed — storms scattered the fleet, and one vessel was taken, with its 60 Hessian Yägers, by an American cruiser, and brought to Boston; some were exchanged at the close of 1778, others not until the end of 1780.

The Markgraf Alexander, of Ansbach Bayreuth, made a treaty with the British government, providing for a subsidy for six years, in return for two regiments, 1,100 strong, one from Bayreuth, the other from Ansbach, with light infantry and artillery in due proportion.

This was the prince who, in 1791, ceded his little territory to Prussia, and spent the rest of his life in England, where he married Lady Craven, dying there in 1806. He was a kindly man, who did his best to relieve his land from the heavy burthen of debts imposed on it by his predecessors.

The Bayreuth regiment, 600 strong, under Col. v. Voigt, consisted of five companies, including one of light infantry, one of Grenadiers, and one of artillery — in its ranks was Döhla, whose diary is full of interesting details. The prince reviewed the regiment at his capital, Ansbach, where it was joined by the Ansbach regiment, Col. v. Eyb, who commanded the brigade. Characteristic is the fact that all went well on the march, until the men were put on boats on the river Main, and then finding themselves uncomfortably crowded, and believing that they were to make the whole journey to America in the same close quarters, they broke out into open disorder and left the boats, declaring that they had sworn to serve on land, but not on water. The people around gave them wine, and the soldiers wandered away in all directions. The light infantry stuck to their colors, and tried in vain to force the fugitives back into the ranks. There was sharp firing and noisy disorder for several hours, until the Grenadier company, under Capt. v. Eckert, charged on the scattered men and finally brought them back, with a loss of 40 men in the Bayreuth regiment.

The prince himself hurried to meet the soldiers, reassured them and accompanied them part of their further journey. The charges of cruelty made against him by recent sensational writers, are met by the fact that Döhla, one of the soldiers, in his Diary, published in 1811, dedicated to one of his comrades, Holper, mentions nothing of the kind.

The prince made handsome gifts to the men to procure comforts for their voyage, and supplied them with tobacco and food and liquor, in addition to the regular supply from the British commissariat. One pound of meat, two pounds of bread, vegetables, rice, meal and wine, with beer and brandy at cost, were good rations, and a special transport, laden with food, accompanied the fleet, and at Portsmouth fresh stores were laid in before starting to cross the ocean.

The German light troops soon rivalled the American riflemen in their sharpness in learning to make use of the advantages of the ground and to avail themselves of every opportunity to gain a knowledge of the movements and strength and plans of the enemy.

Desertion among the Americans was greatly on the increase, and a Hessian officer wrote that almost daily bands of thirty to forty — in one day, indeed, 266 — came into the British lines, some of them bringing their officers along by force.

Brunswick and Amboy were held by the British, but the Americans threatened them on all sides — Cornwallis was too weak to take the offensive, and Howe remained quiet for six months, while an inferior enemy, only twenty-five miles from his headquarters, constantly disturbed his outposts.

At the outset, a large part of the population of New Jersey was loyal, but the British generals changed this by their harsh methods — punishing alike men of all opinions, in their effort to destroy all supplies that might fall into the hands of the Americans.

At first, the Germans were charged with cruelty, but it was found that they were strictly acting under orders, and in the attack on Trenton, an order was found from Gen. Howe to Col. v. Donop, directing the destruction of all supplies that might fall into the hands of the enemy.

Donop and Ewald were good disciplinarians, and their troops were not nearly so much given to excesses as the American militia.

Tired, at last, of a wearisome and trying defensive, Cornwallis decided to act on the offensive, and on April 12th attacked the enemy at Bound Brook. Captain Ewald, at the head of a small detachment, drove the force in front of him into a field fort, which was finally taken by a larger body from the rear. At another time, near Raritan Landing, he captured a force much larger than his own, by a clever *coup de main*. His example so influenced his men, and all under his orders, that there were numerous instances of great personal gallantry and brilliant feats of arms, which won the applause alike of friend and foe.

While Howe and the other high British officers had enjoyed their winter at ease in New York, the troops on the border had been sorely tried. The Waldeck regiment, with a detachment of dragoons, occupied Elizabeth during the hard winter and suffered greatly. On January 5th, a detachment of 55 men, under Capt. Haak and Lieut. Heldring, was taken, and soon after another of 30 men was captured. Withdrawn in January to Amboy, the post was almost nightly alarmed, and it was not taken to Staaten Island until the end of June.

Howe waited for reinforcements and for orders from London, which ordered him to capture Philadelphia and make the southern provinces the seat of war. He asked for 15,000 men and ten men-of-war to carry out the plans, was promised the half, but got 3,000.

On June 3d, the reinforcements reached New York, among them some hundred Hessian light infantry — a much-needed addition—and some German artillerymen. The whole British force was rated at 24,700— enough, said Münchhausen, to drive off the rebels, but not to go right on into the heart of the country.

Howe's plans — or want of them — were sharply criticised by the Germans serving under his command. The capture of Philadelphia was his first business. From the 8th to the 11th of June, he drew together at Amboy his forces — British, Hessian, Ansbach Bayreuth and Waldeck troops, including the Guard and Prince Carl regiments, from Newport; later on, the Germans were placed in an entrenched camp on Staaten Island. His force now joined that of Cornwallis at Brunswick, leaving the Ansbach Bayreuth, Waldeck and Fifty-fifth British regiments, under Maj.-Gen. Campbell, at Amboy.

On the 14th, the army moved from Brunswick in two columns, one under Cornwallis, with Col. v. Donop leading, the other under Heister. The former drove the enemy before him, under Gen. Stirling, but the Americans held their main line and Howe did not venture to attack. He retreated to Amboy on the 22d, and Washington sent a large part of his force in pursuit, which attacked Cornwallis, who, with the Hessian and Ansbach troops, resisted and then drove the enemy; the Ansbach light troops, under Capt. v. Grammont, showing great courage and skill.

Howe had thrown a pontoon bridge across to Staaten Island, when he learned the welcome news of the American advance. He prepared at once to move against them, sending Cornwallis with the right wing, Donop in the advance, Howe with Heister, with the left, to unite and attack the left of the Americans, and seize the heights which they had abandoned.

Howe detached four battalions, with six guns, under Cornwallis, who struck the American force. Vaughan's brigade next joined in the attack. It included the Hessian battalion, made up of the remains of Rall's brigade, after its defeat at Trenton, and was under Lieut.-Col. Kochenhausen — and later under Lieut.-Col. v. Schick and Col. v. Loos — and was attached first to Donop's and then to Stirn's brigade.

The Americans, after a long fight, were driven in disorder back to the hills, with heavy loss — Minnigerode's battalion alone capturing two new guns and eighty prisoners, and its commander received a decoration from his prince, who, on receipt of Knyphausen's report, in September, sent him the reward, which was received in New York in the spring of 1778.

Capt. v. Dinklage, in his diary, says the German loss was a small one. The want of gunners was made good later by the arrival of 164 artillerymen.

Washington at once withdrew to his former strong position, but the British had one substantial gain in the capture of a large amount of fresh provisions.

Howe made a very favorable report to Lord Germain of the conduct of the German forces engaged in this operation. He withdrew to Amboy and gave up his plan for crossing the Delaware, to avoid having the American army in his rear. They pressed him sharply near Amboy, and a strong force was sent out on a reconnoisance towards Elizabeth — including 300 Hessian (Yäger) light cavalry, which had just arrived, but, like the Brunswick dragoons, without horses, which were to be supplied in America; but as this could not be done, they served as infantry.

In New York, Gen. v. Knyphausen commanded, succeeding Heister, who went back to Cassel, nominally on account of his age and infirmities, but really because he could not get on with Howe. With Heister went Col. v. Block and Col. v. Horn, Lt.-Col. v. Schreyvogel, and some invalid officers and soldiers. He was treated with due honor, sailing on a British transport of 10 guns, escorted by a man-of-war. He reached Cassel in October and died there on November 19th. Born in Homburg, Hesse, in 1716, the son of a Hessian captain, he served in his native army and later in that of France, then returned to that of

Hesse, fought in the Seven Years' War, was aid to the crown prince of Brunswick, and was respected alike as a man and a soldier.

## CHAPTER VI.

Howe gave up his plan to march through New Jersey to Philadelphia, and secretly arranged new plans with his brother, the admiral—leaving Clinton in New York, with 600 men. He had 18 regiments of infantry, and of his 16,000 men, over 4,400 were Germans. A part of the Hessian light troops were mounted, but the officers could hardly get the necessary horses.

On July 23d, the fleet of 264 sail started on an eastwardly course, in six divisions; the fifth and sixth carried the Hessians. Taking a southerly course, it reached the mouth of the Delaware on the 30th, but going seaward again after a severe storm, on August 15th it anchored off Cape Charles, in Chesapeake Bay, and after a violent storm, reached the head of Elk, where the forces were at length disembarked.

The army numbered 17,000 men, divided into two corps; one he led, the other, Knyphausen. Howe had three Hessian Grenadier battalions, and the Hessian and Ansbach Yägers; in all, 9,000 men. Knyphausen had Stirn's brigade, and, with the British troops, 8,000 men. A capture of some tobacco-laden vessels gave the men a welcome addition to their scanty supplies.

On the morning of the 28th, a small knot of American officers were seen reconnoitering, and Washington was recognized at their head. Howe started with 3,000 men in pursuit, and captured two officers, who belonged to the volunteer corps of the Marquis d'Armand; one, v. Üchtritz, was a former officer in the Saxon army, who had resigned, to find his fortune in America.

On September 1st, Knyphausen advanced, reaching Iron Hill on the 3d, and the advance, under Cornwallis, with the Hessian and Ansbach light infantry, met the enemy, six hundred strong, under General Maxwell.

There was a sharp struggle, in which Capt. Wreden and Lieut.-Col. Wurmb led their men bravely, finally driving the enemy, with a heavy loss.

Howe praised Wurmb and his officers, and mentioned them in a general order, and gave the men a handsome money reward for their gallantry at Crutchley's Mill.

On the 3d, the two columns united at Newark, and on the 9th again moved separately — Knyphausen going to the left, to the Brandywine, where Washington held a strong position, his left at Chadd's Ford, his right at Dilworth. The passage of the stream was covered by two batteries of light guns, and part of Maxwell's corps was posted in support. General Armstrong was two miles below, to defend another ford. The American force, besides the militia, was 17,000 strong.

The serious nature of the struggle was fully recognized — the British risked being cut off from the fleet and their supplies; the Americans the loss of Philadelphia. Knyphausen was ordered to march, with his division, to Chadd's Ford, and to attack, but not in force, the enemy's left, while Howe and Cornwallis turned his right; this done, Knyphausen was to make a vigorous forward movement, simultaneously with the main body. He marched early on the 11th, and at ten A. M. met a body of 600 riflemen; these he drove back, but they were reinforced and a warm engagement ensued. Knyphausen then moved up the rest of his column on the right and left, the Hessians holding the center. The advance consisted of the English Light Infantry and a hundred men of the German Guards, under Captain Le Long, and, followed by the main body, they moved steadily forward and attacked the Americans with the bayonet, and under a heavy artillery fire finally, about 11 A. M., drove the Americans across the Brandywine.

After keeping up the appearance of action with growing impatience, Knyphausen finally heard the signal that Howe had completed his movement, and at once moved forward, driving Maxwell and Wayne, with the loss of five guns, until they retreated to Chester. Part of Knyphausen's force moved to the left and struck a part of the enemy's right, which had been broken by Howe.

Cornwallis had gone to the left, on the Lancaster road, crossed both branches of the Brandywine, and formed three columns for attack — in the first the Guards, the British Grenadiers, the Light Infantry, and the Hessian and Ansbach troops; in the second, the Hessian Grenadiers and the Fourth brigade; the third was to act as reserve. The advance was formed of the Hessian and Ansbach Yägers and a force under Ewald.

The movement was easily made across the Brandywine—although Ewald says that a hundred muskets and two field pieces could have held them all day, or forced them to find another ford higher up—and moving around the enemy's right flank, came in on the rear of the Americans. After four o'clock the attack was made and successfully, and Howe followed it up with repeated bayonet charges. The English Grenadier battalion and the German Grenadiers lost their track in the thick woods and did not take part again in the action.

Night was beginning, and as Howe had no news from Knyphausen, he decided not to continue the pursuit. Ewald, to his great regret, was obliged to see a force of the enemy quietly fall back in safety, when, with a regiment and a gun, he could have cut it off.

While Howe's two forces had succeeded, it was without any concert of action or knowledge on either side of what the other had done.

Washington reported his defeat to Congress, while

one wing of his army retreated to Chester and the other to Philadelphia.

The Hessian Yägers and Grenadiers, and the Ansbach Yägers, and the Hessian Light Cavalry, just mounted, won great praise for their gallantry. The Hessians lost Capt. Trautvetter, Lieuts. Dupuy, v. Trümbach, v. Lissingen, and v. Baumbach; and the Ansbach Light Infantry lost Lieut. v. Förstner, and many men killed and wounded. Of the eleven guns taken, there were three Hessian guns that had fallen into the hands of the Americans at Trenton.

Captains Ewald and Wreden were decorated, and Bickel was promoted to be a commissioned officer, for their distinguished actions.

Howe did not know how to use his victory, and neglected to turn it to advantage by prompt pursuit.

Lotheisen, a regimental quartermaster, says in his diary, that in Philadplphia he was told that the Americans fled in such disorder that an energetic pursuit would have captured enough to have put an end to the war.

The British were so careless in their advance that it was only owing to Ewald's activity that the American rear-guard failed to drive off in disorder the advance of the pursuing column.

The German military criticism was well expressed by Gen. Ochs, a Hessian who, as a subaltern, had taken part in the battle: " Washington was right to fight for his capital, and that not under its windows, but at a good distance; but he was wrong in trying to put his raw troops forward to fight experienced soldiers on a footing of equality."

Howe remained idle for two days, his patrols gathering prisoners, and on the 13th moved to Wilmington and later to Chester, where the troops lay until October 21st.

Finally, on the 18th, Knyphausen moved towards Philadelphia, and after joining Cornwallis, the column crossed the Schuylkill and drove off Wayne's force. Col. v. Donop was ordered to cross French creek, and sent Capt. v. Westenhagen, who drove the enemy so gallantly as to earn Howe's special praise.

On September 25th, the enemy moved in two columns to Germantown, and Cornwallis, with six British and two Hessian Grenadier battalions, went to Philadelphia and at once threw up batteries on the land and water front.

The British army was weakened by detachments sent in various directions, and Washington, who was in camp on Skippack creek, sixteen miles from Germantown, decided to make an attack.

The British line had its left on the Schuylkill, its center and head-quarters in Germantown. Knyphausen commanded the left, with Stirn, Gray and Agnew. Col. v. Wurmb covered the front of the left wing with his Yägers, at the mouth of the Wissahikon. Gen. Grant commanded the right wing, with its advance thrown well forward.

At 3 A. M. on the 4th of October, the British outposts on the right wing were sharply attacked and finally driven back into the village, where they took refuge in a stone house [Chew's], which they bravely defended, refusing all demands to surrender, and giving Gen. Grant time to bring up his main body, while the Americans became confused and disordered.

Howe himself was promptly on hand, hurried up the Grenadiers of Minnigerode and Donop's regiment, placing a force on the left flank, which was also threatened.

Cornwallis brought reinforcements from Philadelphia and joined in the pursuit of the retreating Americans.

While Howe speaks slightingly of this engagement, the Hessian officers, in their diaries, describe it at considerable length. Lotheisen says: "Münchhausen, of the Guards, was adjutant-general for Howe, and gave the order to the Guards and Donop's regiment, which were under arms, to march to Germantown, where heavy firing was heard. He acted on his own responsibility in doing so — and wisely, for on their arrival the Americans fled, were pursued for three or four miles, the two guns taken in Germantown were re-captured;" and Dinklage, in his diary, speaks of the good fortune of his regiment, the Guards, losing next to nothing, but helping to secure the substantial result.

In the "History of the Hessian Light Battalion," it is claimed that the promptness of the Hessians saved the army and turned a defeat into a substantial victory.

The English — both generals and historians — fail to do justice to the German troops.

Col. v. Wurmb, unlike the British officers, kept strong patrols out on his front and repelled an attack of the Americans.

Howe almost lost his head — he had, it was said, ordered a retreat to Chester, and it was rather a surprise than a battle, which was only saved from becoming a serious disaster by the prompt gallantry of the German troops. Howe's carelessness was the cause —he neglected to pay any attention to Ewald's warning, through Col. v. Wurmb, of a report of an attack by the Americans, and refused to credit a like story told by a captured American.

Howe had made a bad choice for his camp, refused to pay attention to the Hessian warning, and had no connection with his fleet, as the American fleet still held the Delaware.

Washington had attacked in four columns; two he directed on Germantown, the third between Germantown and Philadelphia, to cut off Cornwallis from reinforcements; the fourth was to take him in the rear. The heavy fog interfered and prevented the successful execution of the plan. Detachments were sent to New Jersey, to establish batteries and attack Fort Mifflin, on Mud Island.

On October 21st, Col. v. Donop went on his unlucky expedition to Red Bank. The object was to get control of the Delaware and open it for the British fleet, so as to secure free communication with the army.

Reedy Island was on the Jersey shore, and Fort Mercer stood on it. Col. Christopher Green, a very capable officer, had been sent there by Washington, with a force of Continental troops.

Opposite, on the Pennsylvania side, was Fort Mifflin, on Mud Island, separated from the main land by a narrow channel, and strengthened by war vessels, floating batteries, etc. Some works were thrown up against it and manned by Hessians.

The Americans made several attacks, but were always repulsed by Capt. v. Stamford, with the Grenadier battalion of v. Linsingen.

The English commander determined to seize Red Bank, and gave the order to Donop, an intelligent and bold soldier, and his force included the three Grenadier battalions of v. Linsingen, v. Minnigerode and v. Lengerke, Mirbach's regiment, which had been ordered up from Wilmington, four light companies, including Wangenheim's, a dozen cavalrymen, some artillery and two English howitzers.

Donop recognized the heavy task entrusted to him and asked in vain for more artillery, but Howe said that if Donop could not take the fort, the British would. Donop was angry at this reply and sent back word that the Germans had courage to do any thing, and to his associates he said: " Either that will be Fort Donop or I shall be dead."

On October 21st he left Philadelphia for the last time, made a round-about journey, riding with some artillery officers to reconnoiter. He found that he could approach the fort through a thick wood on three sides undiscovered. The fort was a pentagon, surrounded by a high embankment, and thirty paces in front of the glacis was a strong slashing. A small hill beyond was held with a redoubt. The works were quite extensive.

Donop placed the eight-pound guns and the two mortars on the right, and in support, Minnigerode's battalion and the Light Infantry; v. Mirbach's regiment in the center, v. Linsingen's battalion on the left; v. Lengerke's battalion and some Yägers on the Delaware, to guard against a landing and to protect his rear. Before each battalion there were sappers and a hundred men carrying hastily-gathered fascines, led by a captain.

Donop, at 4 P. M., sent a summons to surrender, with a threat of no quarter, if it was refused, and received a reply that the fort would be held to the last man. As the report was that very few men were seen in the fort, Donop decided to attack at once, and made a stirring address, to which the men replied: "We'll change the name from Fort Red Bank to Fort Donop;" and put himself, with his officers, sword in hand, at the head.

They charged gallantly, but soon found their road broken by deep ditches, and could move only singly; they were met with a sharp fire in front and flank from a covered battery and from two vessels in the river. Still the troops pressed on; v. Minnigerode had taken the outlying redoubt by storm; the Americans at first gave way, but soon stood fast, and before their fire Donop and Minnigerode and many other officers fell, casting dismay on their men.

Col. v. Linsingen succeeded to the command and did all he could to restore order; but the Hessians fell back in disorder. Dead and wounded were abandoned, and v. Linsingen brought the little remnant off under cover of the night, and on the next afternoon reached Philadelphia.

The fault lay with Howe, who had refused Donop's request for more artillery, had not supplied the necessary utensils for a siege — not even sending storming ladders or any means of scaling the walls — had taken no means to learn the nature of the position, and had, as usual, shown too little respect for the enemy.

Col. Greene had wisely acted on the suggestion of the French engineer, Capt. Duplessis, in withdrawing from the unfinished outwork and concentrating his strength in the fort itself — thus, too, misleading Donop, through the report of the small force that held it.

After the repulse, when the officers came out, Duplessis heard Donop's cry for help and at once took care of him. The Americans buried 180 and captured over a hundred wounded.

The Hessians lost 650 in all — among them Col. v. Schieck, Capt. v. Bojatzky, Lieuts. Riemann, Dupuy, v. Wurmb, Hille and v. Offenbach; Col. v. Donop, Capt. Wagner, Lieut. Heymel, and many slightly wounded; while the Americans reported their loss as 32.

The wounded were tenderly cared for by the Americans — Donop, especially, was treated with attention. He died October 29th, in his thirty-seventh year, and was buried with military honors. His death was greatly mourned, both in the army and at home.

Ewald says, in his "Essay on the Service of Light Troops," the attack was entirely unexpected, and if made promptly and in the right way, on both fronts, would have been successful.

Howe determined to gain the fort at any price; sent to New York for reinforcements, gathered at Staaten Island a fleet of 40 transports, with 4,000 men, among them the Bayreuth regiment, and abundant supplies, under convoy of two men-of-war, which reached the Delaware on November 10th, joined one division of Howe's fleet at New Castle, 150 sail, and the other at Chester, 200 sail, while the admiral's great 98-gun ship rode proudly at their head, as they moved up the stream, opening a heavy fire on the fort, and for three days and nights pouring in an unceasing storm of shot and shell.

The Americans abandoned the fort at Mud Island when it was in ruins, crossed the river and retreated to Red Bank, while the British troops were landed and joined Cornwallis in preparation for an attack. Every thing was ready, when, on the night of the 20th, the Americans abandoned and blew up their forts and ships.

Cornwallis sent out troops in pursuit, but finally withdrew again across the Delaware and returned to Philadelphia, entering the city with great military display on the 27th, and taking up position on the fourteen redoubts which covered the approaches on the land side. The Hessians were on the Schuylkill front, the main body quartered in the houses on the Neck, in a region reminding them of their native country.

The Americans tried to tempt the Germans to desert, and Gen. Putnam issued a proclamation in German, to which Captain Emmerick, commanding a German-loyalist volunteer corps, replied in a manner worthy of a German soldier and patriot.

Emmerick had fought bravely in the Seven Years' War, and after the peace, had settled in America. At the outbreak of the Revolutionary War, he returned to Germany, raised a volunteer corps for service under the British flag, and showed courage and skill in his conduct. In 1809 he took a leading part in a conspiracy against Jerome Bonaparte, king of Westphalia, and was executed. His name is still piously cherished by his countrymen as a sacrifice to his love of liberty.

Howe spent the winter with his army in Philadelphia, once making a reconnoisance in force towards Chestnut Hill, Whitemarsh and Edge Hill, trying to find a place to attack the American lines, and at another time across the Schuylkill, leaving Knyphausen in command; but Washington held his position at Valley Forge and prevented any real advance. Howe was greatly blamed for not using his strong force, well equipped and supplied, against the weak body of the Americans, suffering from want of the necessaries of life. Occasional exchange of shots, and some slight skirmishes, were the only active service.

On April 22d, Gen. Clinton relieved Gen. Howe of his command. Clinton himself had been in New York, with a force too small to do more than resist American attacks, such as that of Sullivan, in which the German troops were warmly praised for their gallantry.

Chaplain Waldeck, in his diary, says that one of the captured officers had two brothers serving with the loyalist provincial troops.

Cornwallis divided his force into four corps, to be sent each in a different direction through New Jersey, to capture cattle — as fresh food was growing scarce — and drive the Americans off.

Cornwallis himself, with Gen. Campbell and the Bayreuth and Waldeck Grenadiers, under Captain Seitz, and other troops, crossed from Staaten Island and moved rapidly through Elizabeth, when he struck Putnam's corps and drove it some distance, capturing 500 head of cattle and 1,500 sheep. Seitz covered the rear as it withdrew to New York.

In September, two new Hessian Yäger companies and some Bayreuth recruits joined their regiments. Among the new arrivals was the young v. Ochs, a volunteer, who subsequently became a general, and has left some interesting recollections of his experiences in America.

In October, the Bayreuth and Waldeck regiments were embarked on transports, to go up the Hudson to Burgoyne's relief, but soon after starting, came the news of Burgoyne's surrender, and the Waldeck regiment disembarked at Fort Knyphausen.

A detachment of the Bayreuth regiment, under Capt. v. Eyb, was forced to land and fight its way back to Kingsbridge, to escape the fire of the Americans from the shore.

Finally, the Waldeck regiment was sent to Staaten Island for the winter, and the Bayreuth regiment to the Delaware.

Gen. Clinton himself led a force, partly English, partly German, including the Hessian Grenadier battalion of Köhler, the Ansbach Grenadiers and Trümbach's regiment, and the Hessian Yägers, and landing at Stony Point, marched across country and made a simultaneous assault on Fort Montgomery and Fort Clinton, commanded by General James Clinton and General George Clinton. After a hard day's fight, both were taken — the two commanders and most of the garrison escaping, but leaving a hundred guns, a large supply of provisions and ammunition, and burning their ships at anchor.

The Ansbach Grenadiers and their Captain, v. Eckert, won Clinton's special praise. Eckert was desperately wounded and died in New York.

Lieut. v. Bentheim, of the Hessians, also fell, and the German soldiers, always favorites of Clinton's, were particularly commended by him for their bravery in this brilliant operation.

Razing the forts to the ground, throwing the guns and supplies, that he could not carry off, into the Hudson, he withdrew safely to New York.

## CHAPTER VII.

After a long and severe winter, Gen. Carleton began preparations for the campaign from Canada, which Gen. Burgoyne had planned in London, looking to the union of the two armies at Albany.

Gen. Carleton sent out small bodies of Indians to try to gather news of Howe's army, but with little success.

Gen. Riedesel, in a letter to the Duke of Brunswick, wrote that neither Carleton nor he had the slightest idea of Howe's plan, or of the whereabouts of his army.

Burgoyne arrived from England in May, but with no orders, other than one giving him the command of all operations outside of Canada, thus setting aside Carleton, who, in spite of his successes, was no favorite at court — he had asked for 30,000 men to carry out the plan which Burgoyne was ready to undertake with the small force in hand.

Even Howe was junior to Carleton, and Riedesel saw in this a reason for passing over Carleton in the choice of a leader.

Carleton transferred the command to Burgoyne,

and helped him in every way to prepare for the campaign, and Burgoyne promptly consulted Riedesel.

Carleton was to retain in Canada a force of Brunswick and Hesse Hanau troops, under Lieut.-Col. v. Ehrenkrook. Burgoyne was to take 3,600 Germans in his total strength of 8,000 men.

In June, a fleet of 39 sail brought German recruits and the wife of Gen. v. Riedesel, with her three little children. Her memoirs are among the most interesting and well-authenticated personal narratives of the war, and have endeared her name to many readers of many nationalities.

The army rendezvous was at Cumberland Head; the German corps, in two brigades, the left wing; the first brigade, under Col. v. Specht, the regiments of v. Riedesel, v. Specht, and v. Rhetz; the second brigade, under Col. v. Gall, the regiments Prince Frederick and Hesse Hanau. The Grenadiers, the Light battalion and the Yägers, under Lieut.-Col. Breymann, were the reserve, and the Dragoons were the escort at head-quarters.

The army was moved by boats across Lake Champlain in gallant array, while the Indians moved by land. Burgoyne gave their chiefs a formal reception, and the Germans were formally welcomed as brethren. At Crown Point the army landed, and there found two German families, settled there for many years. The Brunswick chaplain baptized two of the adults, who had for years been without the benefits of the church.

Burgoyne handed the command over to Riedesel, while he pushed forward with the advance, under Fraser.

Fort Ticonderoga was at last uncovered, with its two main works, Fort Carillon and Fort Independence, and an old French redoubt, all well manned with eight and six-pounders, and the old French lines, but the Americans, with their small force, had wisely made their defense within much less ground. Fort Independence had one thirty-two-pounder, six heavy guns, and twelve in its outworks — and palisades and ditches, with an outwork; while a floating bridge connected the two forts, protected by heavy chains. Heavy batteries protected both shores. The garrison of 3,500 men, under General St. Clair, an experienced soldier of the Old French War, was well supplied, and the French had named the fort a "cul de sac," so strong was it by nature and by its defensive works.

On July 1st, the army moved forward in two columns, the left under Riedesel, the right under Phillips. Breymann was with the reserve, and the German Dragoons were in the advance. At the first landing of the leading four German regiments, so little pains was taken to prepare a camp that the men were lost in the woods, and only by morning could they join their colors.

Gen. Phillips, following Fraser's advance, engaged the American outposts, while Riedesel moved at once against Fort Independence.

During the delay in preparing to attack, an American reinforcement, 800 strong, in spite of the Indians, entered the fort.

Captain Gerlach, with a hundred men, was sent on a reconnoisance, to cut off the line to New Hampshire. A battery was placed on a hill commanding both forts and bridge, and the Americans soon abandoned their strong position — Riedesel seizing Fort Independence and placing Breymann's corps there, and Fraser occupying Fort Carillon.

Eighty guns, 1,500 small arms, 5,000 tons of flour, 200 oxen and great stores of all kinds, showed with what precipitation the Americans had withdrawn.

The negligence of the Americans to defend Sugar Hill was heavily punished by the loss of this important post, which the French had defended at the sacrifice of 2,000 lives.

Riedesel was at once ordered in pursuit by land and the rest of the army by water — leaving the Brunswick regiment as part of the garrison to hold Ticonderoga.

Riedesel moved rapidly forward and soon found Fraser engaged. He put his Yägers into action and gave Capt. v. Geisan orders to turn the right flank of the enemy. They soon relieved Fraser, who heartily thanked Riedesel, his old friend in many hard-fought actions during the Seven Years' War in Germany.

Capt. Schottelius was commended, with the other officers, for gallantry in their first engagement.

A Brunswick Grenadier officer reported that of the

enemy, 2,000 strong, over 200 were captured — Brigadier v. Specht says 297.

Riedesel learned the advantage of the American method of fighting in open order, and issued orders to his officers to practice their men in this new system, thus adding a useful lesson to the strict German discipline.

Burgoyne decided to move directly to the Hudson and then to Albany. Riedesel ordered his officers to procure pack horses and relieve the men from the weight of their baggage during the severe marches.

American loyalists reported at the German headquarters, on July 21st, that the Americans had abandoned Fort George. Riedesel and Burgoyne had a long council at Skenesborough, where the Americans had burned the fort and magazine and mills, and destroyed their arms and provisions. Fifty German soldiers were left there to keep open communication between the army in its advance and the magazines at Ticonderoga.

The Americans abandoned Fort St. Anna and Fort Edward and had taken up their position at Stillwater, on the Hudson.

The Hesse Hanau regiment was left at Fort St. Anna, to forward much-needed supplies and establish bakeries and other means of furnishing food for the half-famished men.

August 3d, Burgoyne at last received and returned messages from and to Gen. Howe, and expectation was aroused of an early general engagement.

In the papers of Gen. Schüler von Senden there is a report of the general complaint of the route chosen by Burgoyne and of the unnecessary hardships inflicted on his men by the hard march through the wilderness.

To get a supply of cattle, Burgoyne ordered the Brunswick Lieut.-Col. Baum to make a hurried march to Bennington, partly to gather supplies, partly to make a diversion in favor of Col. St. Leger's movement on Fort Stanwix, by preventing Arnold from sending reinforcements.

Riedesel protested against the operation as being too late — he had suggested it in July — and as made by too small a force. He reported to the Duke of Brunswick that he hardly recognized his own plan, so much was it altered.

Baum was ordered to seize at least 1,300 horses, and the Brunswick Dragoons were ordered to go with him to ride the horses that he was to capture. They were utterly unsuited for the rapid march necessary for success. They were equipped with long, heavy riding boots, with big spurs, thick leathern breeches, heavy gauntlets, a hat with a thick feather; at their side a strong sabretasch and a short, heavy carbine, while a big pig-tail was an important part of this extraordinary costume. The poor Dragoons had already been the laughing-stock of the army, and now they were to carry their supplies with them.

Baum's corps was to consist of 200 Brunswick Dragoons, 40 Light Infantry, 60 Canadians, 140

Indians, and Col. Peters' force of 110 men, but these were replaced by men from the regiments of his left wing and Breymann's corps. Two Hanau guns, under Lieut. Bach, were added. Of the 551 men, 374 were Germans — 360 Brunswick infantry and 14 Hanau artillerymen.

Baum marched on August 11th, from Fort Miller, with Burgoyne's final orders to go direct to Bennington. On the 12th, he met an American force and captured eight men, and took a magazine. He soon reported to Burgoyne that Bennington was defended by a force of from 1,500 to 1,800 Americans, but so loyal that they were likely to retreat. His next message to Burgoyne was for reinforcements, and Burgoyne at once sent orders to Riedesel to order Breymann up — he was thirty miles off.

Instead of help coming, Baum saw the Americans advancing in strong force, and although assured by Major Skene that they were loyalists who would join him, and allowing them to get in his rear and to cut him off from the Canadian volunteers, Provincials and Indians, posted on a neighboring hill, he found himself sharply attacked. He held out for two hours, when his ammunition gave out, he was severely wounded, and finally surrendered.

Col. Stark, the American commander, praised the Germans for their stout resistance.

Breymann was on the way with 333 Brunswick Grenadiers, 288 of Baum's Light Infantry, and 21 artillerymen, with two field pieces, under Lieutenant

Spangenberg. He sent Captain v. Gleissenberg forward with the advance guard of 60 Grenadiers and Chasseurs and 20 light infantry, and then followed quickly, but soon met a large force, at first taken for loyalists. His men fought well, until the ammunition was exhausted, and then, obliged to abandon his guns, he withdrew, with a heavy loss. Captain v. Schlagenteuffel, with 29 Dragoons, were the only Brunswick soldiers that escaped. Baum died of his wounds and was buried, with military honors, in Bennington.

English and Americans both blamed the Germans for this disaster, but Baum and Breymann had acted in strict pursuance of their orders, and Burgoyne himself commended the persoual bravery of both officers and men.

The Americans were greatly delighted with their success, and soon gathered a force estimated at about 14,000, while the English lost so heavily by desertion that Burgoyne ordered the Indians to shoot every deserter, and to scalp, too.

Supplies were very scarce — a Brunswick officer wrote home: " The army is fed with bread made of flour sent from England and with meat salted there, and the difficulty of getting food brought to the front is incalculable."

Riedesel took position, with the regiments v. Rhetz and Hesse Hanau, seven miles from Fort Edward, to open communications with the magazines.

Early in September, Riedesel received word from

Gates of the loss of a number of Germans, shot down in what was thought to be a revolt, but turned out to be only an effort of the prisoners to escape from a falling building.

Lieut.-Col. v. Kreutzburg, who was with St. Leger, reported that the so-called victory at Oriskany was very doubtful, and, through Col. v. Gall, gave a very bad account of the condition of affairs on the Mohawk.

Many of the Indians had left Burgoyne and those from St. Leger then came to the main body, but were of little real help. The American army was strong in numbers and position.

Burgoyne at last advanced, the Germans forming the left wing, and after they had crossed the bridge over the Hudson, it was broken, thus cutting the last tie with Canada. The army was reduced from 10,000 to 6,000, with a very small supply of provisions. The 20 Brunswick Dragoons — all that were left — were mounted, but on very poor footing, for they were in need of every thing. Capt. v. Schlagenteuffet was in command of this, the only cavalry in the army.

Riedesel had shown his sense of the risk to be run in the advance, by sinking two boats at Fort Edward, to be raised and used in case of a retreat.

Burgoyne ordered an advance on the 15th of September, in three columns—the Germans the third, on the left. The route was on the high road from the Hudson to Stillwater. Breymann's corps was the rear guard and had orders to cut the bridges as soon as the army and its supplies were all across.

Burgoyne took the regiments of Specht and Hesse Hanau, under Col. v. Gall, and six guns, and moved forward to reconnoiter. No advance guards, or patrols or pickets, had been sent out — he wanted to strike the rebels on the head. Riedesel and the other generals were with him; 200 men went on to open the road and build bridges; the force moved a couple of miles, then went into camp until roads could be cut through the thick woods, bridges built and entrenchments thrown up; a further advance was made and still nothing was seen or learned of the enemy; on moved the army, and nothing could be heard from one wing to the other.

Burgoyne's advance guard was sharply engaged on the 19th, and when Riedesel heard of it, he reported his disposition of his force — his own regiment, with Pausch's two six-pounders, in support of v. Specht's regiment, which protected the advance guard and workmen.

Two Indians reported that an American regiment was advancing from the left. Burgoyne sent Riedesel orders to attack the enemy on the right, and he at once ordered Col. v. Specht to hold the position on the river, and with the advance, under Capt. v. Fredersdorf, went forward until he had reached a position from which he could see the American army in position and the two forces contending for Freeman's Farm, which was held now by one, now by the other, of the two armies. The Americans were well protected; the English in the open, and their supports not within effective distance — the Americans six times bringing up fresh troops from the woods that covered them. The English ammunition was nearly exhausted, their force heavily wasted.

Riedesel at once moved on the right flank of the enemy, then joined Burgoyne, and Pausch promptly brought up his two guns, which Riedesel posted in support of the English line, already wavering under heavy fire; sending his own regiments against the American position, forcing them to fall back, while Breymann successfully repelled an attack on the right.

The Germans had thus, for the second time, saved the English, and followed up their success by pursuit of the retreating Americans, until Burgoyne ordered them to stop — much to the discontent of the troops, and, according to Gen. Schüler v. Senden, simply because he did not know how to avail himself of the advantage gained for him, and the opportunity of gathering supplies from the rich country in his rear.

The English bivouacked on the field, where Gen. Arnold had necessarily abandoned most of the American wounded.

Not only did the Germans fairly win the honors of this engagement, but Madame v. Riedesel and the ladies with her worked hard to bring succor to the wounded and dying, and thus earned the gratitude of the men for their courage in the midst of the horrors that follow a battle.

## CHAPTER VIII.

The general officers rode over the ground on the day after the battle, September 20th, to find a good position. A redoubt was thrown up on the right, with Breymann's reserve to protect it. On the left was a hill which commanded the whole valley; the Hesse Hanau regiment was posted there.

Burgoyne pitched his camp between the English and German troops, Riedesel placed his on the height on the left. Posts and batteries were put at the openings of the line, a deep ditch protected the front, and heavy trees were cut down to cover the approach from all sides. Pickets were posted well out, and the bridges were defended with earthworks.

The Americans soon converted their position into an entrenched camp, so near that every sound could be heard in both camps; but the British were altogether unable to ascertain the strength of the enemy, which successfully prevented any effective reconnoisance.

On the 22d, Burgoyne received despatches from Howe, and reported to Riedesel that Clinton was moving to attack Gates. Burgoyne determined to remain for eight days, the time for further news from the south, and kept his men at work strengthening his camp.

The Americans did the same thing, and sent out a small force that captured the cattle and guards of the English.

Riedesel sent Captain Gerlach across the Hudson to reconnoiter, ascertain the strength of the enemy, the feasibility of getting away with the artillery, or of an attack on the enemy's right. Gerlach returned the same night, with a report that by help of the bend of the river he had got to the rear of the enemy's right, but that he could see nothing, except that their camp was in two lines, the river on their rear, no bridge, but fords through which patrols passed.

Daily attacks were made by the Americans on the outposts, but by cutting down the woods, preparations were made to resist them successfully. Hardly any patrol was sent out without losing some of its men. Provisions ran short, sickness rapidly increased, discipline diminished under growing hardships, desertion increased, in spite of the dreadful punishment inflicted on the deserters recaptured.

Burgoyne was daily losing popularity and confidence. He did his best to strengthen his magazine and protect his supplies, but on October 16th was obliged to reduce the daily rations to a pound of bread and a pound of meat. The men did not complain, and Riedesel was glad to find how patient they were.

The eight days taken by Burgoyne for news from Clinton had long passed, and he finally took counsel with Riedesel. An enemy four times his strength, in front of him, their position quite undiscoverable, the winter fast approaching — he proposed a flank movement around the left of the Americans and an attack on their rear, leaving 800 men to protect the camp, and it was inspected to see if it could be held for three or four days, but the result was very unsatisfactory — the works were too far apart — and it was decided that if the attack could not be made in one day, it would be better to abandon the camp, cross the Hudson, renew connection with Lake George, and open it with Clinton. This was Riedesel's suggestion and it was approved by the other general officers, but Burgoyne would not hear of a retreat.

On October 6th, the Americans made an attack on the left wing with 600 men and retreated in good order.

On the 7th, Burgoyne ordered 1,500 men to be sent on a reconnoisance, but the Americans met it with a sturdy resistance. Lieut.-Col. Speth, with 300 Germans, in the center, supported by the v. Rhetz and Hesse Hanau regiments, had the brunt of the fight, and Captains v. Fredersdorf, v. Gleissenberg and v. Dahlstierna, and Ensign v. Geyling, were among the wounded, the two Hesse Hanau guns were lost, and the whole detachment barely escaped capture. Breymann and Speth did their best to resist the attack on their position, and Speth, with some other Brunswick officers, fell into the enemy's hands.

The Americans fell back just when they had the key of the position and could have inflicted infinite injury by the capture of the magazine and supplies, although their attack was marked by a bravery that won the applause of the German officers.

At last Burgoyne gave orders for a retreat, and Riedesel was to lead the advance, abandoning about 800 sick and wounded, while preparations were made to cross the Hudson, when Burgoyne suddenly ordered it to go into bivouac, and after a day's delay, and abandoning his camp equipage, tents, etc., again moved forward, while Burgoyne made himself comfortable in his old quarters, Schuyler's house, in spite of Riedesel's earnest warning.

The Americans still pressed on, and Burgoyne, after setting fire to Schuyler's house and other buildings, found his retreat threatened on all sides, his boats and provisions captured, his force under fire, his outposts captured or driven in, and three batteries posted in the rear of his army, his supplies cut off, his troops losing courage and discipline, and the outlook hopeless.

Madame Riedesel and her children set an example of courage in this hour of trial that inspired all who saw her.

At last Burgoyne called Riedesel and v. Gall and his English brigadiers into council. Riedesel advised abandoning guns and baggage, and pledged himself to bring the army to Lake George. His offer was accepted and he urged an instant departure. Delay followed delay, and finally Burgoyne countermanded the order to move.

The next day, the 13th, all was lost. Another council was called, to which regimental commanders, too, were invited, and all agreed that to cut their way out would be a bloody sacrifice, but they were ready to make it. Burgoyne declared that it was too late. He took upon himself the responsibility — for which Riedesel thanked him—and opened negotiations with Gates for the surrender, which finally was agreed upon on the 16th.

Of the 5,800 men included in it, 3,500 were still able to bear arms, and of these the Germans counted 2,431.

Riedesel prepared a memoir, in both German and French, which on the 18th of October was signed by the brigade and staff officers of his command, to be submitted to the Duke of Brunswick and the public. In it he said that his reputation had been sacrificed by others. His friends at home were full of respect and pity and expressed their full confidence.

St. Leger had, in the force he took against Fort Stanwix, the Hesse Hanau Yäger company, under Lieut. Hildebrand, sent from Hanau in May, 1777, and landed in Canada in June and at once sent on this expedition. He lost tents, guns and supplies, and found his way back out of the wilderness as best he could.

Burgoyne was received with great courtesy by Gates, who had on his staff Col. v. Weissenfels, born in Konigsberg and long in the Prussian service.

Riedesel, by his wife's help, saved the flags of his regiments and returned them safely to Brunswick. He encouraged his men and acquitted them of all blame for their misfortunes. The actual surrender was made with the greatest consideration for them.

In Schlözer's Correspondence is a letter from a Brunswick officer describing, in a good-humored way, the contrast between the American army and that which surrendered to it.

The British forces marched by slow stages to Boston, with the loss of only a hundred deserters from the German troops. Madame v. Riedesel shared her husband's hardships.

The regiment Prince Frederic had been left at Ticonderoga, and was reinforced by 150 recruits on the day of the American attack, and successfully repelled it, as well as a second demonstration by a large force, thus saving Canada and the large magazine of supplies gathered for Burgoyne's army from sharing his cruel fate.

## CHAPTER IX.

The German prisoners were encamped on Winter Hill, in wretched barracks, built in 1775 for the American troops engaged in the siege of Boston, badly supplied with even the necessaries of life, officers and men stripped of their personal effects—Gen. v. Riedesel even lost all of his, although guarded at night by the militia, who perhaps helped to take it—and robbed of thirty horses, their private property. In violation of the terms of surrender, by which the officers were promised quarters suited to their rank, three and four were crowded into miserable corners, and Gen. v. Riedesel had to pay heavily out of his own pocket for lodgings in a tavern at Cambridge.

The promises of improvement in the quarters and care of the prisoners were violated. Officers and men did the best they could. The poor fellows were supplied with shoes that cost four silver dollars, at the expense of the officers, who shared their resources with them.

The camp was surrounded by sentries, who forbade all intercourse with Boston, while the officers were allowed on parole a limit of a mile and a half in other directions.

Gen. Heath was in command in Boston—a selfish, rough, rude man, who hardly hid his hatred for the prisoners in his charge. He paid a formal visit to the generals, and invited them to dine with him in Boston. He promised them, in his general order, humanity and kindness, but took no trouble to show them any.

The other German prisoners were scattered throughout Massachusetts, in private families, and the soldiers had to work for their food and clothing.

The winter was a very severe one, every effort was made to induce the men to desert, and especially to get those who were skilled artisans to benefit the Americans by their industry. Every device was adopted to get them to slander their comrades and to forget their duty. Some of them did, indeed, profit by the change, and found brilliant rewards for their new citizenship.

Gen. Riedesel and his officers did what they could to hold their men, but of course had no means with which to make their condition endurable.

Riedesel secured a comfortable house in Cambridge, belonging to a refugee loyalist, and as he was only a mile and a half from Winter Hill, paid daily visits to the soldiers, doing all he could for them. His health was greatly broken by the hardships and exposure of the last few trying months. Some of his officers had secured comfortable quarters, but they were constantly annoyed by the rudeness and brutality of the American officers. Riedesel established discipline in the camp of the prisoners, and secured them the protection of their own officers.

The Commissary department was entrusted by Gen. Heath, at Riedesel's request, to a special officer, Massereau, who made use of every means to enrich himself at the expense of the poor German prisoners. The guinea, which Congress had fixed at 28 shillings, was taken at 90 shillings in paper, and the prisoners could only get the paper at this rate for their gold or silver; the profit was the share of the commissary and the authorities at Boston.

While the British desertions, to the end of December, were nearly 400, the Germans lost only 20.

By the end of January, a much-needed supply of clothing came from New York, to help the men bear the cold weather.

After many efforts to secure the terms promised at the surrender, Congress finally, in the close of March, formally disapproved of them and refused to be bound by them.

The British, too, treated the Germans unfairly, for while many of the officers of the English force were exchanged, not a single German officer was, and Riedesel appealed to Washington, who gave him a kind answer, but reminded him that it was a matter belonging entirely to Sir William Howe. He bribed Massereau with 30 guineas, so as to secure better care for his men.

Burgoyne's release, in April, was conditioned on a deposit of $40,000, and this was made in food and supplies sent from Rhode Island, to the great benefit of the half-starved prisoners of war. Gen. Burgoyne thanked the Germans, through Riedesel, for their services, and promised to report their good conduct to the King of England on his return home.

Riedesel kept his men in good condition by constant exercise, frequent inspection, reviews and other employment, to protect them from the evils of idleness. He and his wife were greatly annoyed by the rude hostility of the Boston men and women of all classes, and even by threats of personal ill usage. He gave his men leave of absence for fixed periods, that they might go into the country and do farm work, both for their health and the little wages they could earn. By April the British had 655 men, the Brunswick force 116, the Hesse Hanau troops 41, off on leave on this plan.

Congress made a formal proclamation, inviting the Germans to desert, and Riedsel protested against it as an abuse of the position of prisoners of war, had the proclamation torn down, and the agents who were trying to persuade the men to desert put out of the camp, and the American officer in charge approved his course, saying that the proclamation was intended only to reach the soldiers in the field.

Lieut.-Col. v. Speth, on account of ill health, was allowed to go to New York, and on his way visited the German prisoners — giving, in a letter of April 28th, a sad account of their condition, starved, sick, ragged, hopeless and despairing.

Near Boston there were repeated examples of ill-treatment — a young Brunswick soldier of the Rhetz regiment, in trying to protect his wife, was brutally killed by half a dozen militiamen, and no punishment was ever meted out to them.

Gen. Riedesel loyally supported Gen. Phillips in his protest against the ill-treatment alike of English and German prisoners, and refused any favor that Gen. Heath showed him and his men. The good supplies sent from Rhode Island were taken by the Americans, who replaced them with their own very poor food, thus inflicting new distress and misery on the unhappy prisoners. Fifty Brunswick soldiers died in four weeks, from the results of bad food and intense summer heat, and the hardships consequent on frequent changes of quarters.

The sight of the British fleet off Boston threw Gen. Heath and the Americans into a state of excitement, and awakened in the prisoners a hope of release, but Howe's plans were all a succession of failures, although he really meant to do something for the men.

As the winter again approached, Burgoyne sent an officer with the promise of a supply of clothing, etc., from Canada *via* New York, but while it was daily expected, Gen. Heath issued an order that the men were to go to Virginia, a march of 650 miles, through a country full of hostile inhabitants, with no provision for health or comfort. Clinton had refused to supply the prisoners, and as Boston was heavily taxed to feed the French troops, it was thought best to send the prisoners southward, where food was more abundant, and where the climate would not be so severe for them.

The Germans were not a little discouraged at the necessity of a long march into a new region. They moved in three divisions, on successive days — the first included the Grenadiers, the Dragoons, and the Rhetz regiment, led by Major v. Mengen; the second the regiments of v. Riedesel and v. Specht, led by Brigadier v. Specht; the third consisted of the battalion of v. Barner, the regiment of Hesse Hanau, and the Hanau artillery, under Brigadier v. Gall. Major Hopkins was the commissary given to the Germans on their march.

Riedesel accompanied the first division for a time, and then returned to Cambridge for money.

The journey was tedious and trying, and the men found great difficulty in getting shelter or food in the thinly populated country through which they moved. Often bivouacking in the woods, without tents or cover, exposed to frost and rain, their condition was a wretched one.

At Salisbury, Gen. Riedesel sent them $70,000 in paper money, which he had secured at Boston on his personal responsibility.

Arrived at Fishkill, on the Hudson, Washington paid them the compliment of his presence, but he also gave them a strong guard, lest Clinton should carry out his threat of releasing them by force — for which purpose he had sent some frigates and troops up the Hudson, hoping to find an opportunity to force the post at Peekskill, and, with the help of royalist citizens, release the prisoners — but nothing of the sort was attempted.

At Newburg, Gen. Riedesel succeeded in sending, through Washington's head-quarters, money to supply the officers with forage for 165 days, and shoes and stockings for the men.

In December, they passed through New Jersey and Pennsylvania—and at Lancaster met a curious reception ; the story had spread that the King of England had given Lancaster to Gen. v. Riedesel as a reward for his services and that he was now come to take possession. The people were greatly excited, and it took some time to convince them of the truth.

On the last day of the year, they reached Virginia, and celebrated New Year's eve in a wild wood, with snow a foot deep, with no shelter and little protection.

By the 15th of January, they got to Charlottsville, where they were finally followed by Riedesel, who had travelled slowly, accompanied by his wife and children. General Gates, who had succeeded to the command of Boston, did every thing to make their journey comfortable, and showed them the greatest courtesy.

In March, 1779, Riedesel reported to the Duke of Brunswick the particulars of their change of quarters from Massachusetts to Virginia.

Riedesel lived like a native farmer, built a block

house, with furniture made on the spot, worked at his own garden, had horses and cattle, and his wife made a capital housewife. The heat was oppressive, and in a short visit to Frederick Springs for relief, he made acquaintance with some of Washington's family.

Few officers were left with the soldiers at Charlottesville, the former being mostly sent to Richmond — it was thought by them with a view to leave the men free to be persuaded to desert and find new and profitable employment in America. Riedesel appealed to Congress and to all others in authority in vain, and, instead of redress, got only evasive answers.

In June, the long-delayed baggage arrived from Canada, but in very bad condition, so that officers and men were really very little better off as to clothing, etc.

In September, Washington sent Riedesel word that he was to be exchanged and should go at once to New York. Turning the command over to Col. Specht, he did what he could for the future comfort of his soldiers and started, with his family and staff and servants, making 16 in all, and 20 horses and a number of wagons. His journey was interrupted by an order from Congress to go to Bethlehem, Pennsylvania, where he was detained for six weeks, with great discomfort—he was suffering, his children were sick, his wife was about to be confined, and he was not allowed even to go to Philadelphia.

When he finally arrived in New York, Clinton

informed him that the exchange had not yet been effected.

Riedesel wrote to the Duke of Brunswick, asking to be allowed to return to his command in Virginia, if the exchange was not completed. He said that in Georgia the British had 1,500 prisoners, and in New York 400 officers, all working hard for an exchange, and that Washington and the army were anxious for it, but Congress was constantly interfering to prevent it, and in a way that showed that no reliance was to be placed upon its promises.

When Riedesel arrived in New York, he found a number of Brunswick soldiers who had escaped and wanted to rejoin their colors, but no one would care for them. Some 50 Brunswick and Hanau soldiers had enlisted with a Captain v. Diemar, formerly in the Sixtieth British regiment, who was trying to raise a volunteer Hussar force, and who was thanked by the Count of Hanau for his kindness to the men, who were supplied by him with clothing and money after their hardships in rejoining their comrades.

After Riedesel's arrival in New York, a partial exchange was made, including 67 officers, with 149 servants, and 113 non-commissioned officers, leaving only 906 men at Charlottesville, and of the Hanau forces, 16 officers and 40 servants were allotted for exchange, leaving 296 men behind. The large proportion of servants was a pretext for getting the non-commissioned officers exchanged. Deprived of officers and non-commissioned officers, the men stood stoutly by their colors, and resisted the temptations held out to them to make their homes in America, with all the rewards offered.

The men made thmselves comfortable in their temporary barracks, surrounded themselves with gardens and such comforts and occupation as they could provide, built a church — with a graveyard, fitted up a theatre, had constant visitors from far and near, and made new life in the desolate little country village.

The men were left for eighteen months without pay, and Congress deliberately repudiated the terms of the convention under which they had surrendered.

Washington stood up stoutly for their rights, but La Fayette justified Congress, on account of English examples of bad faith, particularly at the surrender of Klosterseven, in the Seven Years' War.

## CHAPTER X.

The British ministry was ready to make every effort to end the war in 1778. Parliament voted it all the money needed for fresh allies, and Col. [now General] Faucit again went to the Continent to spend it for the soldiers he hoped to get there. But the reports from America were not of a kind to encourage new supplies, and the only prince who agreed to give his subjects for the British cause was the sovereign of Anhalt-Zerbst. The Elector of Hesse refused to send another corps, and was only finally persuaded to allow the voluntary enlistment of some companies of light infantry.

The Opposition, in and out of Parliament, were active in exciting hostility to these efforts to increase the force sent to America.

It was said that Russia was to lend 24,000 men, Switzerland 10,000, and the Emperor of Fez and Morocco 24,000 Moors, and that other smaller Asiatic sovereigns had promised their help.

The net result was that there went from Cassel 220 recruits and 23 Yägers, under three lieutenants and one ensign, and from Hesse Hanau and Ansbach 660 men, at the end of February, to complete the force already pledged.

In Parliament, the Opposition hurled contempt on the German princes and their troops; but Lord Suffolk retorted: "Who saved the kingdom from a French invasion in 1748? Who resisted the French from 1752 to 1762, and helped England to save Hanover, Brunswick and Hesse from submission and to win at last a satisfactory and honorable treaty? Who have enabled the British to hold their own in America? The German soldiers, who to-day are said to be worthy of no good word."

The German princes took every occasion to reward their officers and men, by conferring orders and distinctions on those who were reported as showing unusual bravery.

On May 11th, 1778, Gen. Howe announced that he was about to return to Egland, and would be succeeded by Sir Henry Clinton. On the 4th, he had held a review of the Hessians in Philadelphia, when seven regiments and fourteen batteries and the Yäger corps were commended for their splendid appearance.

Only twice during the war was such a force, so well drilled, seen together. The occurrence is specially mentioned in a manuscript history of the Hessian Yäger corps, by Capt. Mehlburger.

Festivals followed, one after another. On the 18th of May, the brothers Howe were made 'the special guests of a great display arranged by young Major André, called the Meschianza.

## In the American Revolution.

On the 20th, the corps of Lafayette, reported to be 6,000 strong, showed itself across the Schuylkill, and a great part of the British army was sent out, in three columns — the right and left to cut off their retreat, the center to march through Germantown and attack at once. The whole affair was a failure. The left column saw 3,000 men recross the Schuylkill, with the loss of only ten prisoners and hardly a shot fired — although a good many were drowned. After a rest of two hours, the British marched back again.

The force sent to Germantown was made up of English, Hessian and Ansbach troops. The brigade of Wölwarth was left in Philadelphia — it was afterwards known as v. Bose's, its new commander.

The Yägers moved on the 19th and 20th, through Germantown to Whitemarsh. The complete failure was said to be due rather to the incompetency of an English general than to the treachery to which he attributed it.

On the 24th, Howe embarked with all the honors due his rank. Before going he made special acknowledgment to Wreden and Ewald of the services rendered by them and their light infantry.

Clinton, who succeeded Howe, was deservedly popular with the German soldiers, for he spoke their language, had served in Germany during the Seven Years' War, and had been adjutant to the Duke of Brunswick; so that he and the Germans were friends of long standing.

He prepared at once to evacuate Philadelphia, which

was threatened by a strong French fleet, reported to be at the mouth of the Delaware.

Dinklage, in his diary, on June 3d, noted that for eight days there had been great excitement — every thing put on board the ships; merchants and many families already embarked; the streets, from being like a fair, were empty; all trade ceased, except the sale by auction of furniture set out in the streets; most faces were sad and anxious, but a few showed their hope of better things.

The fleet of 51 sail, with a convoy of men-of-war, carried away the cavalry and the South German regiments, 3,000 in all, to reinforce New York and Newport.

On June 15th, Stirn's and Loos' brigades were sent, with the baggage, through New Jersey, crossing at Gloucester, and camping at Haddonfield, where the rest of the army joined them on the 18th.

As the fleet sailed out of the river, the passage was barred by sinking old hulks. The sick and wounded were left behind, with a letter from Clinton commending them to Washington.

The movement of the British force across the river was largely made in open boats, but the Americans carefully avoided any interference with the retreating force.

On the 19th, the army moved on, in two columns, one under Cornwallis, the other under Knyphausen. With the former were the Hessian Grenadiers and the Guards; with the latter, the two Hessian brigades, v. Stirn and v. Loos, the Hessian and Ansbach light infantry, the Pennsylvania and Maryland loyalists, and the West Jersey volunteers.

On June 28th, the rear guard was attacked at Monmouth, and the advance, under Knyphausen, was also threatened, but he forced his way through.

Clinton found the enemy in large force on his flanks, and finally ordered an attack, driving the Americans from their first and second positions, but stopping when he found he had to deal with Washington and 20,000 men. He had effected his purpose — his baggage trains were in safety, his army concentrated.

The Hessian and Ansbach light infantry, under Wurmb, had been particularly distinguished by their conduct during this trying retreat, where, for three long weeks, they had been constantly under fire from the pursuing force. Lafayette and Pulaski had given them no rest, either day or night, and the Hessians had abundant opportunity for examples of personal valor and military ability.

A young Hessian subaltern, v. Ochs, who had joined as a volunteer in the past September, was so conspicuous that he was at once recommended for promotion, although he did not receive his new commission until two years later, September, 1781, when Wurmb made him his adjutant. This was the soldier who, later in life, as General v. Ochs, wrote his memoirs, in which he dwells on the useful lessons he had learned in the American war.

Captain Ewald, too, was particularly thanked by Clinton.

General Knyphausen showed great skill in protecting the baggage train, which stretched out over a line of twelve miles in length. With all his other cares, he was careful to save his old comrade, Gen. v. Steuben, who owed his life to Knyphausen's command to his men not to fire, when Steuben exposed himself at close quarters.

Clinton's army was only about 13,000 strong, but with the baggage it covered almost fourteen miles, so liberal was the allowance of personal effects — for British officers then moved with an unlimited supply, including mistresses, servants, etc., etc.

When at last the army reached New York, on the 8th of July, it had lost heavily by sickness and desertion — Ewald attributes both to the great hardships of this summer retreat.

The Ansbach and Bayreuth regiments were safely landed on Long Island on June 20th.

---

When France declared war against England in the spring of 1778, it changed the plans of the commander in America, for the French fleet was a new factor.

Clinton decided to strengthen Newport, and sent there, in July, a fleet of seventeen transports and two frigates. The troops landed in Newport, when the German soldiers were sent to Conanicut. The supply of provisions was very scanty and the men were put on short rations.

In New York, little was done, and Col. v. Emmerich undertook a surprise of Putnam's force, which ended very disastrously in the loss of 50 prisoners, and in the constant threat of attack that kept his force at King's Bridge in a state of alarm at all times.

Soon after Clinton's arrival in New York, the French fleet appeared off Sandy Hook, where Lord Howe was guarding the entrance.

The French sailed July 19th, in such haste that, instead of weighing their anchors, they cut their cables, and suddenly appeared off the coast of Rhode Island.

On the night of August 3d, a great fire in New York destroyed many warehouses and 64 dwellings, and a few days later a stroke of lightning exploded the powder on a vessel lying in the harbor and shattered many of the houses on shore.

In September, a fleet arrived from England, with 500 Hessians and 200 Ansbach and 100 Waldeck recruits.

While the troops were idle in New York, watching the movements of the fleets, as they came and went, the Yägers (light infantry) and Col. Emmerich were busy doing outpost duty beyond King's Bridge, constantly engaged with the pickets of Washington's force at White Plains.

An adventurous young Frenchman, Armand, formerly an officer of the French army, at the head of a force of trained sharpshooters and Indians, was constantly looking for occasions to harry the British force.

Emmerich, strengthened by Ewald, was able to give a good account of his force.

Ewald, in his book on Outpost Duties, dwells on his success in outwitting the Indians and giving them a lesson which deprived them of much of the terror they had once inspired in the Germans.

The Americans reproached the English for the use of savage allies, but were themselves glad to get the help of the Stockbridge Indians, who lost heavily in these successive engagements.

On the 23d of September, leaving their baggage in New York, the British army in New York moved out, one column, under Cornwallis, going southward across the Hudson into New Jersey, the other, under Knyphausen, across King's Bridge into Westchester county — this force included four Hessian Grenadier battalions, the Guard and v. Donop's regiments, and some light infantry; the Crown Prince's and v. Wissenbach's regiments followed in supporting distance. Passing Fort Independence, it advanced to the Phillipps house, where Knyphausen made his head-quarters until October 10th. His left and Cornwallis' right were separated by the Hudson, and communication was kept up by boats without difficulty.

On September 30th, Lieut.-Col. v. Wurmb sent out his pickets as usual, between Dobbs' Ferry and Tarrytown, and then ordered Capt. v. Donop, with 70 infantrymen and 20 mounted Yägers, on a foraging expedition. Donop sent Lieut. Bickel on his left to the Hudson, and Lieut. Mertz, with the mounted Yägers, on his right. The latter soon came across some American cavalry, and Donop hurried forward to his support, but Mertz was captured, with quite a severe loss, before the force sent by Donop could come to the rescue, and Donop himself had to retreat to a hill and look out for his own safety.

Early in October, the regiment of v. Seitz was ordered to Halifax, and the officers were handsomely entertained by Clinton. It embarked on the man-of-war Delaware, but as this frigate waited for the fleet which Admirals Byron and Parker were taking against the French, it was not until the 19th that the fleet of 100 sail started.

Instead of a cruise of three or four days, it was not until November 13th that Halifax was reached, and between bad weather, an unseaworthy ship, and a scanty supply of provisions, the German soldiers found this one of their worst experiences.

Clinton organized another expedition for the south, to seize Savannah, which was full of supplies for the American army, and weakly garrisoned. He sent the two Hessian regiments, v. Wissenbach and v. Trümbach, with other troops, making in all a force of 3,500 men, which sailed on November 27th, in a fleet under Commodore Parker, and reached Savannah on the 29th of December.

The German regiments took part in the attack on the American defences, which were soon captured, with a heavy loss on the part of the Americans, who at once abandoned Savannah, and the Hessian regiments were quartered there.

Augusta was soon afterwards taken, and attempts made to capture Charleston, but without success.

The v. Wissbach regiment was particularly distinguished by its capture of an American man-of-war, the Rattlesnake, of 16 guns, in Stono Ferry. On board of her were found guns and flags taken from the Hessians at Trenton. The former were at once handed over to the v. Wissenbach regiment, and the latter were returned to it on its arrival in Cassel. This fact is mentioned in the diary of Reuber, a non-commissioned officer, but he gives no explanation of how these flags, etc., happened to be on a man-of-war.

The v. Trümbach regiment was also very heartily thanked for its good and efficient service in this trying campaign.

At the close of the year, various promotions led to a number of changes in the Hessian regiments. In October, v. Bose, commanding the v. Trümbach regiment, was made major-general, and Col. v. Kospoth, of the Elector's—formerly v. Wutgenau—regiment, was also made a major-general, and the lieutenant-colonels, Köhler, Kurtz and Bremer, were made colonels.

The winter of 1778 was spent quietly at Newport.

The arrival of the French off the coast of Rhode Island aroused the forces there to new activity.

On July 26th, the "Falcon" brought news from Lord Howe and Gen. Clinton, to Gen. Pigot and Commodore Brisbon, that the French fleet had sailed, under Admiral d'Estaing, and might be looked for at any time.

Preparations were at once made for them, and the next day the fleet was seen off the entrance to the harbor, in stately array — twelve line-of-battle ships and four frigates, under the French flag, stretched from Point Judith to Brenton's Neck.

At the same time, intelligence came that danger threatened on the land side, for reports were received that the four New England provinces were organizing an army for the conquest of Rhode Island.

The Ansbach–Bayreuth regiment was brought over from the island of Connanicut, leaving only 50 men on duty there, marched through Newport and encamped at Windmill Hill.

Three ships of the French fleet sailed up the East or Second (or Seconset) River, but meeting a heavy fire from the batteries on the shore, came to anchor off Sachuest Beach.

On the morning of the 30th, the French line-of-battle ships passed the batteries on Connanicut and moved up Narragansett Bay.

The 50 Ansbach-Bayreuth soldiers left on Connanicut evacuated their post, after destroying their guns and ammunition, and rejoined their regiments.

The British frigates lying in the bay took shelter under the shore batteries, and the French opened communication by water with Providence, which soon sent out a fleet of small American vessels.

The three French frigates again sailed up the East River and anchored in front of the battery at Fogland Ferry, where the company of the Ditfurth regiment was stationed at Black Point.

The English men-of-war first sought shelter under cover of the batteries and were then set fire to and exploded in majestic splendor. Capt. v. Malsburg was in command on the land and saw the impressive spectacle. He was shortly reinforced by the Bünau regiment, which was afterwards relieved by the Ansbach regiment.

The British lines were strengthened, and supplies obtained by gathering into Newport all the live stock from the island, leaving only one cow for each household.

Eight British men-of-war were burned and thirteen sunk, in Narragansett Bay, to save them from the French fleet, as it swept on in its strength.

On the 6th of August, Newport was in a state of siege, and on the 8th the French fleet sailed, with its eleven men-of-war, for the harbor, trying to force an entrance under fire, and the remaining British frigates and an East Indiaman were burned, while the troops were drawn together near the town, but the sight of Howe's fleet altered the plans of the French and modified those of the British commander. The

Bayreuth regiment was sent three miles out of town, to meet a rumored advance of the American army.

On the morning of the 10th, Howe's fleet was in sight, but instead of a great sea fight, the two fleets were next seen sailing away.

The American forces retreated after hearing that the French fleet had sailed away.

On the 11th, the Bayreuth regiment took position on Tammany Hill, covering the left flank of the British line.

Three captured American officers reported that an army of 20,000 men, under Sullivan, Greene and Lafayette, was coming to coöperate with the French in the capture of Newport.

On the 15th, the American camps on Honeyman's and Beckham's Hills, some five miles from the town, were plainly seen. The British lines were strengthened with ten main batteries and natural and artificial defences connecting them.

On the 17th, the Americans opened fire, and on the 19th the two lines were sharply engaged, while the Americans strengthened their position and showed a determined front — evidently counting on a prompt return of the French fleet.

Threatened in front and rear, the British position was evidently one of great peril. The French fleet, reduced to 11 vessels, again came to anchor off Point Judith. The British tried to strengthen the spirits of their men — now deserting in large numbers — by reports that Clinton had defeated Washington's army and was on his way to the relief of Newport, supported by Howe's fleet.

On the 22d, the French fleet, finding that the British were still in undisturbed possession of Newport, sailed for Boston, to repair damages.

The Americans still pushed forward their preparations for a regular siege, opening fire from five batteries, but the British replied with great energy, and on the 27th three British frigates sailed into Newport harbor, with the welcome news that Gen. Gray was on his way from New York with 3,500 men on transports.

The Americans withdrew a great part of their batteries to the main land, leaving only three in position on the island.

A general attack by the Americans on the 29th was expected, and Gen. Pigot, hearing that they had evacuated, sent out a force of 2,000 men, including the Ansbach and Bayreuth regiments, to reconnoiter. The advance consisted of 147 men, of different Hessian regiments, under Capt. v. Malsburg. He says, in his report: "The commanding general ordered me to follow the retreating enemy, attack them wherever found, burn the houses of any residents that give false intelligence; reinforcements should be promptly forwarded."

Moving out the west road to Redwood Hill, Malsburg attacked the enemy in its redoubts and driven back, again renewed the attack on the right and drove the Americans from their position. Stopping only to secure help for Capt. Noltenius, who was severely wounded, v. Malsburg pressed on, driving the Americans before him, receiving a slight wound, but keeping on for five miles, until he reached the last American position, when — the supply of ammunition being exhausted — Malsburg put his men under cover behind a protecting wall.

The Americans opened fire from Barrington Hill with three batteries, and Lieutenant Murarius was wounded by it. Malsburg sent him to the rear, and then ammunition coming up, as well as some artillery, renewed the attack, but found the force against him too strong for his small command.

Gen. v. Lossberg arrived at this time, with four Hessian regiments, and sent the Bayreuth and v. Huyne regiments forward to his support.

The Americans, too, were largely reinforced, and outnumbered the British, who finally fell back.

Malsburg had been engaged from 7 o'clock A. M., until 4 P. M., but could not get reinforcements fast enough or numerous enough to help him maintain his advance.

The Americans kept up a heavy fire from their batteries, and finally, on the 31st, were safely withdrawn to the main land. Their abandoned position was promptly occupied by the Ditfurth and Elector's regiments.

Malsburg, in his diary, reports the loss of the Huyne regiment as 87, including Capt. v. Schallern and Capt. Wagner; the latter died of his wounds on the field and was buried with military honors in Newport. The other German regiments sustained heavy losses and were awarded great praise for their conduct.

On September 1st, the British fleet arrived in Newport, with 72 vessels, carrying 4,500 men, Gen. Sir Henry Clinton in command. He issued a general order thanking the troops, especially the Germans, for their gallant defense.

Clinton soon left, and later on Pigot was relieved by Prescott, while the command of the fleet was transferred by Lord Howe — who returned to England — to Admiral Byron, who in turn sailed on the 28th of September.

On October 12th, 400 men of the Ansbach-Bayreuth regiment, including 100 light infantry, arrived, as well as Major v. Dieskau, of the Royal Guards. They had left Ansbach on the 29th of April, were at sea twenty-two weeks, and many of the men had to be sent to hospital on their arrival in New York. Major v. Dieskau returned to Europe, with Lieuts. v. Wagner and v. Molitor, on the 17th of November having received their discharge.

On November 28th, the Ansbach–Bayreuth regiment returned to Newport. The Landgraf (Elector's) and Ditfurth regiments were quartered in the south end of the town, in the houses vacated by the inhabitants. The v. Huyne regiment was quartered on the East road, the v. Bünau on the West road.

The winter was a very severe one; several of the

Hessian soldiers were frozen to death; supplies of all kinds were very scanty, for the French fleet had cut off communication with the main land.

On January 1, 1779, rations were reduced, and changed so as to eke out the small supplies. Later in the month, recruits and convalescents came for the Ansbach-Bayreuth regiment, and with them Dr. Schöpf, of Ansbach, afterwards well known by his work on his travels in North America. Provisions and fuel grew steadily scarcer, until the arrival of the great fleet with supplies from Ireland enabled the men to be properly fed; but many of them suffered from scorbutic diseases, due to their bad food. The loyalist volunteers from time to time brought in supplies of fresh meat, but always at great risk, for the Americans meted out to these loyal countrymen very heavy punishment for their treason.

Major v. Reitzenstein became lieutenant-colonel of the Ansbach regiment, and Capt. v. Seitz, of the Grenadiers, became major, and Capt. v. Molitor was given command of the Bayreuth Grenadiers.

On June 25th, the two Hessian regiments were sent to the force with which Gen. Tryon was to harry New England. During that month, some of the German soldiers were employed making hay, for which they received an extra allowance of three English pistareens from the British commissariat.

In October, Rhode Island was suddenly evacuated, the fruit trees being given to the soldiers, that they might lay in a supply of fresh fruit for the journey.

Many royalists sailed with the fleet of 102 sail, under convoy of three men-of-war. The march out of Newport was a very striking one. Fichtelberger says, in his diary: " All the houses were closed, by General Prescott's order; not a man or woman was allowed to look out of the windows or to be on the street; the patrols were directed to enforce this, under penalty of firing at those whose curiosity might tempt them."

## CHAPTER XI.

At the opening of the spring of 1779, the usual reinforcements were sent out from Germany. On March 11th, the Ansbach-Bayreuth recruits were shipped on three boats down the Main to Hanau and then with the Hanau recruits down the Rhine to Dortrecht. Later in March, the Hessian recruits were sent by the Weser to Bremen. The whole force, numbering 1,300, was shipped on the 23d of May, in a great fleet, under Admiral Arbuthnot, consisting of twenty line-of-battle ships, six frigates, two bomb ships, and three hundred transports.

The troops in New York had a hard winter, with scanty supplies, until a fleet brought a fresh supply of provisions, and poor quarters, into which the men were crowded still more after a fire had destroyed many houses, for they were still mostly of wood.

The forces outside the city, at Kingsbridge, were better off, for they had comfortable huts, nine for each company, and each officer had his own, all surrounded with gardens in which flowers and vegetables were grown. The huts of the subalterns had two rooms, those of the captains three, with windows; behind the huts were stalls for horses, pigs, chickens and other stock ; so that every thing had a peaceful look.

Early in February, Gen. v. Bose arrived from Newport, and resumed command of his brigade, and preparations were made for an early resumption of hostilities.

Gen. Tryon received orders to take an armed force into Connecticut, including the Guards and Emmerich's volunteers. The detachment marched at night and the next day fell upon an American force, drove it from its position, disabled the guns, carried off supplies, burned the village, and retired safely, after a hard march of 65 miles in 40 hours, with no loss, except an old powder cart, abandoned in the mud.

Early in May, the German soldiers left their winter quarters and went into camp beyond Kingsbridge, between the Phillips house and East Chester.

After the loss of Fort Montgomery and Fort Clinton, Washington had established forts at Verplanck's Point and Stony Point, about 60 miles from New York, thus cutting off the Hudson and barring the northern and southern colonies.

Clinton determined to break this barrier, and only waited the return of the British fleet from Virginia, with reinforcements. He brought the Hessian Crown Prince's regiment from Long Island to the Hudson, and with the v. Knyphausen and Lossberg regiments it constituted the v. Hachenberg brigade.

On May 30th, the fleet sailed up the Hudson, and anchoring off the Phillips house, disembarked the troops for the expedition, making a force of 5,000 men — of which the German contingent included the Guards, the Grenadier battalion of v. Linsingen, and 400 Hessian and Rhenish Yägers. The Prince Charles regiment had come with the fleet from the south. Although it counted 70 sail, large and small, and 140 flatboats, there was hardly standing room on deck.

Clinton himself led the smaller division of his troops, which included 100 Hessian Yägers, under Capt. v. Lorey, while there were 300 in the other division, under Gen. Vaughan. The fleet kept up the river — Vaughan, with his division, landing to attack Fort Lafayette; Clinton somewhat further up, opposite Stony Point.

The Americans abandoned their unfinished works during the night, after setting fire to them. Clinton at once took possession, and put some heavy guns in position, with which to open on the fort across the river.

Vaughan attacked from the land side, the Hessian Grenadiers being in his force, while the guns opened from across the river, and the American garrison of three officers and 70 men, surrendered the unfinished Fort Lafayette, and with it three guns.

Clinton returned to New York, leaving the troops in their position, and the forts were strengthened, ditches dug; the orchards and other trees cut down, a garrison of 1,200 men, well supplied, left in the forts, and the rest of the force brought back to New York.

Gen. Wayne at once recaptured Stony Point, and Clinton returning, again evacuated it. On his way up, his 50 mounted Hessians, under Capt. Rau, met and dispersed an equal force of hostile cavalry.

While Clinton operated on the Hudson, General Tryon undertook a second invasion of Connecticut, hitherto little disturbed by the war, in the hope that Washington would abandon his strong position on the Hudson, to come to the relief of the harried citizens. Tryon had only 50 Hessian Yägers in his force of 2,500 men, with which, in nine days, he burned New Haven, Fairfield and Norwalk, returning to New York after a loss of 150 men.

The Americans took their revenge by an attack, on the 18th of August, on the British outpost at Paulus' Hook, to which Capt. v. Schallern, with 50 Hessians, had been ordered. Summoned to surrender, he successfully resisted, with 30 soldiers, the attack of a much larger force, and held his post until it was reinforced.

In May, 1779, Clinton sent a second expediton southward — this time to Virginia. The fleet, under Admiral Collier, consisted of six men-of-war and twenty-two transports, carrying, among other troops, the light infantry of the German Guards and the Hessian regiment Prince Charles. Landing without resistance, Norfolk and Portsmouth and Suffolk were taken and first stripped of all stores and then burned, with 130 large and small vessels, laden with much-needed supplies for Washington's hard-pressed army.

In September, the strong French fleet, under d'Estaing, unexpectedly appeared off the mouth of the Savannah river, and both sides prepared for the siege. The French landed and put in position 53 guns and 14 mortars, and on October 4th opened fire. D'Estaing had landed 5,000 men, and American militia hastened to join him, while Lincoln brought his force, making a total strength of 10,000, the French on the right, the Americans on the left. Opposed to the former were the regiments v. Trümbach and Wissenbach; behind the palisades and traverses, in the center, were the two Hessian regiments.

Count d'Estaing soon wearied of regular siege operations and on the 9th of October did what he ought to have done at the outset, decided to attack by storming the fort, and was finally driven back, with heavy loss.

Col. v. Borbeck, who commanded the Hessians, was warmly praised for his share of the defense.

The French and Americans soon parted company, each charging the other with the failure at Savannah.

Clinton came, with fleet and troops, to capture Charleston, and sent transports to Savannah, with a year's supplies. The Hessians suffered from food and climate and complained bitterly of both.

The regiment of v. Trümbach was sent to Charleston, and that of v. Wissenbach, later v. Knoblauch, remained in Savannah.

Clinton decided, after the failure of the French expedition, to recapture South Carolina, beginning with Charleston, and brought troops from the north for the purpose.

The Hessian Grenadiers were ordered to rendezvous at Sandy Hook, where, on the 22d of December, they joined the fleet; the heavy ice threatened destruction — the Hessian and Ansbach light infantry, under Capt. Ewald, were almost carried down in a transport, and owed their safety to his coolness and presence of mind.

The fleet counted 133 sail, and of the 7,500 men in the expedition, the Germans supplied the Hessian regiments Prince Carl, von Ditfurth and von Huyne, some Hessian and Ansbach light infantry and a force of dragoons.

On December 26th, the fleet sailed right into the teeth of a storm which made the poor soldiers very wretched, and soon scattered the ships, which met a succession of storms, and finally reached a harbor only on the 28th of January, and the point fixed for disembarkation on the 31st. There, at Tybee Island, lay the transport "Polly," with two companies of the Grenadier battalion v. Linsingen, which had been safely landed for two weeks, and were comfortably encamped on the shore.

The voyage was full of hardships — indeed, it was thought great folly to undertake it at that season. Four transports were sunk, many disabled, one captured — in all, nine missing. The hardest fate befel the transport "Anna," with 30 Hessian and Ansbach Yägers and some Hessian artillery; losing its masts, and then drifting helplessly for eleven weeks, with 250 men provisioned only for four weeks, their sufferings were dreadful. At last the Irish coast was sighted, and after fresh horrors, the wrecked hulk made a landing at St. Ives, on the coast of Cornwall, at the end of February; the men were sent to Plymouth in the middle of March, and in August to New York, where they landed again in October, 1780.

The fleet remained at Tybee until February 5th, 1780. The German soldiers made their first acquaintance with the climate and life of the tropics, saw alligators, and enjoyed the game and fish and oysters, of which great quantities were at hand — and their letters are full of the strange sights that met their astonished gaze. Finally, some of the forces were sent to Savannah, others to Bedford — the greater part of the fleet going to Simon's Island, where wild horses were caught and used for wagons and artillery; abundant supplies of fresh provisions were obtained, and the contrast between the narrow quarters on shipboard and the fine old plantations was a very grateful one.

Clinton now sent Captain Ewald, of the Yägers, to reconnoiter the passage of Stono Ferry, which was approached only by a long, narrow causeway, through the marshy ground, with deep water on both sides, protected by part of Pulaski's corps, with boats always on the lookout. Ewald was just the man for the task, and, accompanied by Lieut. v. Winzingerode, he quietly walked out on the causeway, politely greeted the officer in command of the American picket, engaged in pleasant conversation, all the time carefully studying the situation, and returned with a very clear report of the condition of things. As the post was not well guarded, and the gunboat was not in sight, Stono Ferry and John's Island were easily taken possession of on February 14th.

On the 26th, the army quietly moved by Hamilton's Ferry to James Island and to Fort St. John, which the Americans had destroyed the year before. From that point there was a fine view of Charleston, its harbor and the coast beyond.

On the 28th, four American frigates opened fire and obliged the British to move their camp further from the shore, leaving two Hessian Grenadier battalions to watch the enemy, and throw up defensive batteries.

On March 6th, Clinton took possession of Fort Johnstone and began to throw up defenses on James Island, using the works abandoned by the Americans and the so-called Indian forts — rough works of mussel and oyster shells, going back to quite an unknown past.

On March 12th, a fleet of transports arrived with abundant supplies, and on the 17th the Hessian Grenadier battalions fell back from their old camp to a new position.

The Americans had something like 5,000 men in Charleston, covered by hastily-made defenses; in the harbor lay five frigates, a French man-of-war, an old ship, no longer sea-worthy, and a number of small craft.

On March 24th, the Grenadier battalion v. Linsingen moved to Church Bridge, to connect there with the light infantry.

On the 26th, the English commander, with his staff, narrowly escaped capture, going forward to meet the corps of Patterson, coming from Savannah by Purisburg to Randolph Creek. Clinton, without escort, rode out to find them, the road leading for ten miles through a thick wood; about half way was a cross-road, where part of Pulaski's legion was posted. Captain Ewald, with his usual foresight, was on the lookout for danger, and had pointed it out as a proper position for a heavy guard; but his suggestion was laughed at. Clinton passed and repassed the place safely, but part of his staff and some of the baggage of Patterson's corps were captured there shortly after.

On the 28th, the army moved near Ashley river, which it crossed on the 29th, engaging the enemy's outposts — the advance guard of Yägers drawing the fire of the American cavalry on outpost duty and of some 300 riflemen, under cover in the bushes.

A young British staff officer rode up to Clinton with the news of his brother's death and his succession to the peerage, when the poor aid was killed by a shot fired by a negro.

The Yägers hurried up, crossed a marsh, brought up a field piece, drove the enemy out of the works, took possession of them, and the next day the whole army stood within cannon-shot of the defenses of the city.

Charleston was then a city of 1,500 houses and 14,000 inhabitants, of whom nearly one-half were blacks. It lies on the south end of a neck of land, with the Ashley river on the west, the Cooper river on the east; beyond, to the east, is Sullivan's Island, on which the Americans had built some defensive works, opposite Fort Johnson, on James Island, and thus commanding on both sides the entrance to the harbor.

On March 31st, Gen. Clinton undertook a personal reconnoisance of the works and their strength for defense, taking Capt. Ewald, with 20 Hessian Yägers — a task for which he was particularly suited. In the open ground around the town there was, on the right wing of the besiegers, a group of trees, and beyond a narrow dam leading through a marsh; passing this without being seen by the enemy, Capt. Ewald left half of his men concealed in the woods, and with the others crept out on hands and knees until he could plainly see the works. Clinton, with two engineer officers, dressed in Hessian uniforms, then came openly forward, and being taken by the garrison for three of the Hessian patrol, which often came quite as far forward, it did not seem worth while to open fire, thus enabling Clinton and his companions, quite at their ease, to complete their survey.

By April 1st, the batteries were in position in the first parallel, and every day 1,000 men were at work on the trenches, and every night 500 were employed to complete them — the sailors from the fleet taking their share.

Admiral Arbuthnot, as soon as he had landed the troops, tried to force an entrance into the harbor. He passed Fort Moultrie, on Sullivan's Island, on the 9th, under a heavy fire, and lay in front of the city, with most of his men-of-war — breaking through a heavy chain, hung from shore to shore, and as the stately ships slowly sailed on, without firing a shot or taking any notice of the heavy fire from the enemy's batteries, the admiral, in an open boat, coolly took soundings, so as to guide the men-of-war through the dangerous sand banks.

On the 11th of April, Clinton formally demanded the surrender of the town, which Lincoln positively refused. On the 13th, the batteries opened fire from their 24-pounders, and bombs were thrown into the town, setting fire to the houses in different neighborhoods. On the 19th, the second parallel was completed and manned by reinforcements recently arrived from New York.

On the 21st, Lincoln, now cut off on the land side, too, offered to surrender, but as he insisted on being allowed to go with his garrison safely, hostilities were resumed after a two days' suspension for negotiations. On the 24th, the besieged attempted a sortie, but were soon driven back. On the 25th, the Hessians lost heavily in a severe fire on the lines held by them.

On May 6th, the third parallel was completed, and

a dam was cut, letting out the water which had hitherto served as a ditch around the works. The fire from the batteries, now near by, was so destructive that Clinton for the second time demanded the surrender, which was again fruitlessly discussed for two days, when fire was opened at 8 P. M. of the 9th, and kept up until 11 A. M., next day. As every thing was ready for the storming party, Lincoln at last accepted Clinton's terms.

On the 12th, the garrison moved out of the fort and laid down their arms — an English and a Hessian Grenadier company occupied the gates. All the material of war, five men-of-war and many small craft fell into the hands of the conquerors. The garrison that surrendered consisted of American and French troops, twelve infantry regiments, three artillery battalions, and the city and state militia — two major-generals, five brigadiers, 46 staff officers, 145 captains, 162 lieutenants, 41 ensigns, one paymaster, seven adjutants, six quartermasters, 18 commissaries, 329 non-commissioned officers, 137 drummers, and 5,710 armed men; in all 6,609, besides 1,000 sailors.

During the siege, the Hessians and the Ansbach light infantry had distinguished themselves. They had sent every day thirty men and three officers to do duty in the first parallel, to protect the men at work, until sufficient guns could be procured. In parties of three or six they got near to the enemy and, at a distance of 500 paces, their fire was so effective that many of the guns were unmanned, and the riflemen sought in vain to drive them off. When the third parallel was completed, their fire almost silenced the enemy's guns by day; yet the loss was a very small one.

Clinton paid the Grenadiers the somewhat dangerous compliment of giving them white plumes to wear, in reward for their bravery. In his report, he praised the services of Generals v. Huyne and v. Kospoth.

The troops had suffered greatly during the siege, from the want of proper tools, the great heat, the bad water, and the hard work the men had to do; and just after the surrender, the carelessness of an English artilleryman led to the explosion of a powder magazine, causing a large loss of life, including some of the Hessians.

Charleston was then the most flourishing city in the south, and the booty that fell to the troops, according to the custom of the time, was a very great addition to their scanty pay. One of the Hessian officers estimated that the captures on land and sea were worth £300,000. This was divided proportionately among the troops. The regiment Prince Charles, which had captured a laden ship, received the following shares: the colonel, £2,000; lieutenant-colonel, £1,500; the major, £1,200; each captain, £400; each lieutenant, £200; the non-commissioned officers each £40, and every common soldier, £7. A commission of British and Hessian officers was appointed to regulate the distribution, and the duty was a tedious one, as Clinton and Admiral Arbuthnot disputed over the respective claims of army and navy — the latter wanting one-half the value of the captured vessels, although the sailors had taken no part in securing them. To make peace, their claims were granted, but Clinton and Cornwallis transferred their lion's share to the Hessian Yägers and the Hessian and British Grenadiers and light troops, in reward for their large share in the hard work of the siege.

On the 31st of May, part of the force was sent off by sea, leaving Cornwallis, with the Hessian regiments v. Ditsfurth, v. Huyne and v. Trümbach, as part of his force to complete the subjugation of South Carolina.

The fleet left for New York, where the rest of the troops were safely landed — going into quarters on Staaten Island.

The Hessians reported their loss up to the surrender of Charleston at 73 — the Yägers, 7 dead and 14 wounded; the Grenadier battalion v. Lengerke, 4 dead and 33 wounded; the v. Ditfurth regiment, 2 officers and 8 soldiers; the v. Huyne regiment, 5 wounded.

Dr. J. D. Schöpf, the surgeon of the Ansbach regiment, in his "Travels through the United States," volume one, page 53, says: "In 1783, at Princeton, I had the pleasure of meeting many members of Congress, honest and sturdy men, and General Lincoln, a man of clear and strong mind, although his reputation as a soldier had not been increased by his defense of Charleston; he is, however, popular for the good beer he brews on his large property in New England."

The British commander-in-chief anticipated a diversion by the Americans to the northward, and he sent reinforcements to Canada to meet it — including the two weak regiments, Knyphausen and Lossberg. They were ordered in September to embark on transports, mostly old and poor vessels. Col. v. Loos, of the Lossberg regiment, as senior officer in command of both regiments, went on the 12-gun cruiser "King George;" Col. v. Bork, of the Knyphausen regiment, on the ship "Archer;" the smaller vessels were the worst; on the brigantine "Triton" there were no sleeping quarters, and officers and men were obliged to lie down on the floor; the crew, that ought to have counted 18, was only 7, so that the prospect of a northerly voyage at such a season was far from pleasant — the captain of the vessel said he could not be responsible for their safety beyond Staaten Island.

The fleet consisted of 22 vessels, under escort of the man-of-war Renown, of 50 guns, and the soldiers were glad to go to Canada, which was always described in glowing terms.

On the 12th a storm gathered, which broke out in great violence on the 15th, scattering the fleet and doing great damage to the vessels — the Triton suffering the loss of both masts, and the deck almost made untenable by the guns breaking loose. Lieut.-Col. Heymel was sick and unable to give any orders, the captain lost his head, crew and soldiers alike were unmanned by the impending destruction, when Lieut. Wiederhold, the officer who had shown courage in the unexpected attack at Trenton, although an invalid, tried to inspire the men with his own fearlessness ; at first even the well-disciplined Hessians were beyond control — an almost unexampled condition of things — but in answer to his appeal for help in getting the guns out of harm's way, an old sergeant, two corporals and 20 men followed him on deck, and in spite of the dangers from the sea and the guns, at last got matters in better shape, took to the pumps, until they broke, then worked with such means as they could improvise until the pumps were repaired, and did their best to save the ship and their comrades. The captain began to make preparations to take to the boats, but was put under the guard of some of the officers, until it was seen that the boats were unseaworthy, when he was released. The storm gradually subsided, and on the 17th the ship was found to be in latitude 37, somewhere off the coast of Virginia— so far south had she drifted out of her course. A jury sail was set and a flag of distress put up, but the first vessel of the fleet that was seen, on the 20th, took no notice of it. On the 25th, Delaware bay was made, and it was hoped that Sandy Hook would be reached in a couple of days. On the morning of the 26th, two sails were seen, and help from New York was looked for, when it was found they were hostile cruisers under full sail — one of 14, the other of 10 guns; and the Triton, without guns or sails, was forced to surrender, and was taken into Little Egg harbor.

Of the other vessels of the fleet, the Renown lost its main mast, the Springfield all its masts.

On the 21st, the commander, with the approval of Col. v. Loos, headed for New York; they were then at latitude 36. On October 2d, the Renown, King George and Springfield reached Sandy Hook. On October 12th, the Badger arrived, without masts, having on board Captain v. Bockum's and part of Lieut.-Col. Schäffer's companies. It had been in collision with the transport Clementine, and pursued by an American cruiser, only escaping capture by Capt. v. Bockum's decided refusal to surrender. On October 9th, it was again brought to by another American cruiser, of 12 guns, and as v. Bockum had no guns, he had to yield. The cruiser took on board Lieutenant Zoll and Ensigns Henndorff, v. Waldschmid and Cowan, with 20 men, but as Capt. v. Bockum was sick, he was left on the Badger, with Chaplain Oliva. Next day, the cruiser was taken, in turn, by the British frigate Solebay, and the prisoners again set free.

The men on board the Clementine were taken off by two English cruisers, just as she was sinking. The Adamant went down, and of the Guards and

Major v. Lossberg's company of the Lossberg regiment, there were lost Major v. Hanstein, Staff Captains Steding and v. Wurmb, Lieut. Möller, Ensigns v. Zengen, Rathmann and Waldeck. The Molly, with men of the Knyphausen regiment, was captured and carried into Philadelphia, a prize to the shallop Mars, Captain Taylor, who thus took one major, six subalterns, and 156 men — many of them were Hessians, taken at Trenton, and scarcely exchanged before they were again prisoners of war; they were all sent to Reading and were not exchanged until November, 1780.

On October 16th, Col. v. Minnigerode, commander of the Third Grenadier battalion, died in New York. He was an officer of great merit, 49 years old, who had won a decoration and the affection of his comrades and the respect of the British for his military and personal merit. His funeral, on the 22d, was a very imposing ceremony, and he was buried with due honors in the Lutheran churchyard. His successor was Lieut.-Col. v. Löwenstein.

## CHAPTER XII.

When Sir Henry Clinton went south, he left Lieut.-Gen. v. Knyphausen in command in New York, with the two South German and the Hessian regiments as part of his garrison of 6,000 men.

The winter was one of the coldest known, the ships were frozen fast, the garrison reduced to 3,500 men, in order to strengthen Clinton by reinforcements, and Knyphausen looked for an attack, as Washington was at Morristown.

On the 15th of January, a force of 2,700 men, with six guns and two mortars, appeared on Long Island, but as soon as Knyphausen sent 600 men to strengthen the force there, the Americans withdrew, carrying off 600 head of cattle and burning some houses.

On January 25th, a detachment of 300 men, under the Hessian Lieut.-Col. Elbing, went from New York to New Jersey and captured an American outpost and a herd of cattle.

Knyphausen now determined to make another attack, and, on February 2d, sent two companies of

Hessians and some Hessian light infantry, as part of a force, into Westchester county — part of the way on sleighs. The deep snow delayed the march, but the American outpost was captured, after a sharp fight, and the expedition safely returned to King's Bridge. Knyphausen made a full report to Lord Germain on March 27th.

On March 22d, another expedition, with Hessian and Bayreuth troops, numbering 400 in all, with Capt. v. Tannenburg, was sent to Hackensack. It crossed the Hudson in boats and moved through the woods to Hackensack, but the garrison having been withdrawn, the town was given over to plunder, the court-house and some of the best private residences burned, when an American force of 500 or 600 men threatened to capture the invaders and their booty, but just at the right moment Col. Emmerich, with his volunteers, 400 strong, appeared and protected the expedition on its retreat, under fire for six hours, to the Hudson.

Musketeer Döhla says: "We gathered fine plunder, gold and silver watches, silver forks and spoons, furniture, good clothes, fine English linen, silk stockings, gloves and cravats, with other silk, woolen and cotton clothing. My own booty, which I brought safely back, consisted of two silver watches, three necklaces of silver, a pair of women's woolen stockings, a pair of men's summer stockings, two men's and four women's shirts, of fine English linen, two fine table cloths, one silver tablespoon and one silver teaspoon, five Spanish dollars and six York shillings. The rest — eleven yards of fine linen, two dozen silk handkerchiefs, six silver spoons and a silver goblet, all packed up — I had to throw away on our retreat, and leave for the enemy."

The picture is a painful one, all the more as the German discipline was much stricter than the English, and the example of the latter soon influenced their allies in inflicting such personal injuries on the Americans, who complained of them as robbery.

Early in April, a detachment of 100 Ansbach-Bayreuth soldiers brought in a number of head of cattle, with hay and straw.

Knyphausen thus deterred the Americans from any attack in force. He brought the sailors from the ships into the city to do garrison duty, and obliged the citizens to bear arms in its defense. The six wards supplied 40 companies, numbering in all 2,660 men, and these were later on increased to 62 companies, making 5,796 men. The Hessian general was thus able to make a stout defense, and won the thanks of Clinton on his return. If his reputation must suffer from the well-grounded charge of allowing his men to plunder, his excuse is that it was done by order of the British commander.

On May 15th, the companies of the Knyphausen and Lossberg regiments intended for Canada were again embarked. The Lossberg detachment consisted of three companies — those of Col. v. Loos, Lieut.-Col. Schäffer, and Capt. v. Bockum. The

Knyphausen regiment supplied only a company and a half, under Col. v. Bork. Although in the reports from Canada they were spoken of as regiments, they were really not even battalions. They were sent on board under Col. v. Loos, and barely escaped a repetition of their earlier misfortunes. The fleet of 30 sail was again driven before violent storms and only reached Quebec on the 25th of June.

Gen. v. Knyphausen was constantly in receipt of reports of the growing dissatisfaction of the men in Washington's army in New Jersey. The deserters coming into New York amounted on one day to 160, and the stream was a steady one—mostly Pennsylvanians and Jerseymen—who reported that they and their comrades were ready to become loyal subjects again.

Knyphausen determined to make a demonstration in the rich Jersey country, and thus to quicken its people in their returning loyalty. He organized a force of 6,000 men, with Hessian and Ansbach soldiers in it, leaving the Bayreuth and other troops in New York. Besides his other German soldiers, he distributed his 400 Yägers, part of them mounted, among his divisions. His corps was arranged in three divisions — in the first, the Guards, the Elector's regiment; moving out on the night of the 6th, the English commander was wounded, and his place taken by Lieut.-Col. v. Wurmb. The second and third divisions followed promptly, but the Americans met the advance and on the 7th had a sharp contest, reported by Capt. Grau to Gen. v. Riedesel in great detail and precision.

Knyphausen was with the second division, and, while waiting for the arrival of the third division, sent his Hessians and other German forces forward to keep the Americans engaged, and three times driving them back. Washington sent reinforcements, including his own guard, but the Germans, too, were promptly strengthened by Knyphausen, with the Ansbach regiment and some guns, when the Americans withdrew.

Knyphausen kept on until he was near Morristown, where Washington was posted with his main army, and then withdrew in turn and went into camp. His loss had been heavy — 300 dead and wounded. The Guards lost Lieut. Wiederhold, and the Hessians lost 80 men. Major Seitz and Lieut. Ebenauer, of the Bayreuth Yägers, were killed, and the Ansbach regiment also lost sharply. The German Yägers had been under fire for twelve hours and used up all their ammunition. Major du Puy, of the v. Bose regiment, was especially commended and received a decoration from his prince for his distinguished gallantry.

The next morning (the 8th) the Americans again attacked, when the Hessians in three lines resisted stoutly, the first line, under Maj.-Gen. v. Lossberg, advancing, supported by the second line, under Maj.-Gen. v. Hachenberg, until the enemy withdrew.

Knyphausen was quite satisfied that he was mistaken in his opinion of the spirit of the American army, and, ceasing further hostile demonstrations, went into camp.

Ebenauer, who had fallen in this battle, was buried at Springfield, where Washington paid the tribute of his respect and admiration for the courage shown by this officer, and ordered a suitable interment in place of the hurried burial first given him.

While Knyphausen was in New Jersey, Clinton returned, on the 17th, to New York, and sent the Bayreuth regiment to join him. It was put in the second line, on the right wing. The troops lay about two miles from Elizabethtown, without tents, and were soon reinforced by cavalry and artillery. So near were the outposts, that one night an American picket came over in a body — an officer and 30 men.

On June 19th, Clinton came to the front, inspected the men, and ordered Knyphausen to advance. Moving forward the next morning, through Elizabeth, then a place of 300 houses, mostly occupied by Quakers, he captured an American outpost, with three small guns; then pressing on, met and drove a larger force, reaching Springfield. Here Washington had posted some regular troops and militia, under shelter of orchards and outbuildings, a small creek protecting their front. They opened a sharp fire, and Knyphausen posted six twelve-pounders on a hill to drive them off, but Döhla says the Americans did not yield and showed a braver front than he had ever witnessed. The Bayreuth regiment, covering the right flank, made a bayonet charge and finally drove the Americans before them.

In the afternoon, when Knyphausen wanted to renew the attack, the Americans were advantageously posted on high ground, so he quietly withdrew and retreated again, setting fire to Springfield and letting his men plunder it, meaning to cover his retreat; but it was done before the eyes of the American soldiers, and so excited their fury that they pursued the retreating column and inflicted heavy losses. Of the Bayreuth Yägers, Capt. v. Röder and Lieut. v. Diemar were mortally wounded. The Hessian and Ansbach-Bayreuth Yägers were again distinguished for their bravery — under fire for six hours, covering the retreat, they lost a seventh of the whole list of casualties.

The retreat made a march of twenty-two miles, and the men suffered from the fierce heat and hardships. Returned to camp, where the v. Huyne and Ansbach regiments had been left, they were soon called to arms, and again left the camp, marched all night, and retreated still further, to avoid an attack by Washington reported to Knyphausen by his spies and confirmed by the arrival of his troops in the abandoned camp. The galleons lying in the stream covered with their fire the last of the retreating troops on their way back to Staaten Island.

On July 1st, the whole army, consisting of 23 regiments, was again in line from the East river to the Hudson.

Among the reinforcements from Europe, there came a strong body of volunteers, 830 men, enlisted in Hanau, which was not sent to join the other Hanau troops in Canada, but was ordered to Clinton's army. The only report of this organization is in the *Cassel Journal* of 1780. It was apparently attached to Emmerich's command, and is referred to in the *Hessian Army Journal* as a "volunteer corps" attached to the other Hessian forces sent to America by the Elector and Count of Hanau.

Toward the end of July, Clinton organized another strong force of 6,000 men to cut off the French division of Rochambeau, which had landed in Newport, Rhode Island. Admiral Arbuthnot was to support the expedition with his fleet. Included in it were the Hessian Guard regiment, the Grenadier battalion v. Linsingen, and 300 light infantry, under Capt. v. Prüschenk.

After a cruise of a few days on the sound, the expedition was abandoned, partly for want of good management by Admiral Arbuthnot, partly because Washington threatened an attack at King's Bridge. Knyphausen at once moved out to meet it, but as nothing was done, fell back within the entrenchments.

On July 25th, the Hessian Maj.-Gen. v. Huyne died, in New York, and was buried there with military honors.

The Hessian officers, through v. Lossberg, then commanding in New York, joined in expressing their respect for Gen. Patterson, the governor of New York, on his return to England on account of his health, and he returned thanks, with especial commendation of the Hessian troops under his command at various trying times.

During October, the men were again put upon short and poor rations, until the fleet arrived in November, with a fresh supply of provisions.

On October 19th, the troops again went into their winter quarters—the Ansbach regiment in Bloomingdale, the Bayreuth regiment in New York, the Guards in Bloomingdale and Greenwich, stretching along the Hudson for six miles in scattered houses. The Hessian Yägers were sent to Jericho, on Long Island, furnishing a force of 100 men at Morris House, on York Island, which was relieved every six weeks, and late in November the Ansbach regiment returned to New York.

At the end of June of this year, a number of promotions were made in the Hessian corps—Maj.-Gen. v. Mirbach became lieutenant-general; Cols. v. Gosen and v. Biesenroth major-generals, and the latter succeeded the late Maj.-Gen. v. Schmidt as chief of the Prince Charles regiment. In November, Col. v. Bischoffshausen became major-general and the commander of the Guard regiment; Col. v. Wurmb, major-general; Lieut.-Col. v. Schüler, colonel of the Ditfurth regiment; Maj.-Gen. v. Lossberg, of the Mirbach regiment; Major Du Puy, of the v. Bose regiment, was promoted to be lieutenant-colonel; Lieut.-Col. Köhler, colonel of the Second Grenadier battalion, Angenelli; Major v. Ende to be lieutenant-colonel of the Second battalion; Lieut.-Col. v. Schäffer, colonel of the Bunau regiment. Three sergeants and one ordinance sergeant were promoted to ensigns. Captains v. d. Malsburg and v. Dinklage, whose diaries have been quoted in these pages, became majors; Maj.-Gen. v. Knoblauch got the Wissenbach regiment, and Col. v. Benning, the Huyne regiment. In the early part of the next year, Major-Generals v. Hachenberg, v. Bose and v. Lossberg became lieutenant-generals; Lieut.-Col. v. Heymel, of the Knyphausen regiment, colonel of the Donop regiment.

## CHAPTER XIII.

Cornwallis, at the close of 1780, prepared a plan for an expedition into North Carolina, as soon as reinforcements came from the north.

On December 13th, the v. Bose regiment, and 112 Hessian and other Yägers, under Capt. v. Röder, arrived in Charleston, part of a corps of 1,500 men, under Gen. Leslie, who was at once ordered to join Cornwallis, in North Carolina.

The Americans, under Gen. Morgan, were driven by Col. Tarleton, but the latter was completely defeated at Cowpens, a victory which was as important to the American cause in the south as Trenton had been in the north.

Cornwallis was joined by Leslie on January 18th, and after a sharp fight at the crossing of the Catawba, drove the Americans, under Greene, out of North Carolina into Virginia, and then at Hillsborough issued proclamations inviting the royalists to come to his support.

By March 14th, Greene had returned southward, with reinforcements, and on the 15th the two forces met, near Guilford.

The British advance, under Col. Tarleton, which included the Hessian and Ansbach Yägers, the light infantry and cavalry, became warmly engaged, and Cornwallis brought up his force in line of battle—on his right v. Bose's regiment; the light infantry and the Hessian and Ansbach Yägers were on the left.

Greene had posted his army in three lines; the first was broken by a bayonet charge, but rallied on the second under cover of a wood, but at last fell back to the third.

Leslie put the Guards battalion on his right, while the light infantry and German Yägers turned the American right. The Guards battalion broke the American lines, but pushed too far forward, and in the woods could not use the bayonet, and were soon under a heavy fire in front and on flank — and broke in disorder. The fire on the left and center was very heavy, and the v. Bose regiment, under Lieut.-Col. Du Puy, advanced to strengthen the British line, which rallied on it and moved forward again, with the Hessians, to renew the attack. This the Americans could not stand, but pressing forward, the Hessians were attacked in the rear by another force, and forming front to meet it, they were faced on both sides by the Americans and again drove them off.

The gallant conduct of the v. Bose regiment, which decided the favorable issue of the battle for the British, was recognized by the English generals, and openly praised in the New York paper and by the London *Gazette*. The Elector Friedrick wrote, on

September 13th, to Gen. v. Knyphausen: "I have heard, with great pleasure, of the good conduct of the v. Bose regiment, under Lieut.-Col. Du Puy, and of the Yägers, under Capt. Ewald, and request you to make known to these officers and their commands my satisfaction."

This was the first opportunity, since the attack on Fort Montgomery, that the regiment had to show its great bravery. The Hessian Yägers showed their accustomed fearlessness. The v. Bose regiment had heavy losses — Capt. v. Wilmowsky and Lieut. v. Trott died, Capt. Eigenbrod, Lieuts. Schwaner and Geyso were wounded. The sufferings of the wounded left on the battle-field over night were dreadful, while the pursuit was a series of hardships for the Hessian and other German troops, with long marches, streams to ford, and short supplies.

Cornwallis, leaving the wounded at Wilmington, under guard of the Yägers, fell back again to Virginia. Meantime Gen. Arnold, sailing from New York on December 12th, brought a force of 1,400 men, including 125 Hessian Yägers under Captain Ewald. Heavy storms scattered the fleet, which arrived in port in the James river on January 3d, where they seized a strong battery of the enemy and silenced the guns. On the 9th, the other vessels brought the rest of the force.

Cornwallis had ordered Arnold to keep open his communication with the sea, and to call on the loyalists to support him, and if there was no response, to destroy all supplies that could be useful to the enemy. At Richmond, where he first began to do this, he also burned or plundered all shops and houses, thus forfeiting any sympathy he might have hoped to find among the people.

At Fleur de Hundred [Flourde Hundret], Baron Steuben had a force of 7,000 or 8,000 men, to bar the way to Portsmouth. Ewald, with 50 foot Yägers and three companies of rangers, drove in the American outpost, and, with Simcoe's cavalry, forced the advance to retreat, and then entered Portsmouth, the chief depot of supplies of the American army in the south. The Americans made frequent attempts to recover it, but Ewald was always on his guard, and showed such watchfulness and energy that he not only kept the enemy off, but also captured officers with despatches of great value to Arnold.

Ewald's rule was always to attack, and in his book on "War," he lays it down as a maxim that whenever the enemy is met at night, he must be attacked at once and followed by a bayonet charge, so that the leader of the advance can ascertain the strength of the enemy, mask his own, and make his plans for his next movement. Ewald pressed on, through a country so marshy that it was thought impracticable, cut off the retreat of the Americans to North Carolina, and succeeded in breaking their communications southward.

On the 19th of March, the bravery of Capt. Ewald and his men was put to a sharp test. His patrol of one non-commissioned officer and 16 Yägers, near Portsmouth, was met by Gen. Lafayette, with 800 men, on a reconnoisance. Ewald hurried up with another handful of 16 Yägers, and posting his men so as to command the narrow breast of a dam which could only be crossed three abreast, urged them to stand fast. The Americans three times advanced to the attack, in column 300 strong, and were every time repulsed by the 33 Yägers, and finally withdrew, by order of Lafayette. Ewald was wounded, with many of his little band. Arnold had not responded to the call for support, and, angered by Ewald's reproaches, did not even mention him in his report, when Ewald protested and at last secured due recognition for his men.

The Hessians were largely employed, with the other troops, in the ungrateful task of destroying supplies, but on April 25th succeeded in defeating the militia, under Gen. Muhlenberg.

In May, the two South German regiments came from New York, in response to the pressing demand of Cornwallis for reinforcements, and on the 25th were sent to Portsmouth, to join the Hessians.

On June 26th, a force of 300 men, Hessian and Ansbach-Bayreuth soldiers making part of it, made a march of 30 miles, attacked, captured and destroyed an American outpost, taking prisoners, guns and supplies.

Although there was no lack of food, water was scarce and bad, rum was dear, a quart costing half a Spanish dollar, and to make a circulating medium, the Spanish dollars were cut in eight pieces, the pistareens in two and even four pieces.

The Virginians showed a very friendly disposition toward the Germans.

Cornwallis moved gradually toward the coast, to comply with Clinton's orders and to find a good point to keep open communication with him. He sent Ewald with his Yägers, strengthened with an English Grenadier company and a company of rangers and 30 dragoons, to cover his left flank, as he moved across the peninsula to Williamsburg.

The whole American army was reported, by loyal sympathisers, to be in pursuit.

Ewald was usually on his guard for surprises, and says himself, in his book, "On the Handling of Light Troops": "We were never more than a few miles from our own main army, and thought these reports mere inventions, intended to hurry us out of the country," and Tarleton was reported to be within a short distance of their right, when Williamsburg was near at hand. As all danger was thought to be over, the march was stopped, that the men might rest; the 1,200 captured cattle were turned out to graze, the men laid aside their arms and went into improvised camps. Ewald led the advance, but no precautions of even the usual kind were taken, beyond putting advance posts near by — not even patrols sent out.

While all were scattered, there was a sudden sharp

report of firing and a cry, "The enemy is on us." Ewald threw himself on horseback, and hurried out in the direction from which the report came, where he soon met a strong line of the enemy's infantry, moving off to the left. Ewald saw that this was done in order to cut off the roads that led to Williamsburg. As he hurried back, a French officer summoned him to surrender, and captured his orderly. Ewald hurried his men together and ordered Lieut. Bickel to move to the right with the Yägers and fall on the left flank of the enemy. He led the Grenadiers and rangers himself and, without firing a shot, made a bayonet charge on the enemy, while Captain Schenk, with his Hussars, attacked the enemy's cavalry, Lieut. Bickel got on their left flank, and Sergeant Sippel, with some of the Yägers, in their rear.

The Americans fell back into the woods, and Ewald captured 34 of them, with a small loss of his own.

This was the last serious fight of the Hessian Yägers in the American war. From that time on it was only in small hand-to-hand engagements, on outpost duty, that they could show their bravery and their skill as soldiers.

Ewald and his Yägers had won the respect alike of their British allies and their American enemies, not only for their courage, but for their discipline, their coolness, their endurance and their activity.

In spite of the heat, Cornwallis left Williamsburg

on July 4th, crossed the James river on the 7th, and took position at Suffolk.

Lafayette had heard a false report that Cornwallis had crossed on the 6th, and hurried forward with 6,000 men and six guns, to strike his rear, and reaching it — in the belief that the larger part of the British army had crossed — attacked at once.

Cornwallis took v. Bose's regiment, with other troops, and repulsed the Americans, who lost two guns and nearly 200 men, and Lafayette soon gave up the pursuit, or even the attempt to harass the retreating army.

Ewald, in a letter to General v. Riedesel, dated Suffolk, July 20, 1781, speaks of the heavy loss from bad weather and hard marching and fighting, mourns the wounding of Captain Rau, and says he himself had but 46 men left for duty.

On July 16th, all but two of the regiments left Portsmouth and came by water to Yorktown. On the 29th, the German Yägers were brought in big boats, and on the 30th were sent out as the advance, guarding both banks at Gloucester.

Yorktown was a place of 300 houses, mostly of brick, many of them in ruins, and nearly all abandoned. It is on the south bank of the York river, a wide arm of Chesapeake bay. The garrison consisted of 300 militia, which, without firing a shot, withdrew to Williamsburg, 16 miles. The harbor was deep and two miles wide. Opposite, on the north bank, was the little village of Gloucester.

When Cornwallis came to Yorktown, his army was reduced to the Guards, three battalions of light infantry, six British regiments of the line, a regiment of dragoons, two companies of British artillery, a corps of volunteers from South Carolina, six companies of American rangers, a force of sappers, and about 1,400 sailors. His German troops were the two Hessian regiments, the v. Bose and the Crown Prince, the two South German regiments, their artillery, and the Hessian and South German Yägers.

On August 29th, the lines were advanced about a thousand paces, and strengthened by working ou them day and night, but there were only 400 tools with which to put them in condition.

On August 30th, a French fleet appeared, and on the land side Washington approached with his army, including Lafayette and a French corps.

The ships in the harbor were unloaded and their lower tier of guns brought on shore and mounted on the defenses. In front of the camp and the lines, all the roads were blocked and covered by heavy timber. The heat made the work very severe, and the supplies were scanty. The rations were bad ship's stores and very small. Sickness soon ravaged the force with dysentery and fever, which carried off many men. Among the victims, was Lieutenant v. Schuchardt, of the Bayreuth Grenadiers. Heavy thunderstorms and violent hurricanes broke over the camp, often devastating the poor quarters of the men. The French fleet was lying in Chesapeake bay.

In September, many American troops came from Baltimore, and the Americans seized a picket of the Hessian regiment v. Bose, on the right wing, and then withdrew into the woods.

On the 28th, the whole camp was in alarm, from a strong attack of the American forces. Tents were hastily removed and all the baggage taken into the town. This was repeated on the 30th, and some 30 English and Hessians were killed or wounded. At night, all the troops in the camp were quietly moved into the new lines thrown up around the town.

On the 30th, the Americans stormed for three hours a redoubt in front of the right wing, but by help of a frigate lying in the stream were driven back. Among the attacking party were French Grenadiers.

On October 1st, the Americans began to build regular siege works, but had no guns with which to man them.

Two thousand men were at work strengthening the British defenses. Every four hours the commands in the trenches were relieved.

On the 2d, the Americans, who had taken possession of the works abandoned by the English, were heavily cannonaded, and the fire was kept up for succeeding days with bombs and solid shot; this was done steadily until the 9th, but without any return fire. On the afternoon of that day, the first cannon shot on their side came from a battery in the woods, opposite the right wing; it was directed at a redoubt

## In the American Revolution. 209

on a hill near the river, about a mile from the lines. After retreat, the fire became heavier, and a frigate lying in the harbor was set on fire by a hot shot.

On the 10th, the fire of the besiegers was still heavier, and there was no cover that could withstand it.or protect the troops. The last of the inhabitants took refuge in caves dug out in the hills near the river, but these were soon in the range of the fire. The camp was changed and the tents struck.

On the 11th, the fire was still sharper, and 3,600 shots from the besiegers were reported. The destruction was fearful, ships and houses were struck, dead bodies and wounded men were seen on all sides. Bombs exploded in the water, spreading the alarm in all directions, and the ground trembled as with an earthquake. The v. Bose regiment, on the left flank in the second line, was the most exposed; balls and bombs fell from every side, and it had daily the most dead and wounded. The Ansbach-Bayreuth regiment, in the extreme redoubt of the left wing, was also a heavy sufferer. Bombs falling in their camp spread destruction far and wide. To get forage was difficult and dangerous, and the German Yägers lost heavily in serving as escort. Capt. Ewald showed his ability by his success in protecting his men by all sorts of expedients. Ewald led an advance guard of 100 dragoons, 60 Yägers and some rangers, and by moving off on the flank of the column, uncovered a body of French Hussars. He quietly told his commander that foraging had better begin here, and by his firmness was able to withstand the attack of the Duc de Lauzun's legion, with some militia, and Ewald, as rear guard, was successful in protecting the retreat to Gloucester.

On alternate nights, the fire relaxed and then increased. The besiegers attacked the outer redoubts, occupied by Hessian and British troops, and under cover of a heavy fog the French Grenadiers made a successful breach and drove the defenders out, displaying the French flag in close position before the weary garrison. The whole camp was alarmed, and every regiment was ordered under arms. The entire left wing began to fire, out of zeal and curiosity, to give the enemy a warm reception, and with no great result.

During the attack, the French and Americans resorted to a clever *ruse de guerre*, giving commands in German to advance the whole column and to send the batteries to the front—trying to make this diversion appear to be the main attack in force on the center of the position.

On the 15th, the besieged made a bold dash and captured a number of prisoners, forcing the French supports to fly, when the guns were silenced. At night, 250 Ansbach-Bayreuth soldiers were sent to the further redoubt, when the light infantry, which had before occupied it, were sent in shallops across to Gloucester, to draw the fire of the besiegers on that side.

Cornwallis thought that he could still make a bold

sally and escape, but the bad weather prevented his sending more of his troops across. His appeals to Clinton for reinforcements were all in vain, and he saw that resistance was only a matter of endurance; while his fire was maintained, the Americans were steadily pushing their lines close to his front.

On the 17th, the firing opened at daybreak, with increased violence. The light infantry returned from Gloucester, with the report that it was hopeless to try to break through in that direction, as the Americans had strengthened and extended their lines on that side, and a cordon of French Hussars completed the circle.

Cornwallis himself came to the front, studied the situation, and sent a white flag to offer terms of surrender. A second and a third were sent before the firing ceased, thus costing many lives by the delay. The men began to destroy their tents and arms, for they knew that the terms of surrender must be hard ones. While the negotiations dragged on, a powder magazine exploded in the town, doing great damage and costing thirteen lives.

On the 19th of October, Cornwallis surrendered his whole army as prisoners of war. The soldiers, as one of them wrote, were not deprived of their effects, and were treated kindly and fairly, according to the usages of war.

The fifth article of the surrender provided that the soldiers should remain in Virginia, Maryland or Pennsylvania, as nearly as possible in regimental organizations — receiving the same rations as the Continental army. An officer to every 50 men, of the same nationality—English, Hessian or Ansbach —was to remain, on parole, to look after them, and see that they were supplied with clothing and other necessaries.

The Crown Prince regiment was the strongest, and had met a proportionate loss. The Hessian and Ansbach Yägers had also suffered heavily. Ewald had only one-sixth of his original strength. Eighteen German flags and eight batteries were among the spoils that fell to the Americans.

Cornwallis had hardly 4,000 men capable of bearing arms, and he reported to Clinton that the Americans had 8,000 French, as many Continentals, and 5,000 militia.

Just as Burgoyne's surrender largely secured to the Americans their French allies, so that of Lord Cornwallis was mainly instrumental in bringing about the recognition of American independence, and Yorktown was the only great action in which the French had taken an important share.

When the garrison marched out, past the American and French armies, the latter were commanded by Rochambeau, who was surrounded by Lafayette, the Prince of Saarbruck-Zweibrücken [Deux Ponts], and the Prince de Lauzun, all in full uniform, with their decorations. On the right of each French regiment was their white flag with the lilies. Among the French troops were some Alsace regiments. In front of the Americans stood Washington, Gates, Greene and Wayne.

"The prisoners," says one of them, Döhla, in his diary, "looked with wonder on the great force of the enemy, and they saw, with equal wonder, the weakness of our force, a mere handful — not more than one of their daily guard mountings."

Döhla describes the circle of French Hussars into which the prisoners marched to surrender their arms, and the touching sight of Col. v. Seyboth leading his men, he and they all crying at the loss of their weapons.

An officer says the grief and suppressed rage of the old soldiers, thus yielding to those who had been looked on as shopkeepers and farmers, was hard to realize. One old soldier wept like a child; a corporal kissed his gun, then threw it down and cried out, "You can never have as good a master as I was." But he also credits the Americans with great good feeling, while the French, if more soldierly, were noisier and vainer.

Officers were allowed to retain their swords, at the request of the French generals; who also commended the South German regiments as the best.

The prisoners were allowed every reasonable liberty, under guard of the French, who were very friendly. The Americans were not allowed to go into the town, lest the militia might abuse their captives.

On the evening of October 19th, the Bayreuth

Yäger Lieutenant v. Hayden, with 16 men of his regiment, arrived, the only ones left of a command of a 1,000 that had started from South Carolina for Yorktown, and between Hampton and Williamsburg had been scattered by a strong hostile corps, after a sharp resistance.

The troops had abundant supplies, during the siege, both the reserves and the garrison, and for fourteen days an addition to their daily rations of sugar, chocolate and cocoa, just landed from a Dutch merchantman, captured and brought into Yorktown by an English ship.

Of the Hessians and Ansbach-Bayreuth soldiers, only 85 men deserted.

The spoils included over £5,000 sterling in the military chest of the English, and 191 guns and 82 vessels were taken.

The prisoners marched slowly to Williamsburg, then to Fredericksburg, Virginia, passing many homes of German settlers — then on to Frederick, Maryland, where the two Hessian regiments and the Bayreuth Yägers were quartered.

Early in November, the other troops reached Winchester, under an escort commanded by Gen. Muhlenberg, who was very considerate of the comfort of the German prisoners; but, as an officer wrote, the quarters gave poor hope of a comfortable winter—wretched huts of wood and canvass, with no roofs and no beds, miserable chimneys, neither doors nor windows, and in a thick wood. The soldiers were crowded close together, 20 to 30 men in one hut — worse than the pigsties or dog houses in their German homes.

Some of the men were at once allowed to go to work for the neighboring farmers, thus earning comfortable quarters, good living and suitable clothing, while those who remained in the barracks had little of any of the good things promised at the surrender. With money or with articles of value the soldiers could get something — and Major v. Beust borrowed money for his men, at a high rate of interest, from a merchant in Winchester, on his personal pledge and security.

The sick and wounded slowly gathered again at Winchester, complaining that the Americans had kept none of their promises to care for them, and their sufferings and distress were of the most harrowing kind. Those who died soon were the most fortunate.

Congress ordered the troops to Frederick, Maryland, to the great dissatisfaction of the Virginia farmers, who lost their cheap supply of labor in the German soldiers, but the Germans were glad to get away from such hard masters.

On the march through Maryland, the German settlers showed them much kindness, and German speech and friendly hospitality gave them great comfort. Their food, too, improved, and their quarters were two barracks, with 100 huts, built by the English, while nearly all the farmers around were Germans — Swabians. The troops formerly quartered there were sent to Lancaster, Pennsylvania. The two Hessian regiments, the Crown Prince and v. Bose, were quartered in the Poor House, and made fairly comfortable.

By the end of February, provisions ran short, and the officers bought supplies out of their own means, and again in March gave each man a Spanish dollar to help him buy food. Döhla complains of the bad food and the utter want of clothing.

It was not until late in April, that the baggage arrived from New York — and each man got a new ribbon for his queue, that he might keep that in order.

In May, the money due from November to March was paid, and each man received ten Spanish dollars, and with this and the warm weather, the prisoners were more comfortable.

Through death, sickness and desertion, the regiments were greatly reduced. In one night 20 men escaped, but 13 were brought back by an American patrol. Most of them left to escape their weary detention, hoping to get to New York or some other point, where they could rejoin the German forces. The militia revenged themselves by firing on and wounding the prisoners, and a Bayreuth soldier was one of the victims.

On September 1st, Congress ordered all the men of Cornwallis' and Burgoyne's armies, at work on the farms, to report at Frederick. Some of them had become owners of their farms and were married.

These were allowed to ransom themselves for a fixed sum — about 80 Spanish dollars. Those who could not raise that amount, usually found Americans to advance it, and agreed to return it in labor for a fixed term. These were called "Redemptioners," and their bargains had a sort of legal sanction, were made public at church, and generally acknowledged as binding.

The Americans began openly to recruit enlistments among the prisoners, going into the barracks, promising 30 Spanish dollars, hard money, of which eight dollars was paid down, the rest when the recruit joined his regiment. But few of the Germans were tempted, even when the recruiting officers brought music and loose women and liquor, with which to induce the men to abandon their colors and join the American army.

Now and then German settlers came forward to relieve their own kinsfolk by paying for their release from imprisonment, and this soon became an active means for lessening their number.

In September, 300 English prisoners of Cornwallis' army came to Frederick from Winchester, under an escort of an American volunteer corps, made up of all nationalities, among them 40 Ansbach-Bayreuth soldiers, who had been released from imprisonment in Virginia and had then volunteered for the American army.

In March, 1783, the first news of peace reached the camp, and gave rise to great rejoicing, in the hope of early release. An express rider brought the official announcement from Congress, in Philadelphia.

Later on, the rest of the long-delayed baggage came to hand and, on April 1st, the four German regiments received their arrears of pay.

On the 22d, General Lincoln made official proclamation of peace, and it was celebrated by a patriotic demonstration, day and night. The fireworks for the night's display were prepared by Captain Hofmann, of the Bayreuth artillery, and his men; the German musicians played at the ball given in honor of the occasion, and many of the German officers were guests at all the festivities.

In camp there was great rejoicing, too, but when the men cheered for King George, a French captain, in charge, attacked them and mortally wounded four of the German soldiers.

---

The Waldeck regiment went further south than any of the other German troops. It was sent to fight the Spaniards in Florida, as part of the reinforcements sent by Clinton to Pensacola at the end of 1778. With them were the Provincial Loyalists, of Maryland and Pennsylvania — making in all a force of 1,200 men, to coöperate with ten English and two German regiments in the southern provinces.

On October 20th, just two years from their arrival in America, and a year from their hard experiences on the Hudson river, four vessels were assigned to the Waldeck regiment, part of a fleet of 70 sail, under the escort of Commodore Hotham, in the Preston, a 70-gun man-of-war. After a sharp storm, the fleet separated, part carrying soldiers and supplies to Barbadoes and Carolina, the other to Jamaica. On the way there were a number of privateers and cruisers; one was taken, but none of them attacked the men-of-war.

In Jamaica, the Germans saw all the wealth of tropical nature—an earthly paradise, after their long sea voyage. The Waldeck regimental chaplain baptized three soldiers' children born on shipboard — for the soldiers' wives accompanied them; in one vessel there were four of them with children.

On December 31st, the fleet again set sail, and after 3,500 miles of sea voyage, finally reached Pensacola, then a poor village of 200 scattered houses, mostly of wood, with no trace of early Spanish settlement, other than the old stone powder magazine. The defenses on the sea side were sand heaps; on the land side, palisades. Near the town grew great forests, in which it was said there were wild animals—bears, tigers, panthers, alligators and other dangerous creatures, as well as savage Indians. Wild game was plentiful, but of the elements of civilization little was heard. The only English clergyman was at Mobile. Baptism was given only on convenient occasions, and the Waldeck chaplain baptized a child of eight years of age.

From Georgia to Pensacola was a four weeks' journey, and the traveler had to supply tents, axes, covers, and means of living, for there was not a single human habitation to be found on the way.

The Indians were said to be very numerous — one tribe of 20,000 men was on friendly terms with the English. Steurnagel, in his diary, describes them as fearful in war, always killing their prisoners, revenging blood for blood, and skillful in the use of their weapons. The women accompanied them to battle, and sang warlike songs to encourage the braves. Scalps were a regular article of sale, £3 sterling being the fixed market price.

Among these savages, to their great surprise, the Waldeck soldiers found a countryman, from one of their own villages, Königshagen; he had deserted from the army as a youth, and finally joined the Indians, serving as interpreter—his name was Brandenburg, and he was as little of a Christian as his Indian comrades.

The troops were put to work to restore the old Spanish defenses, and owing to the intense heat, they worked at night; patrols were sent out as far as the Mississippi.

On the western coast there was a force of only 500 men, and the Waldeck Grenadiers were sent to reinforce them at Baton Rouge, and they in turn were followed by a company under Major v. Horn and 15 men of that of Col. v. Hanxleden and the company of Capt. Alberti.

The Creek and Choctaw Indians came to Pensacola as allies, the former — women as well as men — well mounted and strong and good-natured.

In August, Don Bernardo Galvez, the Spanish governor of Louisiana, made public proclamation of the independence of the United States, and formally declared war against the British. His force consisted of 2,000 men, against which the British had but small opportunity to prepare.

The Waldeck troops, under Capt. v. Hacke, were at Baton Rouge, but the Spaniards seized a British vessel on the Mississippi, carrying Capt. Alberti's company, 54 men and officers.

The Spaniards attacked the fort at Pensacola, but were twice repulsed, with heavy loss, and then offered terms of capitulation, very favorable to the gallantry of the defenders, which were accepted.

The Waldeckers lost Ensign Noltin, Lieut. Leonhardi, who had distinguished himself at the storming of Fort Washington, and 22 men, besides a number wounded, and surrendered over 200 officers and men.

The news of the capture of Mobile was soon brought to Pensacola, but was received as a trick of the enemy to induce the garrison to leave that post and risk a battle in the open.

Chaplain Waldeck mentions, in his diary, the difficulty of ascertaining the truth and the uncertainty of knowing what to do.

Finally, it was decided to remain in Pensacola — and a fearful storm and an earthquake made their situation more desperate, while the scanty supplies told on the strength of the little force.

On March 5th, 1780, the Waldeck force was part of an expedition sent to relieve Mobile, hard pressed by the Spaniards, and was followed by the Pennsylvania Loyalists and some artillery. It was a march of 120 miles, through an uninhabited wilderness, and all in vain—Mobile had surrendered, and the expedition returned on the 19th, after a trying march.

On March 27th, the Spanish fleet came in sight, 21 sail, and next day it anchored off Pensacola. The Waldeck regiment went to Fort George, and all preparation was made for a siege, when the fleet sailed away on the 30th. The Waldeck force, under Col. v. Hanxleden, was strengthened by the Maryland Loyalists, two companies.

On April 9th, Lieut.-Col. v. Horn arrived, with his two sons and a small body of twenty recruits — they had been a year on the way from Waldeck.

The Chickasaw and other Indians came in large numbers, but they were useless allies, eating and drinking to excess, and doing no work, while the German and English soldiers were worn out with their labor on the new defenses — a new fort was called Fort Waldeck.

The Spaniards crossed the Perdido, but were driven back by the Indians, who stoutly refused to join Galvez, although he had enlisted the help of a good many of the native tribes by his liberal offers.

Chaplain Waldeck reports the greatest difficulty

as to supplies of food—bread and water for breakfast, water at dinner, a pipe of tobacco and more water for supper. Sausages cost $7.00, a pound of tobacco $4.00, of coffee $1.00, a pint of brandy eight hard shillings, rum was a forgotten luxury, and the Indians, in searching for it, plundered the scattered British settlers, pretending that they took them for Spaniards.

Fortune favored the British, as their ships brought in some Spanish merchantmen, with rum, meal, coffee, sugar and other welcome commodities, and a vessel loaded with powder was also captured.

On November 19th, Major Pentzel was sent, with 50 Waldeckers, to the Cliffs, a new post at the entrance to the harbor, and on January 3d, 1781, Col. v. Hanxelden was sent to French Village, on the Mississippi, with some men of his own regiment and 300 Indians and other troops, to drive the Spaniards out of their works. On the 7th, he reached the place and made an attack, the Germans charging at the point of the bayonet, but, without support from the Indians, they were obliged to withdraw, leaving their brave colonel and Lieut. Stirlin dead, and Lieut. Baumbach wounded.

The Spaniards honored the grave of the heroic commander, as a mark of respect for his gallantry.

On March 9th, the Spanish fleet again arrived at Pensacola, with six times the strength of the defense, (not over a thousand men), besides heavy guns and all the means of a regular siege.

A shallop sent out by the British man-of-war Mentor captured a Spanish vessel from Mobile, with the baggage and effects of the Spanish general, and $20,000 in hard money, his fine silver table service, fine wines, and all the utensils of a good kitchen.

On the 11th, the Spanish opened fire on Pensacola, and on the 18th the fleet sailed into the harbor, and on the 23d was reinforced by 16 vessels, with troops from Havannah, but their first attempt at landing was repelled, and even when a counter-attack was betrayed by a catholic Waldeck corporal, who deserted and gave notice, the Spaniards were driven out of their works by the Waldeck troops.

The news of the capture of Charleston was celebrated in Pensacola, which was soon itself exposed to a continuous fire until early in May. Even then treachery helped the Spaniards, for a Provincial officer, who had been broken and driven out of the camp, deserted to the enemy and gave them information where to direct their fire; it soon exploded a powder magazine, costing 52 lives and wounding many more, and utterly destroying the works.

The Spaniards pushed forward in such strength that no further resistance was possible, and favorable terms of surrender were accepted.

The defenders marched out with the honors of war, the officers retaining their swords, and the whole force to be sent by the Spaniards to a British harbor, on parole not to serve against Spain until exchanged; the sick and wounded to be cared for until they, too, could be sent away. New York was the designated harbor.

On June 4th, the troops were put on shipboard, and reached New York at the end of the month. The Waldeck troops, with Captains v. Hacke and Alberti and Lieutenants Strubberg and Brunhardt, also returned from their captivity. They had lost more men by disease than in battle, among them Lieut. v. Goren and Lieut. Alberti, who died in New Orleans in July.

Steuernagel, in his diary, says that Pensacola was defended by 600 men against 22,000, but the actual disproportion was large enough — 800 to 15,000.

---

The war in 1781 was slowly waged in the northern provinces. The reinforcements for the German forces arrived in due time. In the beginning of March, 300 men came for the Ansbach-Bayreuth regiments, under Col. v. Schlammersdorf, of the Guards; they came down the Main to Hanau, where they were joined by the Hanau troops, and later by those from Hesse Cassel; those from Anhalt-Zerbst went to Wangeroge, a little island at the mouth of the Weser, under Gen. v. Rauchhaupt, to avoid desertions— and thence under Brigade-Major v. Weitersheim— making in all 2,988 men; finally arriving in New York in August.

Clinton, who had barely escaped capture early in January, 1781, was persuaded to listen to a report that 800 men in the American force at Amboy would desert, if protected, and sent 2,000 men, including the v. Linsingen Grenadier battalion, a company of Hessian Yägers, and other troops; but fortunately the deception was discovered and the men brought back to their old posts.

General v. Knyphausen had offered pardon to all deserters returning to their colors, and many accepted it, complaining of hard usage with their temporary employers and in the American army.

Clinton gave two guineas, out of his pocket, to two brothers of the Ansbach regiment, who had deserted and now returned.

The force in New York was so reduced that it could do little, but Washington kept it on the alert, and it was obliged to be vigilant and watchful.

Gen. v. Riedesel, then in command at Brooklyn, wrote to the Duke of Brunswick, on June 26th, 1781, a report that showed that he understood the real plan of Washington better than the British commander, who was thus led to sacrifice his best troops, German and English, at Yorktown. Riedesel was satisfied that the English ministry failed to appreciate the important help the Americans were getting from France, and that Washington was planning, by their help, to secure a victory that would help to bring the war to an end, while Clinton and Cornwallis were disputing over their plans and failing to use their force or the fleet to the best advantage in united operations.

Washington, with the French reinforcements from Rhode Island, had over 12,000 men. He threatened Clinton, so as to prevent him from sending reinforcements to Virginia, and meant to inflict heavy punishment on DeLancey's Loyalists. He therefore ordered 800 infantry and 300 cavalry, of his best troops, to move towards King's Bridge and attack DeLancey.

By accident, Clinton had ordered an attack for the same time, the 2d and 3d of July, on the American outpost at Dobbs' Ferry, and to gather all the supplies in reach, sending 200 wagons there to carry them off, and to protect them, 200 Hessian Yägers on foot and 30 mounted, under Capt. Prüschenk; Col. Emmerich, with 100 men, was to go in advance and, when the Americans attacked, to strike them in the rear.

Late at night, Clinton got news that the Americans were in motion, and that Capt. Rau, the leader of a Yäger patrol, had been killed by the advancing enemy. Clinton recalled the whole expedition. Col. v. Wurmb sent back Capt. Prüschenk and his Yägers, and ordered him to recall Col. Emmerich, or to go to his support, if he was already engaged. As the advance, under Lieut. Schäffer, reached Fort Independence, he saw nothing of the enemy, and so reported to Prüschenk.

As a further precaution, a detachment of 18 Yägers, under Sergeant Rubenkönig, an old soldier, was sent out on the right flank to observe. There he met a small body moving up and down; taking them for DeLancey's or Emmerich's men, he spoke to them, and was at once seized and threatened with death if he spoke; but he cried out, warning his men that the enemy were near by, and in the firing, escaped and returned safely. Col. v. Wurmb especially recommended him for promotion, but the close of the war cut off his due reward.*

Lieut. Schäffer, too, was soon under fire and lost many of his men, and Capt. Prüschenk found the enemy in much greater strength than his own, and to cover his retreat, sent Lieut. Fliess, with 30 Yägers, to attack in close order, thus gaining time for his main body, while the Americans were for a time stopped by the bold bayonet charge of the little band, which was able to get off, too, with no great loss.

Col. v. Wurmb came out with the rest of the Yägers and, although much inferior in numbers, even with the reinforcement of the loyalists and 200 men from the defenses at Kingsbridge, attacked the strong line of the Americans and thus freed Emmerich, who had been cut off, and was now able to return and report that Washington himself was advancing with 3,000 men, thus forcing Emmerich to fall back. Wurmb then withdrew to the lines at Kingsbridge,

---

* NOTE.—Rubenkonig is the hero of a late very attractive addition to our slender stock of literature, in a novel, "Forgotten Heroes. A Story of the American War of Independence." By Franz Treller. Cassel, 1892.

and the Americans, after reconnoitering the ground, again quietly withdrew.

The German soldiers lost heavily, but their conduct was heroic, and Prüschenk was rewarded by a decoration, well earned, and by Clinton's thanks, through v. Knyphausen.

Washington repeated his demonstrations, but, in spite of the warning of Col. v. Wurmb, reported by his adjutant, v. Ochs, Clinton refused to credit their statement that all this was merely done to keep Clinton fast in New York.

In August and early in September, the Prince Charles regiment, the four Hessian Grenadier battalions, 400 Hessian and Ansbach Yägers, and other troops, were sent on board ship, landed and again loaded, ready to go to Cornwallis' help in Virginia, and finally kept in the harbor of New York, losing precious time, on one pretext or another — as that there were not enough carpenters to repair the English fleet, when the soldiers could easily have supplied all that were needed. Even when oncé on board, the transports were again held at Staaten Island and the troops once more disembarked, to be reviewed by Prince William, later William the Fourth. Then the 6,000 men were again put on board, and then, on the 18th, on the fleet of 24 men-of-war, which finally sailed to Chesapeake Bay, arriving there on the 28th of October, and at once getting ready to meet the French fleet, when a small boat put off from Cape Charles for the admiral's ship.

Then orders were given to move, and the fleet promptly put out to sea again — for news had been received that Cornwallis had surrendered nine days before.

Returning at once to New York, head winds and seas kept the crowded ships outside, and the men came near starving; but supplies were brought them from the city, and finally, on the 14th of November, the troops were again landed and quartered in very poor temporary quarters on Long Island.

## CHAPTER XIV.

Although the surrender of Cornwallis was the real end of the war, the British government did not admit it, Parliament renewed the grant for the allied troops, and the German recruits were forwarded as usual.

On June 10th, 1782, the transport fleet of 15 vessels, escorted by three men-of-war, sailed with Hessian, Hanau, Brunswick, Ansbach and Zerbst recruits.

Col. v. Hatzfeld led 900 Hessians, the eighth regular reinforcement — consisting of Yägers, artillerymen and infantry — leaving Cassel on April 10th. Their route lay through Prussian territory, and in spite of the report that Frederic the Great would not allow German recruits for America to go through his kingdom, or that he exacted the same duty that was paid on cattle sent to England, no effort was made to interrupt their march — indeed, their number was increased by Prussian soldiers deserting to join the new recruits.

Arriving in Halifax in August, the men were disembarked, on the report of a large French fleet near by; but it proved to be a British transport fleet, with 1,500 men and provisions for the army.

Meantime, the German soldiers in and near New York were kept busy with preparations for military operations. The Guards and Prince Charles regiments were quartered in new barracks, which they quickly surrounded with earthworks.

Dinklage says, in his diary, that New York was converted into a regular fortification — on every side defenses, trees all cut down, the beautiful avenues and orchards all gone — the work of years destroyed in a day.

There was little real work for the soldiers, but they were kept busy protecting the refugees — men who joined no regular military organization, neither the regular nor the provincial loyalist troops, but fought for their own hand, singly, and in defiance of all rules of war, and were bitterly hated by the Americans, who pursued them relentlessly.

On May 1st, Gen. Clinton published the official declaration of negotiations for peace and ordered all hostilities to be suspended. He was soon relieved by Gen. Carleton, now Lord Dorchester, who came rather to make peace than carry on war, and who at once recalled to New York the troops in the south, at Charleston and Savannah.

The German soldiers shared the general dissatisfaction, and one of their officers wrote home: " Our conquests in America avail nothing. We must give up this country; for though we have conquered it, the spirit of the Americans remains unbroken."

Lieut.-Gen. v. Knyphausen returned home, and

was succeeded by Lieut.-Gen. Lossberg, in command of the Hessians. He and Clinton sailed together, after receiving every mark of respect from the Germans — and Dinklage says, in his diary, that v. Knyphausen went with the affection and respect alike of the English and Hessian and American soldiers.

The report of Admiral Rodney's great victory over Admiral Grasse led to renewed reports that peace was not agreed on and that the war would be renewed, and on September 15th, Maj.-Gen. v. Wurmb led three brigades and a force of cavalry out on a great foraging expedition. But this was the last military demonstration against the enemy, and not a shot was fired. The men were exercised and manœuvred mostly in brigades, just as in peace times.

The Hessian Yäger corps had enjoyed its first quiet summer on Long Island, and now went into winter quarters there.

The three Hessian regiments left in Charleston, South Carolina — separated for years from their fellow soldiers serving in the north — led a miserable life, with no sort of opportunity for military distinction. Left there by Clinton in May, 1780, they did little but police duty, protecting the town against a threatened attack of the French fleet at one time, and at another against a conspiracy on the part of some of the patriotic Americans to secure the help of the negroes in an attempt to overturn the British command; until, in October, 1782, the garrison was put on board a fleet of transports and, after joining the other troops from Georgia, sailed for New York, landing there, after a stormy passage, on December 1st, when the Hessians joined v. Bunau's regiment, in Brooklyn, and went into winter quarters there. Most of the Hessian soldiers were put into tents and suffered great hardships during the winter.

By May, nearly all the Hessian and Ansbach-Bayreuth prisoners of war were returned to their commands in New York. Many were delighted at the prospect of returning home, but a goodly number preferred to stay in America, and permission was freely given to all who chose to make their home there.

The royalists were first supplied with transportation and it was not until July that the troops could be embarked, for the fleet had over 9,000 flying royalists to take on board.

Carleton carried on negotiations for the exchange of prisoners with great zeal, and the last lists provided for the surrender of 5,826 men held in Philadelphia, of which number 806 were Germans and 326 loyalists or provincials, and as Congress would not allow these to remain in the country, they were the first to be sent to New York.

Carleton did his best to settle matters, and his work was completed when peace was finally agreed on at Versailles, on November 3, 1783.

## CHAPTER XV.

### EVENTS IN CANADA, FROM 1777 TO 1783.

After Burgoyne left Canada on his campaign which ended so ingloriously, there was little of importance in that province to influence the war.

Gen. Guy Carleton, who was left in command, showed characteristic prudence in handling his small force, scattered through the vast region entrusted to him. His force included 669 Brunswick and Hesse Hanau soldiers — 6 captains, 12 lieutenants, 48 non-commissioned officers and 600 private soldiers, under Lieut.-Col. v. Ehrenkrook, a capable officer, soon after made a brigadier.

The spirit of unrest was spreading rapidly, and Carleton showed great skill in avoiding any open quarrel with the dissatisfied elements. He strengthened the defenses, manned them as well as he could, kept up communication with all his posts and strove to do his best in his isolation.

When the news of Burgoyne's disaster reached him, Carleton sent 324 of the Brunswick and Hanau soldiers, under Capt. v. Zielberg, to Trois Rivieres, to be ready to lead the advance in any movement southward.

In July, Lieut.-Col. v. Kreuzburg arrived, with three new Hanau Yäger companies, which remained in Canada. It was a thoroughly disciplined body of men, well trained in firing and other exercises, and a welcome addition to Carleton's forces. They had started from Hanau in May, to be sent to Burgoyne, but arrived too late.

Late in November, the Brunswick troops went into winter quarters near Sorel, the Hanau troops near Berthier, the light infantry (Yägers) on the southeast side of Montreal, but they were kept constantly moving, going as far as Lake Champlain, over the snow, on patrol duty. The officers were mostly quartered in private houses, and the men were often cut off from them by bad weather for days at a time.

The posts stationed in block-houses were still more dreary, and the German soldiers complained of the dreadful dulness. Only in March was it broken by the sudden arrival of the governor, with orders to the soldiers to concentrate, in view of the report of an American attack, but as it proved a false rumor, the men returned to their quarters.

Carleton hurried to Quebec, to restore order there, and Brigadier Ehrenkrook was sent to the parish of Terrebonne, to quiet an outbreak there.

In May, a regiment of Anhalt-Zerbst soldiers arrived. In September, 1777, the Duke of Anhalt-

Zerbst had made a treaty with England, in which he agreed to furnish a regiment of 1,160 men, to serve for six years. Enlistments were carried on in Zerbst very successfully. The Duke was a strange character, envious of the fame of Frederic the Great, with one passion—fine soldiers—and he raised 2,000 men, with 11 colonels. After the Seven Year's War, he was made an imperial field marshal, by the emperor, although he lived in Switzerland as a private citizen.

On the conclusion of the treaty, he received $300,-000, under these stipulations: that for every soldier not returning, he was to get $44; three wounded men should be counted as one dead man. The men were to receive the same uniform and rations as the English soldiers. The officers were to be paid 12 pence, the non-commissioned officers 8 pence, the private soldiers 5 pence, per day. All sorts of refugees from other parts of Germany, and indeed of Europe, were attracted and enlisted—good care being taken to prevent their escape. But to get officers it was necessary to advertise in the papers, and in this way two brothers from Brunswick, Barons v. Rauschenplatt, became, one, the elder, colonel, the other major, of the new regiment.

The regiment consisted of
First battalion, Major v. Piquet,
  Yäger troop, Capt. Keppenau, 50 men,
  Grenadier company, Maj. v. Piquet, with 1 captain, 3 lieutenants, 1 ensign, 10 corporals, 4 musicians and 166 men.

First Musketeer company, Col. v. Rauschenplatt,
Second Musketeer company, Prince August Schwarz-
   burg-Sondershausen,
   Each company consisted of 4 officers, 2 sergeants,
      10 corporals, 5 musicians, 146 men—in all, 334.
Second battalion, commander, Maj. v. Rauschenplatt,
   Yäger troop, Lieut. Jaritz, 50 men,
   Grenadier company, Capt. v. Wintersheim, 50 men,
   First and Second Musketeer companies, Major v.
      Rauschenplatt and Capt. Gogel,
same strength as the First battalion.
   The regimental staff, 44 strong,
   Artillery and train, 20 strong,
   Staff adjutant, Lieut. v. Möhring,
   Adjutant First battalion, Lieut. Littchau,
   Adjutant Second battalion, Lieut. Vierermal,
   Regimental quartermaster, Pahnier,
   Regimental surgeon, Dr. Pakendorff,
   Regimental chaplains :
      Lutheran, Braunsdorf,
      Reformed, Naumann,
      Catholic, Backer.
   The regiment brought out 34 soldiers' wives, who served as washerwomen. It included 1,164 men— each battalion 550. In five months it was ready to move. About 900 men were new recruits, the rest were old soldiers.
   Col. Faucit mustered the regiment into the British service in January, 1778, and in February it left Zerbst, after a warning from the colonel against

desertion. Nevertheless, the Prussian recruiting agents got a number, and to escape them, a roundabout march was made through Leipzig, Weissenfels and Hannover to Stade, but there were desertions all the way and open outbreaks, both with the soldiers and civilians. One officer died of his wounds. At one place, it was said 130 men left, at another a lieutenant and 50 men — often 8 to 10 went off at once, but at last the regiment reached the sea coast 1,119 strong, and were quartered on a little island belonging to the Duke of Anhalt-Zerbst, until they could be put on board ship.

Leaving port on April 26th, they reached Quebec in the end of May, but as General Carleton had no official news of this much-needed reinforcement, he refused to receive it or allow it to land, and for three months the poor fellows had to stay on shipboard, while the quartermaster travelled to London and back with the necessary papers. Finally allowed to land, they were kept in Quebec until the men could recover their health and get a fair share of training and discipline.

Late in June, Carleton was relieved by Haldimand as governor of Canada, who was waited on by the German officers in Quebec.

In July, 31 Hanau artillerymen arrived and, with 60 men drawn from the German forces, were assigned to and served with the British forces.

In September, 470 men of the Brunswick troops came, under four officers — Captains Stöder, Weiss,

Ruff, and Lieut. Corves — as recruits. The officers soon returned to Germany.

Brigade-Major v. Papet notes, in his diary, the return of two expeditions — one under Major Carleton, nephew of the general, the other under Johnson — which spread destruction across a wide stretch of country, burning and carrying off supplies for 8,000 men, driving women and children off to New England, and spreading the hatred of Great Britain far and wide. The English excused these Indian methods of warfare by the necessity of protecting their long frontier and of intimidating the Americans, so as to prevent their making reprisals in kind.

The troops were not sent into winter quarters by Gen. Haldimand until the middle of January, 1779. The battalion of Ehrenkrook was distributed as follows: Capt. v. Zielberg at Rivieres, Capt. v. Plessen at Champlain Parish, Capt. v. Schlagenteuffel at Point du Lac, and the commander's own company at Trois Rivieres; the battalion of v. Barner: Lt.-Col. Barner's company at Riviere du Loup Parish, Capt. v. Hambach's at Vanrenil, Capt. Thomä's at Masquinonge, Capt. Rosenberg's at St. Culbert. The Prince Charles regiment, under Lieut.-Col. Prätorius, long since recalled from Ticonderoga, was quartered in and around St. Hyacinthe.

The cold was so bitter that the Second battalion, on its march across Lake St. Peter, under Captain Thomä—Lieut.-Col. Barner being sick—lost 14 men and two soldiers' wives killed by the cold, and 30 men had their limbs frozen. Thomä was court martialled, and escaped on the plea that the proper clothing had never been issued; but he had been warned of the danger of exposing his men at such a season. Brigadier v. Ehrenkrook at once sent an officer to inspect the troops, who reported 15 dead, 2 lost, 15 severely, 23 slightly ill, from the effects of the exposure incidental to the literal execution of orders. Gen. Haldimand showed great sympathy, sent the best physicians, ordered the men to be cared for, and had them brought to the hospital at his own head-quarters, at Trois Rivieres.

Papet, in his diary, describes the bad condition of Barner's battalion. Many of the officers were sick, and nearly the whole battalion made unserviceable, and quite unable to make any resistance to an enemy or to do any military service effectively.

In February, placards were posted at Trois Rivieres, inviting the Canadians of French blood to return to their allegiance to the King of France—signed in his name by Count d'Estaing, dated Boston, October, 1778—but they produced little result. Investigation fixed the responsibility on a bookseller in Montreal, where the placards were also posted.

In July, the provision and troop fleet arrived in Quebec from Cork, which it had left in April, bringing Lieut.-Col. v. Speth, Ensign Häberlin and 25 Brunswick soldiers, who had been exchanged at Halifax the year before and spent the winter there. A body of Hanau recruits also arrived — dressed in

French uniforms, blue with red facings, which they had been obliged to buy with their own money. An English privateer had captured a French vessel, laden with French uniforms and supplies, and as they were sold cheap, the poor fellows who had been exchanged prisoners, were glad also to exchange their old rags for new French uniforms, for the sake of decency and comfort. To their French uniforms were now added English muskets and cartridge boxes, which gave them a very soldierly air. They were glad to rejoin their comrades, and gave a sad account of the hardships of their long imprisonment.

On July 30th, a soldier of the Rhetz regiment rejoined his comrades, after having escaped and gone through infinite suffering to prove his loyalty to his colors. He was one of 44 men brought to Albany in October, 1777, and at first imprisoned there, then distributed among the farmers, for a period of ten months, for their food and lodgings. When the harvests were over, they were asked to enlist, and as they all refused, they were again sent to the prison in Albany. At last a commissary, a German, got them passes and had them set free. Then some of them were persuaded to join a royalist force under Butler, and were able to get by way of Niagara to Montreal, where they showed their discipline by rejoining their respective commands.

A fifth body of Hanau recruits came in August, on a fleet of 36 ships, which brought provisions, etc.

Lieut.-Col. v. Speth now, as senior officer, resumed

command, relieving Lieut.-Col. v. Ehrenkrook, who had kept the German troops together in one brigade. He remained as battalion commander.

At the end of August, Brigadier v. Speth inspected the German troops and directed the oldest soldiers to be invalided and sent back to Germany.

In September, Lieut.-Col. v. Kreutzburg took a Yäger detachment of a captain, two lieutenants and 100 men, to Montreal. A report had been spread that a force of 7,000 men were on the way to Niagara. The Fifth Hanau company, under Capt. Hugget, who had lately arrived, joined the Yägers and marched to Fort Niagara. Wittgenstein's company was sent to Carleton Island, in the St. Lawrence river, where it falls out of Lake Ontario. Captain Hambach, with his company of Barner's battalion, was ordered to Montreal on October 1st.

A British fleet, leaving England in May, reached the St. Lawrence river in September. Of the 14 transports, two were filled with Brunswick troops; they were put on smaller vessels and taken to St. Ann's, whence Brigadier v. Speth led them to Trois Rivieres. They included 1 staff officer, 9 subalterns and 263 men. They were in old uniforms, which were replaced by new ones, as were those of the Anhalt-Zerbst regiment, and all were supplied with tents sent from England.

The governor issued from the depots in Canada for each man a pair of breeches, a pair of shoes, a blanket, and also a pair of gloves, to protect them through the winter. These were a gift from the Queen of England.

Maj. v. Cleve, of the Brunswick troops, reported to Gen. v. Riedesel that there were in Canada at this time 2,185 Brunswick and 306 Hanau soldiers, besides the Yägers. They were carefully provided with good quarters for the winter, to avoid a repetition of the disasters of the last winter — the staff and Ehrenkrook's battalion at Berthier, v. Barner's battalion at Montreal, the Prince Frederick regiment at its old post, sending one company to St. John, and an officer and 50 Yägers to Isle aux Noix. Lieut.-Col. v. Kreutzburg, with his Hanau Yägers, was sent to La Prairie and other villages, as far as St. Francis.

The Wittgenstein company remained at Carleton Island, the Hanau detachment at Quebec, under Captain v. Schill.

An officer and 30 Hessian Yägers were part of a detachment sent, in April, 1780, to Lake Champlain.

In June, Lieut.-Col. v. Kreuzburg, with his entire Hanau corps, was ordered to Quebec, leaving one officer and 50 men on Carleton Island. Lieut.-Col. v. Ehrenkrook and his battalion were brought into the lines at Trois Rivieres. The German troops worked on the defenses at Quebec. Two companies of the Prince Frederick regiment were quartered at Fort St. John, and 114 men must work every day on the works, which had been injured by a fire. The v. Barner battalion was sent to Quebec, and went into camp there, drawing tents from the English supplies.

Quebec was strengthened, on the report that two French fleets were preparing to attack it. Col. v. Kreutzburg objected to his men working on the fortifications, on the ground that they were exempt from such duty, and they were afterwards employed on long expeditions, which was much more to their liking.

At the end of June, reinforcements for the v. Lossberg and v. Knyphausen regiments arrived, under Col. v. Loos, who was soon made brigadier and, with his men, stationed at Quebec.

In July, the Brunswick infantry exchanged stations with v. Ehrenkrook's battalion, which occupied the tents vacated by the former.

The fearful heat made provisions scarce and the summer as trying as the winter had been. Desertions became very frequent among the Germans — not worse than among the Americans, of whom a captain and 150 men at one time came into the British lines.

Eight men of the Brunswick companies deserted together, but were pursued and brought back by the Anhalt-Zerbst regiment. The fault lay largely with the poor quality of recent enlistments in Germany.

At the end of August, in the camp at Quebec, there were the brigade of v. Loos, Hessian troops; the Hanau regiment, under Capt. v. Schöll; the two Brunswick companies of the v. Ehrenkrook battalion.

Col. v. Rauschenplatt commanded his own regiment, the Hanau Yägers and the Hanau and Hessian artillery. The news of the promotion of Brigadier v. Speth to be colonel was received along with that of the death of the Duke of Brunswick.

In September, the Hanau Yäger company made part of Col. Carleton's force on an expedition below Quebec.

In October, the German troops were sent to winter quarters, in villages some forty miles from Quebec, where no Germans had hitherto been stationed, but they were afterwards sent to their old stations — the Ehrenkrook battalion at L'Assomption, v. Barner's at Montreal, the Hanau detachment, under Capt. v. Schöll, at St. Anna, the Hanau Yägers, under Kreuzburg, at St. Valier, one company in Quebec, the v. Knyphausen regiment at Berthier, the v. Lossberg on Isle Orleans.

The handful of Brunswick dragoons had a hard time of it, scattered among the other troops, wearing their old cavalry equipment, until v. Speth got them fitted out more suitably.

The hot summer was followed by a winter of high prices for grain; straw rose from three or four piasters to 30; the dwelling houses were robbed of their thatched roofs to give the straw to the cattle, but many starved, and the vegetation was destroyed by worms and caterpillars.

A conspiracy of Johnson's men to imprison and kill the British officers was detected and prevented.

The provision fleet was eagerly expected; instead came the news that, after being scattered by storms at sea, of the 63 vessels intended for Canada, out of 150 which left Portsmouth in May, a portion had been attacked in the Gulf of St. Lawrence in August by three French frigates. At the end of the month, a fleet of 65 vessels reached Quebec, with two years' supplies and some Brunswick recruits.

Gen. v. Riedesel came at the end of September, having been exchanged, with many of his officers, and 900 German soldiers, after a hard voyage from New York. He brought 5 Brunswick staff officers, 16 captains, 24 subalterns, and 400 men; the rest were Hesse Hanau and Anhalt-Zerbst troops — recruits brought from New York to join their regiments. Before Riedesel arrived, Capt. v. Schlagenteuffel had reached Canada, with 70 Brunswick soldiers, who had bought their own release from the Americans; their worn out uniforms were exchanged for English uniforms, bought by their commander. Riedesel brought the rest of the Dragoon regiment and a battalion which Major Lucke had organized in New York, of the Brunswick soldiers he found there.

Riedesel and his family were warmly welcomed by Haldimand and they became warm friends. The German officers, Papet and others, spoke highly of Haldimand in their letters home.

Riedesel at once resumed command of the German troops and reorganized them, equalizing, as far as possible, the proportion of officers and the number of

men. On the 20th of October, he assigned the officers as follows:
(1) Dragoon regiment, Capt. v. Schlagentuffel,
(2) Prince Frederick regiment, Lieut.-Col. Prätorius,
(3) v. Rhetz regiment, Lieut.-Col. v. Ehrenkrook,
(4) v. Riedesel regiment, Lieut.-Col. v. Hille,
(5) v. Specht regiment, Major v. Lucke,
(6) Light battalion, Lieut.-Col. v. Barner.

There were six regiments, or rather battalions, of Brunswick troops, a half regiment of Hanau troops, a battalion of Hanau Yägers, two half regiments of Hessians, the Anhalt-Zerbst regiment.

Riedesel, at Clinton's request, suggested to Haldimand that he should lead an expedition of 4,000 men across Lake Erie to Virginia, to attack the Americans on the rear.

But Haldimand, instead, sent small expeditions to Vermont and to Oswego, and both returned at the end of September, without result, for 3,000 Americans had promptly rallied to drive the former off.

The order for winter quarters was issued early in October, assigning the German troops, under Gen. Riedesel, from Besancourt to Point au Fer, on the north shore of Lake Champlain; those under Brigadier v. Speth at Montreal; the Hanau Yägers to Parish Chateaugay, and the royalists, under Major Nern, to Vergere.

The Brunswick corps, by the end of the year, had lost, by death and desertion, 405 men, and the total, including the prisoners, showed a strength of 3,898 men.

The fear of insurrection kept the soldiers busy as armed police, and the prisons were soon full of suspects and men accused of treason or sympathy for the enemy.

As early as 1777, many Canadians, thought guilty of conspiracy, were taken to the cathedral and with ropes around their necks forced to listen to a long high mass and then to ask pardon of the king, church and God.

To maintain the good feeling of the loyalists, all were promptly paid for supplies furnished, and the German soldiers were particularly commended for their good conduct to the citizens.

Naturally, Canada was the refuge of all loyalists sent out of the American colonies, and Montreal and Quebec were full of them, so that life was made as attractive as possible.

Gen. v. Riedesel had general charge of the military posts and defenses, and was anxious lest the French should try to regain their old foothold. Indeed, in July, 1780, the French ministry seriously considered sending 6,000 men, under Rochambeau, from Newport, to make a demonstration of the kind. Riedesel suggested sending spies down the Connecticut to Springfield and Hartford, to ascertain and report what preparations were making, and whether the French were in force at Hartford. It was not known that the French, under Rochambeau, had marched to Virginia in September, with a part of Washington's army — thus showing how tardily news reached Canada.

Not until the middle of June, 1782, did the troops leave their winter quarters. The Anhalt-Zerbst regiment, the companies of the Lossberg regiment and of the Hanau troops, under Capt. v. Schöll, went into camp at Point Levi, opposite Quebec, under Maj.-Gen. v. Loos. Two companies of the Lossberg regiment, lost in the storm of 1779, were replaced by newly-arrived recruits, at Halifax. The missing officers were already replaced.

Riedesel spoke in the highest terms of the German troops in Canada. He wrote to Gen. v. Knyphausen, in September, 1781: "Not a single difficulty has occurred between them and the inhabitants, and Gen. v. Loos has gained the affection alike of the German and English soldiers."

Gen. Carleton, when he succeeded Clinton, at once directed Gen. Haldimand to strengthen all of his defenses, and the German general, in spite of failing health, was active in carrying on the work. During the summer, his five German regiments completed the defenses of Isle aux Noix; British and German soldiers working side by side, in heat and cold and rain.

The works, constructed of stone, were built with casemates, and were to be completed by the middle of the next summer.

Isle aux Noix was the key to the command of Lake

Champlain from the south. Fifty Hanau Yägers were posted at River la Colle.

In October, Lieut.-Col. v. Mengen arrived in Quebec with some of the exchanged officers from Virginia. Riedesel went to Quebec to welcome them. Later in October, Major v. Maiborne brought more from New York. After Mengen's arrival, the Grenadier battalion was reorganized by help of men from the four infantry regiments.

At the end of October, the orders were issued for winter quarters — the Dragoons at St. Antoine, the Grenadier battalion at Berthier, the v. Rhetz regiment at Sorel, St. Dennis and St. Charles, the Riedesel regiment at Sorel, the Specht regiment at St. Francois, the Light battalion v. Varner at St. Sulpice.

Haldimand showed Riedesel the last instructions from Carleton, advising him that Congress wanted to drive the Indians out of their territory, and to prolong the war, in the hope of securing the cession of Canada and Florida.

Writing in September or earlier, from New York, Carleton said the Americans would attack Canada in October, and that communication must be kept open with Halifax, to secure the prompt forwarding of reinforcements lying or arriving there and quite useless at that place. Riedesel complained that Carleton had not sent orders to Halifax directly to forward the reinforcements.

The fifth Brunswick detachment of recruits had arrived at the beginning of the year in Canada; the sixth was on its way, and Riedesel sent his adjutant to the Penobscot to meet it; so that at the end of the year it numbered 2,830 men, including 129 officers and 25 subalterns; there were still 1,137 prisoners of war. Many officers were now exchanged or borne on the active list.

Riedesel ordered a number of his soldiers to practice the use of snow-shoes, and the patrols, looking like Eskimos in their winter garb, were learning the use of snow-shoes, to the great amusement of the natives, to whom they were a second nature.

On the report of a hostile movement from Albany, Riedesel ordered Lieut.-Col. v. Kreuzburg to send a detachment of Yägers and dragoons to Isle aux Noix, and a company of the v. Rhetz regiment to St. John, all on snow-shoes.

Riedesel himself, in spite of bad health, personally inspected the posts from Sorel. At St. John he heard that the Americans had started in February, and early in March reported it to Haldimand, but the real state of the case was soon ascertained. A French Col. Villet had undertaken to surprise Fort Niagara, but was forced to retreat, with a loss in prisoners and deserters.

In March, rumors of peace began to spread, but the doubt as to the future of Canada made it necessary to act very cautiously.

On March 22d, Lieut.-Col. v. Ehrenkrook died, at Trois Rivieres, and was buried with military honors, and the officers who had gathered for his funeral were, by his direction, entertained at a handsome dinner, paid for by him.

In April, Haldimand received news of the peace, through a vessel coming from the east, although the treaty had been published in Philadelphia.

On the 26th, he received from Carleton official word that hostilities had ceased, by virtue of an agreement of January 20th. Riedesel said the news was received with great regret, which he shared.

In June, Riedesel received from Gen. Carleton the king's orders to send all the German soldiers home; the Brunswick troops to go first, and only the prisoners in New England to be left. They had seen little fighting since Burgoyne's surrender, but they had done much hard work.

A Hessian officer, describing the Hanau Yäger corps, said: "Although seeing little real war, they had led a wholesome life in the Canadian woods, rivalling the Indians in their long marches, hunting and fishing, and enjoying life much more than the German soldiers at home or in the southern armies."

The scattered forces could not well be brought together. Some of the last recruits were in New York, some in Newfoundland. The prisoners of war in Pennsylvania were sent directly to Europe.

Riedesel sent Lieut. Reineking to take those that were brought to New York directly to Germany, asking Carleton to help him with money and other necessaries, and Carleton reported to Riedesel that they had started in June.

The prisoners taken at Bennington were still in Massachusetts; Major Baurmeister was sent to Philadelphia to arrange with Congress for their return home.

## CHAPTER XVI.

The German soldier could gain little glory in the war now ended, but he had shown himself brave, patient, well disciplined and trustworthy. He had gained practical experience and useful lessons in new methods of warfare, which proved useful in subsequent campaigns.

Gen. Valentini, an able soldier and a good writer on military matters, said of the Hessians: "Of all the troops sent against France in the later wars, the soldiers from Hesse Cassel showed the highest military skill, endurance, good spirit, and a true love of war; even in uniform, he was ready to turn his hand to any labor; he showed the good lessons learned in America, and was the last to complain of having been sent there in British pay—for it was a capital school of war, and the men who returned profitted by their experience, and those who stayed behind had nothing to regret."

The American war was of infinite use to the German soldiers. Ten years later, they applied the lessons learned there in defending their own country, and the best officers and the best soldiers in the war with France were those who had served in America.

Dömberg, Langen, York and Gneisenau were capital examples of the lessons learned in America, applied in the Prussian army to its great advantage, for those who had fought in the Seven Years' War were now gray-haired veterans.

The Americans naturally, perhaps, in the heat of the contest with Great Britain, exaggerated every thing that was said about the Germans — their numbers, their losses and their actions.

Adjutant Henel, in 1778, wrote from New York, complaining that the reports published in Germany made the same mistake.

Even as faithful a writer as Cooper, the novelist, was unjust to the German soldiers serving in America. Against his romantic abuse, let us put the plain statement of the Hessian Major Pfister, in his account of the Hessian Yägers in the American war, from 1776 to 1784. He says: "In spite of false reports, the Hessians served well, both on foot and on horseback, and were respected alike by British and American soldiers, for their bravery and good conduct."

In an essay, presumably by Ewald, published in 1789, the author says: " Five years after the close of the American war, few people know the brilliant part played by the Hessian corps in America, and history has failed to do them justice. The outcome of that war was the result of the bad management of the

British government, and not the fault of British soldiers, or their allies, the Germans."

Their losses are not easily ascertained. Ventrurini says there were

|  | Sent to America. | Lost. |
|---|---|---|
| Hessians | 16,992 | 6,500 |
| Brunswick | 5,723 | 3,015 |
| Hanau | 2,422 | 981 |
| Ansbach-Bayreuth | 1,644 | 461 |
| Waldeck | 1,225 | 720 |
| Zerbst | 1,160 | 176 |
|  | 29,166 | 11,853 |

Gen. v. Ochs estimates that of 12,000 Hessians sent to America, and 4,000 to 5,000 recruits afterwards sent out, between 6,000 and 7,000 did not return; but besides the loss in seven campaigns, a large number voluntarily remained in America after the war.

Gen. v. Schlieffen says that their actual loss was much less than in the European campaigns — 1,800 actually killed out of nearly 30,000 was no great proportion.

Major Pfister says the far larger proportion of the men sent to America were volunteers, and so the larger proportion of those that did not return stayed in America voluntarily. The Germans did not desert in as great number as the English and American troops, but after the war was over, they decided to make their homes in America.

Most of the recruits sent to the Hessian forces were volunteers from Hanau, and they had joined just for the purpose of going to America and staying there, and they were quite justified in doing so.

Of Hessian officers there fell, to the end of 1777, Col. Rall, Lieut.-Col. Scheffer and Lieut.-Col. Brethauer, Majors v. Weitersheim, v. Hanstein, v. Dechow and Matthias; there died Cols. v. Heringen and v. Riess, Lieut.-Col. Lange (on the way over) and Maj. v. Bentheim.

To the close of 1778, Heister only reported twelve casualties, and of the five general officers of Germans in America, all returned safe home again.

Many of the soldiers who remained in America did so with the consent of their officers. The Duke of Brunswick reduced his standing army at the close of the war, and gladly gave their men and officers leave to stay in America. Of 115 Brunswick officers, 7 were killed in battle, 12 died, and 7 remained with leave — a total of 26 — and this in spite of long and weary imprisonment, which enabled them to make an intimate acquaintance with the country, and with the wish of their own sovereign to have them stay.

Equally untrue is it that the Hessian invalided soldiers were treated cruelly by their own sovereign. The Invalid battalion at Cassel was increased in 1781 by two companies and up to the close of the war by three, so that it made eight companies and formed a regiment, and was not reduced to a battalion until 1784.

## In the American Revolution. 259

Gen. v. Ochs, who was himself in the Hessian service in America, says the men were particularly well cared for, both in war and in peace — much better than in the war with France, later on.

Ewald, too, had personal experience, and attests the fact that there were no great losses or hardships.

The average ration of the British soldier was much better than that of the German soldier at home, and in America they shared it together.

---

When the war was over, Congress offered the German soldiers every advantage, in case they remained in America. The British government, too, made liberal offers of land in Nova Scotia — free transportation, 300 acres, free from taxes for twelve years, etc.; but only a few accepted them.

In July, 1783, the Hanau, Waldeck and Zerbst recruits left New York, followed in August by the Ansbach-Bayreuth and the First, and later the Second Hessian divisions. The Hessian Yägers, for want of transportation, did not sail until late in November.

The First Hessian division, under Maj.-Gen. v. Kospoth, consisting of the regiments Knyphausen, Ditfurth, Prince Frederick, Bose, Borbeck, Bunau, Benning, Knobloch, and the Grenadier battalion Angenelli, sailed August 15th, reaching home in October and November. The Hanau volunteers went directly home.

The troops, as they arrived in Cassel, were received by the Elector.

The Second division, under Maj.-Gen. v. Wurmb, sailed in November, reaching England only at the end of December. Scattered by storms, the transports landed at Plymouth and Deal and Portsmouth and Dover and Chatham, wherever and whenever they could make a harbor, for provisions were running short, and some were obliged to run into Irish ports for fresh supplies.

Finally landed in Chatham, they were comfortably quartered in barracks there. They were inspected by Gen. Tryon, the former governor of New York, in March, and he entertained the Hessian officers at a splendid dinner, for, as Lotheisen notes in his diary, he had always been a special friend of the Hessians.

Leaving England in April, they reached Germany at last, and being freshly equipped, were received by the Crown Prince and were reviewed by the Elector, with every mark of honor and gratitude for their good service.

The Hessian Yägers were also welcomed by the Elector, on their return to Cassel, in May, after a long detention in England.

The other German regiments were released from captivity in May, 1783, at Frederic, Maryland, their officers rejoining them. Döhla says, in his diary, that the people — and especially the women — were very sorry to bid them good-bye. Chaplain Wagner, of Ansbach, preached his last sermon. Capt. Quesnoy's company of 102 men was reduced to 33, and many others in the same proportion. They were brought in boats across the Susquehanna and bivouacked at Lancaster, then reached Philadelphia, where the men revolted at being quartered in the jail. After a four days' rest, they went through Bristol, Trenton, Princeton, to Staaten Island, marching 236 miles in 13 days, and on Long Island went into their old quarters, got new clothes, wigs and queues again, just as of old.

Col. v. Seyboth rejoined his regiment on the 22d of June — now reduced to one-third of its original strength. The King gave them new breeches, the Queen new blankets.

At last came the order, and the 450 men were embarked on three frigates — such wretched ships that they were soon scattered, reaching port in August and September, and then the men sailed in 14 transports and two frigates — 1,500 in all, Brunswick, Hessian, Anhalt-Zerbst and Waldeck soldiers — and not until the 20th were they mustered and paid. The men not natives of the particular little state with whose force they were serving, received traveling expenses, some as much as two guineas, to carry them to their own homes. They were all supplied with good and abundant food, but their pay was at once reduced to the German rate. The troops were heartily welcomed at their homes, received free entertainment, and were treated with marked honor by their princes and by all the authorities.

The German forces in Canada were soon collected in Quebec, where Riedesel arranged for their transportation — he and his family going on a special vessel.

The troops were specially inspected and reviewed, as they arrived in Quebec, embarked under salutes, and sailed early in August, making a fleet of sixteen sail for the first, and eight for the second, division. Together they numbered 105 officers and 1776 men and 64 soldiers' wives. The general had the best ship, which reached England in eighteen days — the others later on.

Riedesel and his wife received every mark of distinction in London from the court and nobility.

The Brunswick and Hanau prisoners of war, 484 men, came with the First Hessian division — after six years of helpless captivity. They were the first German soldiers to reach home — and the next were the exchanged prisoners from New York.

Gen. v. Riedesel rejoined his forces and marched at their head into Brunswick early in October, and was welcomed by the Duke with every honor—it was a real triumphal progress. They numbered 2,618, of whom 112 were officers. The greater part were discharged, but 163 of the handsomest men were sent to the Duke's Prussian regiment. Officers and soldiers were officially authorized to remain in America.

All these German soldiers were received on their return home with honor and in a way that showed the popular appreciation of their service in America.

It was a duty which they had done bravely and well, and there was no evidence that they were looked on as hirelings. Their heroic deeds were matter of constant mention, and were preserved in songs and popular sayings that are still traditions, but never was there any reason for failing in due honor to them.

# NOTES.

On February 8, 1783, the Duke of Brunswick issued an order directing the reduction of his army, and giving the officers and men permission to remain in or return to America, and granting those who did so six months' pay. Each captain was to receive an allowance, on being retired, of $15; a first lieutenant, $8; a second lieutenant, $6.

In April, 1783, Lord North wrote to Gen. v. Riedesel in reference to the return home of his force, thanking him and them for their services.

Notice of the Hessian Yäger corps, by Major Pfister:

Col. v. WURMB, after Donop's death, commander; Lieut.-Gen. 1806; died 1813.

Maj. v. PRÜSCHENK, commanded the Yägers in the Netherlands in 1793; died in 1800, a Major-General.

Maj. PHILIPP V. WURMB, 1806, Maj.-Gen.; died 1808.

Capt. v. WREDEN, died a Colonel in 1791.

Capt. JOHN EWALD, the original organizer of the

Yäger corps, won great reputation in the American war; in 1788 was made Lieut.-Col. in the Danish service and raised the Holstein Yäger corps; became a nobleman, a Lieut.-General, General in command of Holstein, and died in 1813.

Capt. HEINRICHS, became a Lieutenant-General in the Prussian army and died in 1834.

Fr. Ad. JULIUS V. WANGENHEIM, First Lieutenant and Captain, originally in the Gotha service. (Wrote a capital book about the trees in America.)

DeMESSEY, MONTLUISANT and DE FASQUIEL, three Frenchmen, who refused to fight against their countrymen in America; the first was discharged in 1781; the second entered the army only to get to America; was discharged, tried to join the American army, was seized and sent to England; the third got his discharge.

Capt. JOHN SCHÄFFER, became Lieut.-General and Minister of War in Darmstadt, and was ennobled as "Schäffer v. Bernstein."

JOHN CONRAD FLIESS, Second Lieutenant, became Colonel of the Dutch Crown Prince regiment in 1816.

ADAM LUDWIG OCHS, Second Lieutenant and Adjutant, 1781; 1809, Brigadier-General (in Spain); 1810, General of Division (in Russia); died 1823, as Major-General; author of a capital book on "The Formation of Light Infantry."

Sir GEORGE HANGHER(?), Lord Coleraine, Captain, 1778; Major-General, died 1840.

---

Of the Hanau Yäger corps:
CARL V. KREUTZBURG, Lieut.-Colonel, Colonel; in the campaign of 1792, commanded the Hessian Yäger corps; died 1796.

# APPENDIX.

The Hessian troops sent to America in 1776:
1. The Guard regiment . . . . . Col. v. Wurmb.
2. " Prince Charles regiment . . Col. Schreiber.
3. " v. Ditfurth regiment . . . . . Col. v. Bose.
4. " v. Trümbach regiment,
   Col. v. Bischoffshausen.
5. " v. Donop regiment . . . . . Col. v. Gosen.
6. " v. Mirbach regiment . . . . . . Col. Loos.
7. " v. Wutgenau regiment . . Col. v. Kospoth.
8. " Crown Prince regiment, Col. v. Hachenberg.
9. " v. Lossberg regiment. . . Col. v. Lossberg.
10. " v. Knyphausen regiment . . Col. v. Borke.
11. " Grenadier Regiment Rall . . . Col. v. Rall.
12. " Garrison Regiment v. Wissenbach,
    Col. v. Horn, Col. v. Borbeck.
13. " v. Huyne regiment . . . . Col. v. Huyne,
    Col. Kurtz.
14. " v. Bünau regiment . . . . . Col. v. Bünau.
15. " v. Stein regiment . . . . . . . Col. Seitz.
16. " First Grenadier battalion, Col. v. Linsingen.
17. " Second Grenadier battalion, Lt.-Col. v. Block.
18. " Third Grenadier battalion,
    Lt.-Col. v. Minnigerode.

19. The Fourth Grenadier battalion, Lt.-Col. Köhler.
20. Two companies Field Yägers . . Col. v. Donop.
21. Three companies Field Artillery . . Col. v. Eitel.

The first organization was as follows:

First Division:
Lieutenant-General v. Heister.

First Brigade,  
Maj.-Gen. v. Mirbach.  
Regiments,
- v. Mirbach,
- v. Donop,
- v. Wutgenau,
- Crown Prince,

Grenadier Battalion v. Block.

Second Brigade,  
Maj.-Gen. v. Stirn.  
Regiments,
- The Guards,
- Prince Charles,
- v. Ditfurth,
- v. Trümbach,

Grenadier Battalion v. Minnigerode.

Second Division:
Lieutenant-General v. Knyphausen.

First Brigade,  
Col. v. Lossberg.  
Regiments,
- v. Huyne,
- v. Stein,
- v. Knyphausen,

Grenadier Battalion Köhler.

Second Brigade,  
Maj.-Gen. Schmidt.  
Regiments,
- v. Lossberg,
- v. Wissenbach,
- v. Bünau,

Grenadier Battalion Köhler.

In a letter of July, 1776, to the Duke of Brunswick, Gen. v. Riedesel complains that Gen. Carleton insisted on the German soldiers being trained, as were his English troops, on the French system of open order in thin lines, and adds that he means to teach his men to secure the shelter and protection of the trees in their advance, just as do the Americans, and to be able to meet them in fighting in the woods on equal terms.

---

In a letter to Gen. Burgoyne, Riedesel sketched a plan for making the army mobile, by seizing horses for transportation of both men and stores, and thus moving rapidly enough to get advantage of its superiority in numbers and equipments. Acting in part on this suggestion, Burgoyne issued orders to Lt.-Col. Baum, instructing him that the objects of his expedition were to ascertain the inclination of the population, to secure horses, and a supply of cattle, wagons and food; he needed 1,300 horses, in addition to the number required to mount Riedesel's dragoons. The order was issued on August 9th, 1777, and was based on the notion that the work could be easily done in a fortnight.

---

In a letter (in cipher) to the Duke of Brunswick, in 1777, Riedesel reported the difficulties growing out of the change of command in Canada, and said that Carleton was violently excited against Lord George Germain, and meant to call him to account in Parliament. He also complained of Burgoyne as demanding more from Canada than it could possibly supply. All this made Riedesel's position very uncomfortable.

Reports were rife that Howe did nothing but gamble, and that the majority of the officers were ruined by high play. Plundering was the rule, and New Jersey was said to be laid waste.

Howe's lines were so far extended that it was impossible to hurry reinforcements to Trenton. But for the unfortunate affair there, the people, worn out by their suffering, would have forced Congress to submit to the Crown, but that success changed the feeling of the rebels.

The letter said that, in spite of wearying slowness, of the mistakes made in every direction, if General Howe held the Delaware and gained any advantage on the rebels, and reached Albany by the middle of August, every thing would be improved, "but we can hardly hope to get back to Germany in 1778. The intrigues and misunderstandings in the army are very violent, and I am afraid that the union with Gen. Howe will prove a source of new difficulties."

---

In an order to the Brigadiers and staff officers of his corps, Gen. v. Riedesel, while complimenting them on the bravery and good conduct of the men, urges the necessity of instructing them to fight in open order, to secure the shelter of trees or cover of any kind, and only to fire from that position, except when meeting the enemy in the open, then to fire and attack at once with the bayonet, in close order,

## In the American Revolution. 273

for then the enemy will give way at once. Then, too, officers and men must be prompt in going to the assistance of any part of the force that may be engaged, so as to give it promptly the help of numbers.

The recall of Gen. Heister was due entirely to the influence of Gen. Howe with the British government, which insisted on the change. Heister criticized Howe's operations in the fall of 1776, in a way that made the latter bitterly hostile.

In December, long before the affair at Trenton, Lord Suffolk, Secretary of State, wrote to the Hessian representative in London, asking that the Elector of Hesse would insist on Gen. v. Heister's absolute obedience to Howe's orders.

In January, 1777, he writes: "Gen. v. Heister is worse than useless, and his presence at the head of the German soldiers in the field is a constant source of anxiety and trouble." Again on January 7th, 27th, and February 4th, he returns to the matter, and urges Gen. v. Schlieffen, the Hessian representative in London, quietly to secure the recall of Gen. v. Heister, so that the command might fall to Gen. v. Riedesel, who was entirely satisfactory. He very unfairly tried to put the responsibility of the defeat at Trenton on Heister, whose reports, however, showed that it was entirely Howe's own fault in leaving a force far beyond supporting distance. However, the pressure put on the Elector, who was then in Italy, was so great that he finally recalled

Heister, courteously, and saying that it was only for a time, and to have his advice, etc., but it excited a great deal of comment at home and abroad.

In Holland, particularly, it was discussed in very plain terms, for the Dutch hated the English, and the German princes who helped England.

Schlieffen wrote to York, the British minister in Holland, to try to put some restraint on the freedom of the Dutch press, and York replied that the statement had better come from Cassel, and be made public in the English papers, when it would be copied into those of Holland.

There was no question of Heister's military capacity, but only his disposition to submit to Howe.

In July, 1779, the Count of Hanau wrote to Captain v. Diemar, thanking him for a letter of April 3d, from New York, giving a report of the Hanau troops still in captivity. The sovereign of Hanau said these were his best soldiers, and his heart was full of love and pity for them; he hoped Washington would soon exchange them. For his own part, he begged for frequent reports of their condition, as everything that concerned them was of the greatest interest to him.

NOTE ON THE BATTLE OF TRENTON.—The battle of Trenton served a good purpose, in enabling those who were hostile to the employment of German soldiers in the British service in the American Revolution, to put them in the worst light. There is a letter, purporting to be written by the Elector of Hesse Cassel, Frederick the Second, to the commander of the Hessian troops, which has often been commented on. It purports to be an answer to a letter of December 27th, 1776, reporting that of 1,950 Hessians engaged in the battle, only 300 escaped, and that 1,650 were killed, wounded or captured. The Elector says the English list gives only 1,455 casualties. If that were so, he would lose 160,000 florins—he would get only 483,450 florins, instead of 643,000. The British treasury would not pay for 100 wounded the price of dead soldiers. The Elector expresses his discontent with Major Mindorf for escaping with 300 men from Trenton, and for losing only 10 during the whole campaign.

This letter is pronounced, by good authority, an impudent forgery. It purports to be signed by the Count of Schaumburg and Prince of Hesse Cassel; but there never was any such person — it is a confusion of the Crown Prince of Hesse and the Count of Hanau. There was no such officer as Count Hohendorf, to whom the letter is addressed, and there was no Major Mindorf. General v. Heister was the commander.

The report purports to be dated December 27th— as if a commander could, on the day after such a battle as that at Trenton, have given all the particulars! The answer is dated February 8th; but at that time it took letters five to six weeks to get to London, and this letter had to go to Rome.

It was first printed in St. Louis, in 1845, in the newspaper *The Reveille*, and it was soon reprinted in Germany, where it has often been cited.

Friedrick Kapp attributes it to a French source, and thinks it may have been forged by Mirabeau, one of the busiest of French pamphleteers, and published in Holland. Mirabeau and Abbè Raynal were doing their best to oppose the alliances with the German powers as strengthening the English force.

The fact is that Gen. v. Heister's first report is dated New York, January 5, 1777, and is addressed to Gen. v. Schlieffen, in London; in it he says a brigade of Hessian soldiers, under Col. Rall, was attacked in Trenton, N. J., by an American force, ten thousand strong. Only 291 men saved themselves by flight; the rest were killed or captured. All the staff officers of the brigade and Col. Rall were mortally wounded. The fifteen flags and six guns of the three regiments were taken. He attributes the disaster to Rall's want of judgment and coolness. The Elector's answer was April 7th, in letters to Gen. v. Heister and Gen. v. Knyphausen—he regreted that such a responsible post should have been entrusted to Rall, who was not entitled to it by seniority or service. He directed a strict investigation of the conduct of the surviving officers, especially of Lieut.-Col. Scheffer, that the fault might be laid on those who deserved it. The court of inquiry was appointed, and on January 11th exonerated these officers, and later, in the spring and summer of 1778, the staff officers Scheffer and Mathäus, and the captains of engineers, Pauli and Martin, the staff captain, Baum, and adjutant, Biel.

A LIST OF THE OFFICERS OF THE HESSIAN CORPS SERVING UNDER GENERALS HOWE, CLINTON AND CARLETON, 1776–1783.

## AUTHORITIES.

The principal sources from which the following list was compiled, besides the material in Eelking, are:

I. A List of the General and Staff Officers, and of the Officers in the several Regiments serving in North America, under the Command of His Excellency General Sir William Howe, K. B., with the Dates of their Commissions as they Rank in each Corps and in the Army. Philadelphia: Printed by Macdonald & Cameron, a few doors above the Barracs-Office, MDCCLXXVIII.

II. The same. New York: Printed by James Rivington, etc., MDCCLXXVIII.

III. A List * * of the Officers in the several British, Foreign and Provincial Regiments, serving in North America, under the Command of His Excellency, General Sir Henry Clinton, K. B. * *
New York: Printed by Macdonald & Cameron, etc., 1779.

IV. Gaine's Universal Register; or, American and British Kalendar, for the Year 1780. New York: Printed by H. Gaine, etc.

V. Mills & Hicks' British and American Register, with an Almanack for the Year 1781. * * New York: Printed by Mills & Hicks, etc.

VI. Gaine's Universal Register * * for the Year 1782. New York: Printed by H. Gaine, etc.

VII. A List of the Officers of the Army serving * * under the Command of His Excellency, Sir Guy Carleton, K. B. * * For the Year 1783. New York: James Rivington, MDCCLXXXIII.

VIII. Adam Friedrich Geisler's des jüngern Geschichte und Zustand der Königlich Grosbrittannischen Kriegsmacht zu Wasser und zu Lande von den frühesten Zeiten bis an's Jahr 1784. * * Dessau und Leipzig, 1784.

From the newspapers published in New York city and Philadelphia during the British occupation, and other sources, some additional matter has been collected, most of which has been embodied in the foot notes. The list is necessarily imperfect, as scarcely any information can be found about the composition of the Hessian regiments during 1776 and 1777.

A roster of the Brunswick officers will be found appended to Eelking's Leben der Riedesel, Leipzig, 1856.

# A LIST OF THE HESSIAN CORPS NOW IN AMERICA.

*His Excellency the Lieutenant-General and Commander-in-Chief.*
[1]Leopold Philipp von Heister, 1777–1778.
Baron Wilhelm von Knyphausen, 1778–1782.

*Adjutant-General.*
Major Carl von Baurmeister, 1778, 1780, 1781, 1782.

*Aides-de-Camp to the Commander-in-Chief.*
Major Carl von Baurmeister, 1779.
[2]Capt. William Faucit, May, 1776–'81.
[3] " Hon. Henry Phipps, 1778.
[4] " George Beckwith, 1779–1782.
 " von Doernberg, 1781, 1782.
 " Marquard, 1782.
Lieut. Marquard, 1778–1781.
 " von Heister, 1778.
 " von Barsewitz, 1778–1783.
 " Crammond, 1779–1781. [Eelking, Captain.]
 " von Metzner, 1779.

---

[1]On the 19th of November last, died at Cassel, Lieutenant-General Philip von Heister, in his Britannic Majesty's service, Knight of the two Hessian orders, the Golden Lion and Military Virtue The occasion of his death, was an inflammation in his lungs, which carried him off in four days, in the sixty-first year of his age.—*Gaine's New York Gazette*, February 9, 1778.
[2]Of His Britannic Majesty's Third Regiment of Foot Guards.
[3]Of His Britannic Majesty's First Regiment of Foot Guards.
[4]Of His Britannic Majesty's Thirty-seventh Regiment of Foot Guards.

*Secretary.*

H. Motz, 1778–1782.

*Lieutenant-Generals.*

Lieutenant-General Baron Friedrich Wilhelm von Lossberg, 1782, 1783.
A. D. C., Captain Meltzheimer, 1782, 1783.
Lieutenant-General von Bose, 1782, 1783.
A. D. C., Lieutenant Henel, 1782, 1783.
Lieutenant-General Max. von Dittfurth, 1782, 1783.

*Major-Generals.*

Major-General Stirn, 1778, 1779.
A. D. C., Lieutenant von Westerhagen, 1778, '79.
Major-General von Mirbach, 1778.
A. D. C., Captain Schotten, 1778.
Major-General Schmidt, 1778, 1779.
A. D. C., Lieutenant Becker, 1778, 1779.
Major-General Baron von Lossberg, 1778–81.
A. D. C., Lieutenant Meltzheimer, 1778–81.
Major-General von Bose, 1778–81.
A. D. C., Lieutenant Volpert, 1779–80.
A. D. C., Lieutenant Henel, 1781.
Major-General von Huyne, 1778–80.
A. D. C., Lieutenant Hoeckert, 1779.
A. D. C., Lieutenant Roepenack, 1780.
Major-General Heinrich Jul. von Kospoth, 1779–83.
A. D. C., Lieutenant Marquard, 1779–83.
Major-General Friedrich von Hackenberg, 1780–83.
A. D. C., Lieutenant Grau, 1780–83.
[1]Major-General Friedrich Adolph Riedesel.
A. D. C., Lieutenant Cleve,
A. D. C., Lieutenant Freeman.

---

[1] In command of the District of Long Island.—" Robertson's Orderly Book," November 22, 1780.

Major-General Uphraim von Gosen, 1781–83.
 A. D. C., Lieutenant von Westphal, 1781–83.
Major-General Hans von Knoblauch, 1781–83.
 A. D. C., Lieutenant Knoblauch, 1781–83.
Major-General Carl Ernst von Bischausen, 1781–83.
 A. D. C., Ensign von Sacken, 1781–83.
Major-General Friedrich W. von Wurmb, 1782, '83.
 A. D. C., Lieutenant Wiederhold, 1782, '83.
Major-General Johann August von Loos, 1783.

*Brigadier-Generals.*

Brigadier-General Johann August von Loos, 1782.
Brigadier-General Carl W. von Hackenberg, 1780.

*Quarter-Masters General.*

Lieutenant-Colonel von Kochenhausen, 1778–81.
Lieutenant-Colonel du Puy, 1782.

*Deputy Quarter-Masters General.*

'Captain Martin, 1778, '79.
Lieutenant de Gironcourt de Vomecourt, 1781, '82.

*Majors of Brigade.*

Major du Puy, 1778, '79.
Captain von Willmousky, 1778–80.
Captain Werner, 1780, '81. .
Lieutenant Führer, 1782.

*Deputy Majors of Brigade.*

Lieutenant Werner, 1778, '79.
Lieutenant Führer, 1778–81.

*Judge Advocate.*

—— Motz, 1778, '79, '81, '82.

---

[1] Died in New York, May 27, 1780 —*Gaine's New York Gazette*, June 5, 1780.

*Chaplains.*
Reformed—Bingell, 1778.
          Becker, 1779–81.
Lutheran—Heller, 1778, '79, '80, '81.
*Provost Marshal.*
Lieutenant Riedell, 1778–82.
*Wagon-Masters General.*
Ruppersberg, 1778, '79.
Schade, 1781, '82.
*Commissariat.*
¹Counsellor of War and Commissary-General John George Lorentz, 1778–81.
*Paymasters General.*
Carl Schmidt, 1778–80.
Richard Lorentz, 1781, '82.
*Commissaries of Stores.*
John Ebert, 1778–82.
—— Lorenz, 1782.
*Assistant Commissary General.*
Richard Lorentz, 1779, '80.
*Commissaries.*
Sroppel, 1778.
Rysch, 1778.
Frebell, 1778.

HOSPITAL.
*Purveyors.*
Franz Gelan, 1778, '81, '82.
Ludwig Schmidt, 1778, '81.

---

¹Died of apoplexy, aged 68, in New York city, June 29, 1781.—*Gaine's New York Gazette*, July 2, 1781.

### Clerks.

Schmidt, 1781.
Massot, 1781, '82.
Schaeffer, 1781.

### Physicians.

Dr. Lukhardt, 1778–82.
Dr. Estarch, 1778.
Dr. Alirhalis, 1780.
Dr. Michaelis, 1781, '82.

### Surgeons General.

—— Amelung, 1778–81.
Carl Bauer, 1778–81.

### Commissaries.

Marsol, 1778.
Schaeffer, 1778–81.
Chartier, 1778.
Massot, 1781.

### Chaplains.

Schrecker, 1779, '81, '82.
Becker, 1782.
Beck, 1782.

### Surgeons.

—— Müller, 1779–81.
—— Girard, 1779–81.
August Bauer, 1779–82.
—— Wagner, 1779–81.
—— Claus, 1779–81.
—— Brand, 1779.
—— Amelung, 1782.
—— Fleck, 1781.

### Apothecaries.

Rudolph, 1779, '80.

Schirmer, 1779–82.
Gunther, 1779.
Hierman, 1781, '82.

*Cooks.*

Welgehausen, 1781.
Sander, 1781.

---

BATTALION OF GRENADIERS LINSING, 1778–1781.

*Lieutenant-Colonel.*

von Linsing, 1778–81.

*Captains.*

¹von Stamfort, 1778.
von Malet, 1778, '79, '81.
von Webern, 1778, '79, '81.
von Plessen, 1778, '79, '81.
²August von Westerhagen, 1778.
¹Ernst von Eschwege, 1778.
von Dinklage, 1779, '81.

*Lieutenants.*

³de Buy [1777.]
¹Prodemann, 1778.
Friedrich Henrich von Groening, 1778, '79.
¹von Baumbach, 1778.
¹Waitz von Eschen, 1778.
Philo von Westerhagen, 1778.
Proecke, 1778, '79.
Kleinschmidt, 1779.

---

[1] Wounded at Red Bank.—Eelking, vol. 1, page 222.
[2] Wounded at the passage of the Bronx, October 28, 1776.—*Gaine's New York Gazette*, March 17, 1777.
[3] Wounded at Brandywine.—*Pennsylvania Ledger*, March 4, 1778.

### First Lieutenants.
von Schuler, 1779, '81.
von Hegeman, 1781.
Schraidt, 1781.

### Second Lieutenants.
von Ende, 1778, '79, '81.
von Hartleben, 1779, '81.
von Hanstein, 1779, '81.
von Verschuer, 1779, '81.
Kersting, 1779, '81.
Dunker, 1779, '81.
von Wangenheim, 1781.

### Adjutant.
Kleinschmidt, 1781.

### Quarter-Master.
Wilhelm Broeske, 1778, '79, '81.

### Surgeon.
George, 1778, '79.

NOTE.—See note at end of the Mirbach Regiment.

---

TWO GRENADIER COMPANIES HESSIAN GUARDS.

### Captains.
| | |
|---|---|
| Webern, 1783. | Oct. 9, 1768. |
| Plessen, 1783. | Apr. 4, 1775. |

### First Lieutenants.
| | |
|---|---|
| Hantleb, 1783. | Mar. 5, 1779. |
| Hanssein, 1783. | Mar. 6, 1779. |

### Second Lieutenants.
| | |
|---|---|
| Wangenheim, 1783. | Feb. 19, 1779. |
| Eptingen, 1783. | June 3, 1782. |

## BATTALION OF GRENADIERS LENGERCKE, 1778–81.

*Lieutenant-Colonel.*
von Lengercke, 1778–81.

*Captains.*
von Wurmb, 1778.
von Eschwege, 1778, '79.
[1]von Oreilly, 1778, '79, '81.
von Gall, 1778, '79, '81.
von Willmousky, 1779.
Vogt, 1781.
Reuting, 1781.

*Lieutenants.*
Roll, 1778.
von Eschwege, 1778.
Kauffmann, 1778.
Spangenberg, 1778.
Donop, 1778.
Freyenhagen, 1778.
Schwaner, 1778, '79.
Ernst, 1778, '79.
Butte, 1778, '79.
von Westphal, 1778, '79.
Berthod, 1778, '79.
Hausmann, 1779.
von Kospoth, 1779.

*First Lieutenants.*
von Trott, 1778, '79, '81.
von Kospoth, 1781.
Hausmann, 1781.
Reiss, 1779, '81.
von Leliva, 1779, '81.

---

[1]To be Town Major of New York city, *vice* Captain Reuting, who resigns.—*Gaine's New York Gazette*, November 30, 1778.

*Second Lieutenants.*
von Kospoth, 1781.
von Geyso, 1781.
von Losberg, 1779, '81.
Hartmann, 1781.
*Adjutant.*
von Kuntzch, 1781.
*Quarter-Master.*
Spangenberg, 1778, '79, '81.
*Surgeon.*
Reinhard, 1778, '79.

---

BATTALION OF GRENADIERS MINNIGERODE,
1778, 1779.

BATTALION OF GRENADIERS. LOWENSTEIN, 1781.

*Lieutenant-Colonels.*
[1]von Minnigerode, 1778, '79.
Friedrich Heinrich von Schuter, 1780.
von Lowenstein, 1781.
*Captains.*
[2]Wachs, 1778, '79, '81.
[2]Stendorff, 1778, '79.
von Munschhausen, 1778.
Wilhelm von Biesenroth, 1778, '79, '81.
Mondorff, 1779, '81.
Klingender, 1781.
*Lieutenants.*
Gebhard, 1778.

---

[1]Wounded at Red Bank.—*Pennsylvania Ledger*, March 4, 1778. Died at New York, October 16, 1779 He was a Knight of the "Order of Merit."—*Gaine's New York Gazette*, October 25, 1779.

[2]Wounded at Red Bank.—Eelking, volume 1, page 222.

von Haller, 1778.
Heymell, 1778.
Heinrich Hille, 1778, '79.
Vaupell, 1779.
Marquardt, 1779.
von Gluer, 1779.

*First Lieutenants.*

Toepffer, 1778–81.
von Winzingerode, 1778–81.
Zinck, 1778–81.
Kimm, 1779–81.

*Second Lieutenants.*

von Rabenau, 1778–81.
von Geyso, 1778–81.
Ernst Briede, 1779–81.
Desoudres, 1779–81.
von Hoben, 1781.
von Romrod, 1781.

*Quarter-Master.*

Ungar, 1778–81.
Spangenberg, 1779.

*Surgeon.*

Franck, 1778, '79.

*Adjutant.*

Hille, 1781.

NOTE.—See note at end of the Mirbach Regiment.

BATTALION OF GRENADIERS KOEHLER, 1778.

BATTALION OF GRENADIERS GRAFF, 1779–1781.

*Lieutenant-Colonel.*

Koehler, 1778.
Graff, 1780, '81.

### Majors.

Graff, 1779.
¹Platte, 1782.

### Captains.

Hessenmueller [Hessemueller, *Eelking*], 1778,'79,'81.
²Neuman, 1778, '79, '81.
Wilhelm Bode, 1778, '79, '81.
Hohenstein, 1778, '79, '81.
Mertz, 1781.

### Lieutenants.

von Romrodt, 1778.
Justi, 1778.
Brauns, 1778.
Hupeden, 1778, '79.
Mertz, 1778, '79.
Anton von Dalwigk, 1778, '79.
Munchhausen, 1778, '79, [Muehlhausen, 1779, *Eelking*], '81.
³Oelhaus, 1778, '79.
Studenroth, 1778, '79.
von Romrodt, 1779.
von Treyden, 1779.

### First Lieutenants.

von Dalwigk, 1778, '79, '81.
Waldeck, 1778, '79, '81.
³Fritsch, 1778, '79, '81.

### Second Lieutenants.

Schenck, 1781.

---

[1]The command of the Fourth Battalion of Grenadiers, late Colonel Graff's, is conferred on Major Platte, regiment Beunau.—*Gaine's New York Gazette*, September 2, 1782.

[2]Wounded at Fort Washington, November 16, 1776.—*Gaine's New York Gazette*, March 17, 1777.

[3]Wounded at the siege of Charleston.—*Gaine's New York Gazette*, June 12, 1780.

von Lahrbusch, 1781.
Jung, 1781.
*Ensigns.*
Wiederhold, 1781.
Schimmelpfennig, 1781.
*Adjutant.*
Brauns, 1779, '81.
*Quarter-Master.*
Bauer, 1778, '79, '81.
*Surgeon.*
Henry Koch, 1778, '79.

REGIMENT DU CORPS, 1778–1783.
*Major-Generals.*
Baron von Losberg, 1778.
Carl Ernst von Bischausen, 1782, '83.   Nov. 1, '80.
Friedrich Wilhelm von Wurmb, 1782, '83.  Nov. 2, '80.
*Colonels.*
Friedrich Wilhelm von Wurmb, 1778–81.
Otto Christ. Wilhelm von Linsing, 1783.  June 5, '78.
*Lieutenant-Colonel.*
Otto Christ. Wilhelm von Linsing, 1782.  June 1, '66.
*Majors.*
Biesenroth, 1778.
Ludwig Friedrich von Stamfurth, 1779–83.  May 8, '77.
August Eber. von Dincklage, 1782, '83.  Nov. 5, '80.
*Captains.*
August Eber. von Dincklage, 1778.
Waldenberg, 1778, '79.
Carl Reinh. von Motz, 1778, '79, '81–83.  May 23, '72.

*In the American Revolution.* 295

Christ. Matt. Le Long, 1778, '79, '81-83. Feb. 26, '76.
Friedrich Melchior von Milkau [von Abilkan, *Eelking*], 1778, '79, '81-83. Feb. 29, '76.
Christ. Friedrich von Urff, 1778, '79, '81-83.
              Nov. 23, '76.
Friedrich Heinrich von Groening, 1781-83.
              May 14, '80.
Carl von Zenge, 1782, '83.     Jan. 30, '81.
Johann Mar. Meltzhaimer, 1782, '83.  Mar. 1, '81.

*Lieutenants.*

Heinrich Hegemann, 1778, '79.
Johann Mar. Meltzheimer, 1778, '79.
Heinrich Ernst, 1778, '79.

*First Lieutenants.*

Christ. Bode, 1778, '79, '81-83.   Dec. 24, '77.
August Wilhelm von Ende, 1782, '83.  Mar. 7, '81.
Just. Ernst, 1782, '83.      Mar. 8, '81.

*Second Lieutenants.*

Carl August Kleinschmidt, 1778, '82, '83. Feb. 2, '76.
Caspar von Groening, 1779, '82, '83.  Nov. 23, '76.
Philipp Peter Ludemann, 1779, '81-83. Dec. 24, '77.
Johann Anton Germar, 1781, '82.   May 14, '80.
Just. Ernst, 1781.
Bernhardt Wilhelm Wiederhold, 1781-83. May 15, '80.
Max. Ludwig von Helmold, 1782, '83.  Mar. 7, '81.
Christ. Friedrich von Lacken [Sacken], 1783.

*Ensigns.*

Philipp Peter Ludemann, 1778.
Johann Anton Germer, 1778, '79.
Bernhardt Wilhelm Wiederhold, 1778, '79.
Max. Ludwig von Helmold, 1779, '81.
Christ. Friedrich von Sacken [Lacken], 1779, '81, '82.
              Oct. 22. '77.

Caspar Theo. von Dalwigk, 1779, '81–83. Nov. 12, '77.
Heinrich von der Litt, 1779, '81–83.   Mar. 26, '78.
von Heimel, 1782.                      Feb. 12, '81.
de Cornberg, 1782, '83.   Feb. 12, '81, Feb. 13, '81.
de Stamford, 1783.                     Mar. 9, '82.

*Adjutant.*

Caspar von Groening, 1778, '79, '81–83.

*Quarter-Master.*

Jacob [or John] Lotheisen, 1778, '79, '81–83.

*Judge-Advocate.*

Witte, 1778, '79, '81–83.

*Chaplains.*

Schrecker, 1778.
Wiedermann, 1777.
Crepon, 1782.

*Surgeon.*

Friedrich Waldeck, 1778, '79, '81–83.

---

WUTGENAU, 1776 [Eelking].

REGIMENT LANDGRAVE, 1778–83.

*Major-Generals.*

von Bose, 1778.
Heinrich Jul. von Kospoth, 1782, '83.   Sept. 26, '78.

*Colonels.*

Heinrich Jul. von Kospoth, 1778.
Heinrich Walrab von Keudell [Budell? Eelking],
   1779–83.                            Dec. 25, '77.

*Lieutenant-Colonels.*

von Romrodt, 1778.
Friedrich von Hannstein, 1779–83.      Dec. 24, '77.

*In the American Revolution.*

### Majors.
Friedrich von Hannstein, 1778.
von Ahrenberg, 1778, '79.
Friedrich von Eschwege, 1781–83.   Sept. 20, '79.

### Captains.
¹Meddern [1776].
Mondorff, 1778.
Hohlefeld, 1778.
Gren Minne, 1779–81.
²Friedrich Ernst de Muenchhausen, 1779, '82, '83.
                                                  Mar. 31, '76.
Johann Jacob Vogt, 1778, '79, '82, '83.   Feb. 22, '77.
Adam Bauer, 1779.
Wilhelm von Eschwege, 1779.
Ludwig Eberhard Murarius, 1781–83.   Apr. 15, '79.
Johann Con. Ernst, 1781–83.          Sept. 30, '79.
Peter Volpert, 1781–83.              Oct. 1, '79.
August von Kospoth, 1783.            Nov. 7, '81.

### Lieutenants.
¹Lowensfield [1776].
¹von Lendow [1776].
Adam Bauer, 1778.
Juliaa, 1778.
³Ludwig Eberhard Murarius, 1778, '79.

### First Lieutenants.
⁴Peter Volpert, 1778, '79.

---

[1] Wounded at Fort Washington, Nov. 16, 1776.—*Gaine's New York Gazette*, March 17, 1777.

[2] Aid-de-Camp to Sir William Howe, 1777.—*Macdonald & Cameron's Army List* for 1777.

[3] Wounded at Rhode Island, August 29, 1778.—*Almond's Remembrancer*, volume VII, page 36.

[4] His rank is determined from the Army List of 1781, where he appears as First Lieutenant in the temporary Battalion of the Grenadier der Lengercke.

August von Kospoth, 1778, '79, '82.   Feb. 24, '77.
Ludwig von Kospoth, 1778, '79, '82, '83.  Dec. 24, '77.
Carl Goddeus, 1783.                   Apr. 1, '82.

*Second Lieutenants.*

Carl Goddeus, 1778, '79, '81.         May 8, '76.
Franz von Ende, 1778, '79, '81–83.    Feb. 23, '77.
Carl von Seelhorst, 1779, '81.
Friedrich von Kospoth, 1782, '83.     Dec. 13, '78.
Philipp Wagener, 1781–83.             Feb. 13, '79.
Adolph Friedrich de Zanthier, 1781–83. Sep. 30, '79.
Julius von Klingsohr, 1783.           Mar. 9, '82.
Eugen Benjamin von Kliest, 1783.      Mar. 10, '82.
Georg von Rosing, 1783.               Mar. 11, '82.
Carl Philip Hannstein, 1783.          Mar. 12, '82.

*Ensigns.*

Franz von Ende [1776].
Carl von Seelhorst, 1778.
Friedrich von Kospoth, 1778, '79.
Carl von Billingsleben, 1778, '79.
Philipp Wagener, 1778, '79.
Adolph Friedrich von Zanthier, 1778, '79.
de Micklaskewitz, 1779.
Julius von Klingsohr, 1779.
Eugen Benjamin von Kliest, 1781, '82.  May 1, '78.
Georg von Roosing, 1781, '82.          Nov. 8, '78.
Carl Philipp von Hannstein, 1781, '82. Nov. 14, '79.
von Berglassen, 1781–83.               Nov. 15, '79.
Carl Schoenewolf, 1781–82.             Nov. 16, '79.
de Nolden, 1781–83.                    Mar. 21, '80.
August von Papenheim, 1781–83.         Apr. 7, '80.
Munschausen, 1783.                     June 1, '81.

*Adjutants.*

Peter Volpert, 1778.

In the American Revolution.

Julius von Klingsohr, 1781, '82.           Feb. 26, '78.
August von Pappenheim, 1783.
*Chaplain.*
Stern, 1778, '79, '81–83.                  Aug. 15, '76.
*Quarter-Master.*
Bockewitz, 1779, '81–83.                   Jan. 1, '78.
*Judge Advocate.*
Meisterling, 1778, '79, '81–83.            Mar. 10, '76.
*Surgeon.*
Ohlhaussen, 1778, '79, '81–83.             Sept. 23, '71.

---

REGIMENT HEREDITARY PRINCE, 1778–1783.
*Major-Generals.*
Stirn, 1778.
[1]Friedrich von Hackenberg, 1782, '83.    Sept. 19, '79.
*Colonels.*
[2]Friedrich von Hackenburg, 1778, '79.
Friedrich von Kochenhausen, 1782, '83.     Dec. 26, '77.

---

[1]Last Wednesday died, at the age of sixty-one, FREDERIC BARON DE HACKENBERG, Major-General in the service of his Serene Highness the Landgrave of Hesse, and Knight of the Most Honourable Order, *Pour la Virtue Militaire*. He with great probity, and steady courage, served the House of Hesse Cassel forty-two years, ever having the glory of his Prince and the British Nation, the constant ally of his Serene Highness, immediately at heart. He was hospitable, candid, good natured; in short, he always proved himself a true Philanthropist. He was universally beloved, and it may be truly added that few have left the world more generally regretted, by the Military, and the Citizens of New York, than the late amiable General le Baron de Hackenberg. His remains, with the usual marks of distinction due to Nobility, and all the Military honours, were, on Thursday, deposited in the Lutheran Church vault, Frankford street, attended by a very numerous, affectionate and truly mournful procession.—*Gaine's New York Gazette*, September 1, 1783.

[2]To be Brigadier-General.—*Gaine's New York Gazette*, July 12, 1779.

*Lieutenant-Colonels.*
Friedrich von Kochenhausen, 1778, '79.
¹Matthew von Fuchs, 1781–83.　　　Sept. 19, '79.

*Majors.*
Matthew von Fuchs, 1778–80.
¹Peter Melick Waldenberger, 1781–83.　Sept. 19, '79.

*Captains.*
¹Ludwig Friedrich von Gall, 1778, '79, '81.
Christoph Laun, 1778, '79, '81–83.　　$\begin{cases} \text{Feb. 28, '74.} \\ \text{Feb. 28, '77.} \end{cases}$
Heinrich Friedrich Wachs, 1782, '83.　Mar. 2, '74.
von Schaller, 1778, '79, '81, '83.　　Feb. 26, '77.
¹Kümmell, 1778, '79, '81–83.　　　Mar. 1, '77.
Adolph Fr. von Eschwege, 1779.
¹Herman Christoph Gebhard, 1779, '81–83.
　　　　　　　　　　　　　　　　Nov. 15, '77.
Joachim Kimm, 1782, '83 [Grimm—Eelking, volume
　II, page 252].　　　　　　　　Nov. 2, '80.
Friedrich Wilhelm von Haller, 1783.　Mar. 9, '82.

*Lieutenants.*
Friedrich von Eschwege, 1778.
von Boyneburg, 1778.

*First Lieutenants.*
Friedrich Wilhelm von Haller, 1779, '81, '82.
　　　　　　　　　　　　　　　　Nov. 10, '77.
Ernst Wolfe Briede, 1783.　　　　Feb. 10, '82.
Andreas Ludwig Descoudres, 1783.　Mar. 9, '82.
¹Bauer.
¹Kummel.
¹Gebhard.
¹Grimm.

---

¹Surrendered at Yorktown.—*Eelking*, volume II, page 252.

### Second Lieutenants.

Ernst Wolfe Briede, 1778–82.   Feb. 1, '76.
Andreas Ludwig Descoudres, 1778, '82.   Feb. 2, '76.
'Ernst August Westerhagen, 1778, '79, '81–83.
 Feb. 3, '76.
'Ernst Wilhelm Andersohn, 1778, '79, '81–83.
 Feb. 26, '76.
Friedrich Graw, 1778, '79, '82, '83.   Feb. 22, '77.
'Friedrich von Keudell, 1779, '81–83.   Dec. 24, '77.
'Rhein Fried. Ungewitter, 1781–83.   Dec. 13, '78.
'Jacob Diedrich Pfaff, 1781–83.   May 28, '80.
Georg Ludwig Motz, 1783.

### Ensigns.

Friedrich von Keudell, 1778.
Rhein Friedrich Ungewitter, 1778, '79.
Jacobus Diedrich Pfaff, 1778, '79.
'Georg Ludwig Motz, 1778, '79, '81, '82.   Feb. 23, '77.
'Christian von Hoening, 1778, '79, '82, '83.
 Apr. 21, '77; Apr. 25, '77.
'Valentine Schoenewolff, 1779, '81–83.   Dec. 24, '77.
Descoudres, 1782, '83.   Nov. 8, '80.
Winicke, 1782, '83.   Jan. 9, '81.
Ludwig, 1782, '83.   Mar. 23, '81.

### Adjutants.

Kimm, 1778.
Christian von Hoening, 1779, '81–83.

### Quarter-Master.

'Ludwig, 1778, '79, '81–83.

### Judge-Advocate.

Plumque, 1778, '79, '81–83.

---

[1]Surrendered at Yorktown.—*Eelking*, volume II, page 252.

*Chaplain.*

[1] Hausknecht, 1778, '79, '81-83.

*Surgeons.*

Avemann, 1778, '79, '81.
[2] Francis Aug. Baur, 1783.

---

REGIMENT PRINCE CHARLES, 1778-1783.

*Major-Generals.*
Schmidt, 1778.
Carl Uphraim von Gosen, 1782, '83.   June 12, '80.

*Colonel.*
Johann Wilhelm Schreiber, 1778-83.   June 21, '76.

*Lieutenant-Colonels.*
Georg Eman. von Lengerke, 1782, '83. { June 19, '76.
                                       { May 28, '78.
Wilhelm von Loewenstein, 1778-80,    { June 22, '76.
  '82, '83.                          { June 1, '78.

*Majors.*
Carl August von Kutzleben, 1778-83.   Feb. 25, '77.
Wilhelm von Wilmousky, 1782, '83.     Sept. 22, '79.

*Captains.*
Wilhelm von Wilmousky, 1778.
Johann Jacob Fischer, 1778-83.        Jan. 28, '77.
[3] Heinrich Wilhelm Reuting, 1778, '79, '82, '83.
                                      Jan. 29, '77.

---

[1] Surrendered at Yorktown.—*Eelking*, volume II, page 252.
[2] Surrendered at Yorktown and died of his wounds.—*Ibid.*
[3] Resigned the Town Majorship of New York city.—*Gaine's New York Gazette*, November 30, 1778.

Friedrich Adolph Neuber, 1778, '79, '81-83.
Feb. 23, '77; ——, '79.
Johann August Gerstman, 1779, '81-83. Nov. 11,'77.
¹ Theodor Hart Harkert, 1779, '81-83. Apr. 14, '78.
Balthasar Spangenberg, 1781-83. Nov. 18, '79.
Martin Beckers, 1781-83. Feb. 8, '80.

*Lieutenants.*

Hartel, 1778 [Theodor Hart Harkert].
Johann August Gerstman, 1778.
Heinrich Schmidt, 1778.
Ferdinand von Trott, 1778, '79.
Balthasar Spangenberg, 1779.

*First Lieutenants.*

Johann Philip Schmidt, 1783. Feb. 1, '76.
Ludwig Otto Carl von Dornberg, 1783. Feb. 2, '76.
Carl Georg Rhein. von Trott, 1782, '83. Dec. 13, '78.
Johann Carl W. S. von Westphall, 1782, '83.
Feb. 8, '80.
Wilhelm Carl Ludwig von Geyso, 1778, '79, '82, '83.
Oct. 1, '80.

*Second Lieutenants.*

Heinrich von Trott, 1781, '82. Feb. 1, '77.
Carl Wilhelm Christ. Friederich von Trott, Jr., 1783.
Feb. 1, '77.
Barthold Kroll, 1781-83. Nov. 12, '78.
Friedrich Adolph Martin Becker, 1782, '83.
Dec. 17, '78.
Carl Wilhelm von Trott, 1782, '83. Nov. 1, '80.
von Eptingen, 1783.

*Ensigns.*

Barthold Kroll, 1778, '79.

---

¹ Died on August 7th, 1783, and was buried in St. Paul's Churchyard, New York city.—*Gaine's New York Gazette*, August 13, 1783.

Friedrich Adolph Martin Becker, 1778, '79.
[1] von Bouilly, 1779.
Carl Wilhelm von Trott, 1778, '79, '81.
Philipp Peter Schmidt, 1778, '79, '81–83.  Feb. 22, '77.
von Eptingen, 1781, '82.  Jan. 13, '78.
Christoph Roesing, 1779, '81–83.  June 18, '78.
Apell, 1783.  Mar. 25, '82.

*Adjutants.*

Hartel, 1778 [Theodor Hart Harkert].
Christoph Roesing, 1779.
Friedrich Adolph Martin Becker, 1781, '83.
von Eptingen, 1782.  Jan. 13, '78.

*Quarter-Master.*

Heinrich Pfaff, 1778, '79, '81, '82.  Apr. 20, '56.

*Judge-Advocate.*

Plumque, 1782.

*Chaplain.*

Hausknecht, 1782.

*Surgeon.*

Bauer, 1778, '79, '81, '82.  Jan. 28, '76.

REGIMENT DITTFURTH, 1778–1783.

*Lieutenant-General.*

Mil. Max. von Dittfurth, 1782, '83.  May 26, '71.

*Colonels.*

Max von Westerhagen, 1778–83.  May 8, '77.
Friedrich Heinrich von Schuler, 1782, '83.
May 24, '78.

---

[1] Discharged at his own request, by the Landgrave of Hesse.—*Robertson's Orderly Book*, November 21, 1780.

*Lieutenant-Colonels.*
Friedrich Heinrich von Schuler, 1778, '79, '81.
            May 24, '78.
Ernst Leopold von Bork, 1782, '83.  Nov. 3, '80.

*Majors.*
Ernst Leopold von Bork, 1778-81.
Friedrich Wilhelm von Malsburg, 1782, '83.
            Nov. 2, '80.

*Captains.*
Ludwig Reichell [Berchell, *Eelking*], 1778, '79.
¹ Engerding, 1778, '79, '81.
Nicholas Frederick Klingender, 1778, '79, '82, '83.
            Mar. 4, '74.
Friedrich Wilhelm von Malsburg, 1778, '79, '81.
Wilhelm von Malsburg, 1779, '81-83. Nov. 12, '77.
Heinrich Hugo Scheffer, 1781-83.  Feb. 9, '80.
Georg Ernst Topfer, 1782, '83.    Nov. 3, '80.
² von Rabenau, 1782.
Arnold Wilhelm von Haller, 1783.  Sept. 7, '81.

*Lieutenants.*
Wilhelm von Malsburg, 1778.
Heinrich Hugo Schaeffer, 1778, '79.
Wilhelm L. Franz von Dittfurth, 1778, '79.
Christian von Bose, 1778, '79.
Franz Ferdinand von Bardeleben, 1778, '79.

*First Lieutenants.*
Carl Levin Marquard, 1783.     Feb. 2, '76.

---

¹ On the 13th of June last, died at Charles-Town, South Carolina, Capt. EDDERGING, of the Hessian Regiment of Dittfourth, greatly regretted as a good officer and much lamented by those who were acquainted with his private character.—*Gaine's New York Gazette*, August 6, 1781.

² Died in New York, November 30, 1782.—*Gaine's New York Gazette*, December 2, 1782.

Arnold Wilhelm von Haller, 1782.   Feb. 8, '80.
von Rabenau, 1782.   Nov. 1, '80.

*Second Lieutenants.*

Arnold Wilhelm von Haller, 1778, '79, 81.
Carl Levin Marquard, 1778, '81, '82.   Feb. 2, '76.
Leon Wilhelm von Trumbach, 1778, '79, 81–83.
   Feb. 3, '76.
Adolph Frederick Duncker, 1779, '81–83.
   Feb. 22, '77.
von Bardeleben, 1781.
Georg Hermann Vultejus, 1781–83.   Apr. 10, '78.
Peter Christopher Firnhaber, 1782, '83.   Feb. 8, '80.
Heinrich A. von Schachten, 1782, '83.   Feb. 9, '80.
Friedrich von Buttlar, 1782, '83.   Mar. 7, '81.
Heinrich Lorey, 1782, '83.   Mar. 7, '81; Mar. 8, '81.

*Ensigns.*

Dunker, 1778.
Georg Hermann Vultejus, 1778.
Peter Christopher Firnhaber, 1778, '79, '81.
Heinrich A. von Schachten, 1778, '79, '81.
Strasser, 1778, '79, '81.
Friedrich von Buttlar, 1779, '81, '82.
Heinrich Lorey, 1781.
' Carl Wetzell, 1781–83.   Mar. 21, '80.
Friedrich Lange, 1782, '83.   July 10, '80.
Carl von Buttlar, 1782, '83.   Jan. 27, '81.
Amabilis von Zehmen, 1782, '83.   Mar. 1, '81.
Wilhelm von Brunn, 1782, '83.   Mar. 2, '81.
Franz Martins, 1782, '83.   Mar. 28, '81.
Buttlar, 1783.   Mar. 9, '82.

*Quarter-Master.*

Cornelius Wende, 1778, '79, '81–83.

---

Died at Charleston, South Carolina, August 25.—*Rivington's Gazette*, October 2, 1782.

*Adjutant.*
Georg Hermann Voltejus, 1779, '83.
*Surgeon.*
Limbergen, 1778, '79, '81–83.

---

REGIMENT LOSBERG, SENIOR, 1778–1783.
*Lieutenant-General.*
von Losberg, 1783.   Oct. 25, '72.
*Major-General.*
Johann August von Loos, 1783.
*Colonels.*
Franz Schaeffer, 1783.   June 7, '77.
[1] Johann August von Loos, 1778–82.   May 22, '78.
*Lieutenant-Colonels.*
Franz Schaeffer, 1778–82.   Jan. 24, '76.
von Losberg, 1782, '83.
*Majors.*
Lewis Aug. von Hannstein, 1778–82.   Feb. 24, '77.
Ernst Eber. Altenbockum, 1782, '83.   { April 5, '77. / Nov. 7, '80.
*Captains.*
[2] von Benning.
[2] von Reise.
[3] Ernst Eber Altenbockum, 1778, '79, '81.
Johann Reid Mondorff, 1782, '83.   Feb. 20, '76.
von Steding, 1778, '79, '81, '82.   Feb. 25, '76.
von Wurmb, 1778, '79, '81, '82.   Feb. 24, '77.

---

[1] See *New York Historical Society Collections*, 1875, p. 113.
[2] Killed at Trenton.—*Eelking*, vol. I, p. 130.
[3] Wounded at Trenton—*Eelking*, vol. I, p. 130.

Friedrich Wilhelm Krafft, 1779, '81–83. Dec. 26, '77.
Marquard, 1782, '83.           Mar. 21, '80.
Ernst Christian Schwabe, 1782, '83.   Feb. 1, '81.
Jacob Biel, 1782, '83.          Feb. 2, '81.
Heinrich Hegeman, 1782, '83.    { Feb. 15, '81.
                                { Feb. 18, '81.

*Lieutenant.*
[1] Kimm.

*First Lieutenants.*
[2] von Wurmb [1776].
Friedrich Wilhelm Krafft, 1778.
Keller, 1778.
von Münchhausen, 1782, '83.    Aug. 17, '76.
von Hoben, 1782, '83.    Nov. 9, '80; Nov. 11, '80.
Henry Reim Hille, 1782, '83.    Nov. 12, '80.
[3] Hermann Heinrich Georg Zoll, 1782, '83.
                                Nov. 9 and 19, '80.
William von Uslar, 1782, '83.   Nov. 21, '80.

*Second Lieutenants.*
von Stoben, 1778.
von Gluer, 1778, '79.
[4] Schwabe, 1778–81.
Jacob Biel, 1778–81.
Hermann Heinrich Georg Zoll, 1778–81.
Moeller, 1778, '79, '81, '82.   Feb. 3, '76.
von Hoben, 1779, '80.
Franz Grebe, 1781, '83.         Nov. 7, '80.
C. von Waldschmidt, 1781, '83.  Nov. 10, '80.
Georg Kress, 1781, '83.         Nov. 11, '80.
Carl Friedrich von Luder, 1781, '83.   Nov. 13, '80.

---

[1] Killed at Trenton.—*Eelking*, vol. I, p. 130.
[2] Wounded at Fort Washington, November 16, 1776 —*Gaine's New York Gazette*, March 17, 1777.
[3] Wounded at Trenton.—*Eelking*, vol. I, p. 130.
[4] Wounded at Trenton.—*Eelking*, vol. I, p. 130.

*Ensigns.*

Franz Grebe, 1778, '79, '81.
von Zeugen, 1778, '79, '81, '82.  Feb. 2, '76.
² Hennendorff, 1778–81.
C. von Waldschmidt, 1778, '79, '81.
Georg Kress, 1778, '79, '81.
Rathmann, 1778, '79, '81, '82.  Apr. 24, '77.
Stendorf, 1779.
von Roven, 1779, '81–83.  Feb. 26, '78.
Gottlieb Waldeck, 1779, '81, '82.  July 15, '78.
Carl Friedrich von Luder, 1781.
Recordon, 1781–83.  Aug. 1, '79.
Zoll, 1782.
Mueller, 1782, '83.  Apr. 2, '80.
Stegmann, 1782, '83.  Oct. 26, '80.

*Adjutant.*
Jacob Biel [or Piel], 1779–83.

*Quarter-Master.*
John Heusser, 1778, '79, '81–83.

*Surgeon.*
Oliva, 1778, '79, '81–83.

---

REGIMENT LOSBERG, JUNIOR, 1782, 1783.

*Lieutenant-General.*
Baron Friedrich Wilhelm von Losberg, 1782, '83.
  Mar. 7, '81.

*Colonel.*
Carl Christoph von Romrod, 1782, '83.  Dec. 24, '77.

---

² Transferred to the Third Battalion, New Jersey Volunteers, as Ensign, Feb. 5, 1782.—*Von Kraff's Journal*, New York Historical Society's Collection, 1882, p. 170. *Rivington's Army List, 1783.*

310        *The German Allies*

### Lieutenant-Colonel.
Hans von Biesenrod, 1782, '83.        Dec. 26, '77.

### Major.
Emanuel Ernst Anton von Wilmousky, 1782, '83.
                                       Feb. 22, '77.
Carl Leopold Bauermeister, 1782, '83.  Feb. 26, '77.

### Captains.
Ludwig Maive von Mallet, 1782, '83.    Oct. 16, '68.
Johann M. Rothe, 1782, '83.            Nov. 16, '76.
Ludolph Rodemann, 1782.                Dec. 27, '77.
Carl von Toll, 1782, '83.              Dec. 28, '77.
Friedrich August Broeske, 1782, '83.   Jan. 6, '81.
Johann C. Schraidt, 1782, '83.         { May 25, '81.
                                       { Dec. 26, '77.
Johann Reid Rodeman, 1783.

### First Lieutenants.
Lewis Wilhelm August von Boyneburg, '1782, '83.
                                       Jan. 6, '81.
Carl Friedrich Rueffer, 1782, '83.     Sept. 5, '81.
Johann Georg Wissemuller, 1783.        Mar. 25, '82.

### Second Lieutenants.
Johann Georg Wiesenmueller, 1782.      Dec. 24, '77.
Friedrich von Biesenrod, 1782, '83.    Dec. 25, '77.
W. V. Buelzingsloerven, 1782, '83.     Dec. 26, '77.
Ehrhard von Drach, 1782, '83.          Dec. 27, '77.
Hieronymus Berner, 1782, '83.          Dec. 28, '77.
Georg Bern Kersting, 1782, '83.        Dec. 29, '77.
Rudolph Wilhelm Duncker, 1782, '83.    Dec. 30, '77.
Ludwig Martin Wiscker, 1782, '83.      { Jan. 1, '81.
                                       { Jan. 6, '81.
Carl von Ehrenstein, 1783.             Mar. 9, '82.

### Ensigns.

Carl von Ehrenstein, 1782.     Oct. 18, '77.
Heinrich Lange, 1782, '83.     Dec. 24, '77.
Friedrich Fey, 1782, '83.     Feb. 13, '78.
von Bode, 1782, '83.     Dec. 2, '79.

### Chaplain.

Virnau, 1782.

### Judge-Advocate.

Hynemann, 1782.

### Adjutant.

Carl Friedrich Rueffer, 1782, '83.

### Quarter-Master.

August Schmidt, 1782.

### Surgeon.

Conrad Gechter, 1782.

---

## REGIMENT KNYPHAUSEN, 1778–1783.

### Lieutenant-General.

Baron Wilhelm von Knyphausen, 1778–83.
                                           Sept. 22, '75.

### Colonel.

[1]Heinrich von Borck, 1778–83.     Jan. 20, '76.

### Lieutenant-Colonels.

Carl Philipp Heymell, 1778–81.
von Knyphausen, 1782.

### Majors.

[1]von Dichow [1776].
Johann Friedrich von Stein, 1778–83.     Feb. 27, '77.
Georg Wilhelm von Biesenroth, 1783.     May 6, '77.

---

[1] Wounded at Fort Washington, Nov. 16, 1776. *Gaine's New York Gazette*, *March 17, 1777.*

*Captains.*

¹Arnold Schlemmer.
²Barkhausen [1776].
Ludwig Wilhelm von Lowenstein, 1778, '79, '81.
Georg Wilhelm von Biesenroth, 1782.   Mar. 29, '62.
Schimmelpfennig, 1778, '79, '81–83.   Feb. 9, '76.
Christoph Philipp Reuffurth, 1779, '81–83.
                                  Feb. 24, '76, Dec. 24, '77.
Jacob Baum, 1778, '79, '81–83.   Feb. 21, '77.
Andreas Wiederhold, 1781–83.   Nov. 12, '78.
Vaupell, 1781–83.   Nov. 16, '79.
³Hon. Bennet Wallop, 1781–83.   April 23, '80.

*First Lieutenants.*

Vaupell, 1778.
Heinrich Friedrich Zinck, 1782, '83.   Feb. 22, '77.
Christian Sobbe, 1782, 83.   April 5, '77.
⁴John F. William Briede, 1782, '83.
                                  ——, 1777; Feb. 6, '81.

*Second Lieutenants.*

Christoph Philipp Reuffurth, 1778.
de Terry, 1778, '79.
Andreas Wiederhold, 1778, '79.
Wilhelm Heymell, 1779.
Ludwig von Romrodt, 1778, '79, '82, '83.   June 13, '74.
von Bassewitz, 1778, '79, '82, '83.   June 10, '75.
Johann Heymell, 1782, '83.   Feb. 1, '76.
Fuhrer, 1778, '79, '82, '83.   Feb. 2, '76.

---

¹*See* Regiment de Seitz.

²Killed at Fort Washington, Nov. 16, 1776.  *Gaine's New York Gazette, March 17, 1777.*

³To be Major of Brigade of Provincial Forces, Nov. 5, 1780.—*Robertson's Orderly Book.*  Fourth son of John Viscount Lymington, grandson of the first Earl of Portsmouth, born Jan. 20, 1745, died Feb. 12, 1815.—*Foster's Peerage.*

⁴Wounded at Fort Washington, Nov. 16, 1776.—*Gaine's New York Gazette, March 17, 1777.*

*In the American Revolution.*

Zinck, 1782, '83.                           Feb. 22, '77.
Geysow, 1782.                               Feb. 22, '77.
Christian Sobbe, 1778, '79, 82, '83.        April 5, '77.
Johann F. Wilhelm Briede, 1778, '79–81.
                                            1777, Feb. 6, '81.
August or Anton von Lützow, 1781–83.        Nov. 16, '79.
von Ruger, 1781–83.                         Mar. 1, '80.
Wilhelm von Drach, 1782, '83.               Mar. 24, '80.
Heinrich Zimmermann, 1782, '83.             Sept. 5, '81.
Heinrich Ritter, 1782, '83.                 Sept. 6, '81.

*Ensigns.*

¹Fuhrer, 1778.
August or Anton von Lützow, 1778, '79.
Wilhelm von Drach, 1778, '79, '81.
Heinrich Zimmermann, 1778, '79, '81.
Heinrich Ritter, 1778, '79, '81.
Ferdinand Ungar, 1781–83.                   Feb. 25, '78.
Wilhelm von Müller, 1781–83.                Mar. 1, '80.
Ronneberg, 1782, '83.                       Nov. 1, '80.

*Quarter-Masters.*

Mathias Müller, 1778, '79, '81.
Lewis Schmidt, 1782.
Pausch, 1783.

*Chaplain.*

Wilhelm Bauer, 1778, '79, '81–83.

*Adjutant.*

Christian Sobbe, 1779, '81–83.

*Surgeon.*

Wilhelm Pausch, 1778, '79, '81, '82.

---

[1] His portrait was fixed to the gallows in New York as a deserter, Oct. 1, 1781.—*Von Krafft's Journal, New York Historical Society's Collections, 1882.*

REGIMENT MIRBACH, 1778–1781.

*Major-General.*
von Mirbach, 1778.

*Colonels.*
von Block, 1778.
Carl von Romrodt, 1779–81.

*Lieutenant-Colonels.*
¹von Schieck [1776, '77].
Hans Moutz von Biesenroth, 1779–81.

*Majors.*
von Willmousky, 1778–81.
²Bauermeister, 1778, '79.

*Captains.*
Endmann, 1778.
Schotten, 1778.
David Reichhold, 1778, '79, '81.
Rothe, 1778, '79, '81.
Rodemann, 1779, '81.
von Toll, 1779, '81.

*Lieutenants.*
von Toll, 1778.
Schraydt, 1778, '79.
Wilhelm August von Boyneburgh, 1778, '79.
³Carl Friedrich Rüffer, 1778, '79.

*First Lieutenants.*
Broetke, 1781.

*Second Lieutenants.*
Wiesenmüller, 1779, '81.
Hans Friedrich von Biesenroth, 1779, '81.

---

[1] Killed at Red Bank.—*Eelking, vol. 1, p. 222.*
[2] A. D. C. to Sir Henry Clinton, 1779–82.
[3] Wounded at Red Bank.—*Eelking,* volume 1, page 222.

von Bulzenflöwer, 1779, '81.
Ehrhard von Drach, 1779, '81.
Hieronymus Berner, 1779, '81.
Martin Ludwig Wisker, 1781.
von Boyneburgh, 1781.

*Ensigns.*

Wiesenmüller, 1778.
Hans Friedrich von Biesenroth, 1778.
von Bulzenflöwer, 1778.
Ehrhard von Drach, 1778.
Hieronymus Berner, 1778.
Martin Ludwig Wisker, 1779.
Carl von Ehrenstein, 1779, '81.
Heinrich Friedrich Lange, 1779, '81.
Ungar, 1779.
Fey, 1779, '81.

*Adjutant.*

Carl Friedrich Rüffer, 1779, '81.

*Chaplain.*

Fernau, 1778, '79, '81.

*Quarter-Master.*

August Schmidt, 1778, '79, '81.

*Judge-Advocate.*

Heinemann, 1778, '79, '81.

*Surgeons.*

Conrad Taecher, 1778, '79.
Gechter, 1781.

NOTE.—The following officers belonging either to the Regiment Mirbach or the Grenadier Battalions of Minnigerode or Linsing or to the Jager Corps, to which cannot now be ascertained, were killed at the attack on Red Bank: Captains von Brogatzky and Wagener, Lieutenants Riemann, du Puy, von Wurmb, Hille, von Offenbach, and Heymel.

Lieut. Gottschalk was severely wounded at the same attack.

REGIMENT STEYN, 1778.
REGIMENT VON SEITZ, 1779–1783.

*Colonel.*
Franz Carl von Seitz, 1778–82.  Feb. 28, '74.

*Lieutenant-Colonels.*
¹Arnold Schlemmer, 1778.
Carl von Kutzel, 1780–83.  Feb. 3, '76.
[*Army rank*, Col., Nov. 3, '80.]

*Majors.*
Graff, 1778.
Ludwig von Schallern, 1779–83. Regt., April 13, '77.
[*Army rank*, Lt.-Col., Nov. 6, '80.]
Johann Newmann, 1782, '83.  Nov. 8, '80.

*Captains.*
Friedrich Platte, 1778.
Johann Newmann, 1778.
von Ende, 1778, '79.
G Langenschwarz, 1778, '79, '81–83.  Sept 7, '75.
Andreas Sandrock, 1778, '79, '81–83.  Mar. 12, '76.
Wilhelm Bode, 1778, '79, ,81–83.  Mar 13, '76.
Christian Münch, 1781–83.  Dec. 14, '78.
Wilhelm Justi, 1781.
Andreas Oelhaus, 1781.
Henklemann, 1781.

---

¹ On Wednesday last died, at 52 Years of Age, after four days' Illness, of an Inflammatory Fever, Lieut. Colonel Arnold Schlemmer, a Native of Hershfeld, in the Landgrave of Hesse, he served his Serene Highness, the Landgrave, thirty-eight years, particularly in the Campaigns of Bavaria, In 1742, 1743, 1744, 1745; in Scotland, in 1746; in Holland, in 1747, 1748; in England, in 1756; with the Allied Army in Germany, from 1757 to 1762, and in 1776 to the Day of his Death in North America; from a just sense of his great military Abilities, his Prince promoted him from the Rank of Captain, in the Regiment of his Excellency General de Kniphausen, to that of Lieutenant Colonel in the Regiment de Seitz, just before the Embarkation of that Corps for this Continent; he has left a Widow and one Son, an Infant. His Remains were on Thursday last interred with the military honours due to his Rank; he was as brave a Soldier, and as respectable a Gentleman as ever existed.—*Gaines' New York Gazette*, August 5, 1778.

*Lieutenants.*
'Swein [1776].[1]
von Romrodt, 1778.
Vilmer, 1778
Buebach, 1778.
von Freyden, 1778.
Christian Münch, 1778, '79.
Henklemann, 1778, '79
von Lahrbusch, 1778, '79

*First Lieutenants.*
Wilhelm Justi, 1778, '79, '82, '83.      Feb 23, '77.
Andreas Oelhaus, 1778, '82, '83.         Dec. 24, '77.

*Second Lieutenants.*
Johann Knies, 1779, '81–83.              Feb. 23, '77.
Georg [or Johann Heinrich] Fenner, 1779, '82, '83.
                                        Dec. 26, '77.
Rhein. Jung, 1782, '83.                  Nov. 12, '78.
Ludwig Friedrich Wilhelm von Boyneburgh, 1781–83.
                                        Dec. 13, '78.
Vieth, 1781, '82.                        Dec. 13, '78.
Johann Paul, 1781–83.                    Dec. 14, '78.
Johann Koerber, 1782.                    Nov. 1, '80.
Conrad Stolzenbach, 1782.                Mar. 7, '81.

*Ensigns.*
Bernhard Sturtz, 1778.
Albus, 1778.
Georg [or Johann Heinrich] Fenner, 1778.
Rhein. Jung, 1778, '79.
Vieth, 1778, '79.
Ludwig Friedrich Wilhelm von Boyneburgh, 1779.
Johann Paul, 1779.

---

[1] Killed at Fort Washington, Nov. 16, 1776.—*Gaines' New York Gazette*, March 17, 1777.

318                The German Allies

Johann Koerber, 1779, '81, '83.        Jan. 2, '78.
Conrad Stolzenbach, 1779, '81.         Feb. 26, '78.
Emanuel Maus, 1781–83.                 Dec. 13, '78.
Georg Langenschwartz, 1781–83.         Dec. 15, '78.
Petri, 1781–83.                        Feb. 13, '79.
Otter, 1782.                           July 10, '80.
Hunerdorf, 1782.                       Mar. 7, '81.

*Adjutants.*

Johann Kneis, 1778, '79.
Georg [or Johann Heinrich] Fenner, 1781, '82.

*Quarter-Master.*

Spangenberg, 1778, '79, '81–83.

*Judge-Advocate.*

Franke, 1778.

Kummell, 1778.

*Surgeon.*

Hellmerich, 1778, '79, '81–83.

---

REGIMENT WISSENBACK, 1778–1780.

REGIMENT KNOBLAUCH, 1781–1783.

*Major-General.*

Hans von Knoblauch, 1782, '83.        Feb. 19, '80.

*Colonel.*

Friedrich von Borbeck, 1778–80, '82, '83.  July 11, '80.

*Lieutenant-Colonels.*

von Kilzell, 1778, '79.
Friedrich von Borbeck, 1781.

### Majors.

Johann Georg Seelig, 1778–80.
Johann Otto Goebell, 1780–83.     Nov. 12, '78.
Johann Christian von Ende, 1781–83.   June 12, '80.

### Captains.

Oswald, 1778.
Germer, 1778.
Gunthermann, 1778, '79, '81.
Georg Hoenstein, 1782, '83.     Mar. 6, '76.
Jacob Boediker, 1778, '79, '81–83.   Mar. 20, '76.
Hupeden, 1778, '79, '82.     July 15, '78.
Wilhelm Heinrich Hegemann, 1781–83.  Nov. 15, '79.
Johann Anton von Darwigk, 1781–83.  July 10, '80.
Samuel Waldeck, 1783.     Mar. 28, '81.

### Lieutenants.

Stippich, 1778.
Kleyensteuber, 1778.
Conrad Koerber, 1778, '79.
Wilhelm Heinrich Hegemann, 1778, '79.
Resing, 1778, '79.
Lotz, 1778, '79.
Biermann, 1778, '79.

### First Lieutenants.

Ludwig Knoblauch, 1782, '83.   Mar. 21, '80.
Christoph Goebell, 1782, '83.   Mar. 22, '80.
Georg Schenck, 1782, '83.     Nov. 1, '80.
Johann Christoph Koerber, '81–83.  Mar. 7, '81.

### Second Lieutenants.

Christoph Goebell, 1778, '79, '81.
Johann Christoph Koebler, 1779.
Koerber, Jr., 1781.
Heinrich Abel, 1781–83.     June 16, '79.

Carl Ludwig Gessner, 1781–83.     Nov. 16, '79.
Bernhardt Justi, 1782, '83.       Mar. 21, '80.
Rud. Reinhard Dick, 1782, '83.    Sept. 15, '80.
Peternell, 1782, '83.             Nov. 2, '80.
Heinrich Stückradt, 1782, '83.    Nov. 3, '80.
Friedrich Cordemann, 1782.        Mar. 7, '81.
Schimmelfennig, 1783.             May 25, '81.

*Ensigns.*

Georg Schenck, 1778.
Koerber, Jr., 1778, '79.
Carl Ludwig Gessner, 1778, '79.
Heinrich Abel, 1778, '79.
Bernhardt Justi, 1778, '79, '81.
Mathæus, 1779.
Rud. Reinhard Dick, 1779, '81.
Weissenborn, 1781.
Peternell, 1781.
Heinrich Stückradt, 1781.
Schimmelpfennig, 1782.            June 1, '80.
Johann Dietrich, 1782, '83.       Nov. 1, '80.
Simon Vockeroth, 1782, '83.       Nov. 2, '80.
Andreas Wagener, 1782.            Mar. 11, '81.
Hartmann Scheuber, 1782, '83.     Mar. 12, '81.

*Chaplain.*

Grimmel, 1779, '81–83.

*Adjutants.*

Conrad Koerber, 1778, '79.
Carl Ludwig Gessner, 1783.

*Judge-Advocate.*

Schanz, 1779, '81–83.

*Quarter-Master.*

Pfluger, 1778, '79.

*Surgeon.*

Krupp, 1778, '79, '81–83.

REGIMENT WOELLWARTH, 1778.

REGIMENT TRUMBACH, 1779, 1780.

GRENADIER REGIMENT MARQUIS D'ANGELELLI, 1781–1783.

*Lieutenant-General.*

Louis d'Angelelli, 1781, '83.     Mar. 4, '77.

*Colonels.*

von Woellwarth, 1778.
Johann Christoph Kochler, 1779–81.    Sept. 18, '78.
Halzfeld, 1783.     Mar. 7, '82.

*Lieutenant-Colonel.*

Johann Wilhelm Endemann, 1781, '83.    Nov. 8, '80.

*Majors.*

Mathæus, 1778, '79.
[1] Johann Wilhelm Endemann, 1779–81.
Johann Jost, 1780.
Johann Eckhard Bode, 1782.     Mar. 9, '80.
Friedrich Wilhelm Bode, 1783.     Nov. 9, '80.

*Captains.*

Coecking, 1778.
Goebell, 1778, '79.
Feetz, 1778, '79, '81.
Staebeli, 1779, '81.
von Griesheim, 1781.
Johann Adam Bauer, 1781–83.     Apr. 10, '78.
Giesell, 1781.     Oct. 6, '78.
Greg. Salzmann, 1779, '81–83.     Nov. 17, '79.
Friedrich Heinrich Widekind, 1781–83.
    Nov. 20, '79.

---

[1] Wounded at Stono Ferry, S. C., June 30, 1779.—*Almon's Remembrancer*, vol. 8, page 302.

Johann Chr. Mülhausen, 1781, '83.   Nov. 8, '80.
Carl von Dalwigk, 1783.   Mar. 7, '82.

*Lieutenants.*

Staebeli, 1778.
Greg. Salzmann, 1778.
[1] Friedrich Heinrich Widekind, 1778, '79.
[1] von Griesheim, 1778, '79.

*First Lieutenants.*

[2] De Muy, 1779, '81.
Carl von Dalwigk, 1781.   Nov. 16, '79.
Wilhelm Studenroth, 1781, '83.   Nov. 8, '80.
Carl Andreas Kienen, 1781, '83.   Nov. 9, '80.

*Second Lieutenants.*

Carl Andreas Kienen, Sen., 1778, '79, '81.
Carl Andreas Kienen, Jr., 1778, '79, '81.
Wilhelm Studenroth, 1779, '81.
Wernicke, 1779, '81.
Christoph Friedrich Goebell, Sen., 1781, '83.
   Mar. 21, '76.
Eberhard, 1781.   Oct. 6, '78.
Gippert, 1781.   Oct. 7, '78.
Boppe, 1781.   Dec. 25, '78.
Eschtnith, 1781.   Dec. 26, '78.
Liebrecht Fleck, 1779, '81-83.   Nov. 16, '79.
Georg Broetke [or Bœske], 1781, '83.   Nov. 17, '79.
Wilhelm Boecking, 1781, '83.   Nov. 8, '80.
Friedrich Georg Mathæus, 1781, '83.   Nov. 9, '80.
Joseph Heinrich Wiederhold, 1781, '83.   Nov. 11, '80.
Heinrich Pauly, 1781, '83.   Mar. 7, '81.
Goebell, Jr., 1783.   Mar. 8, '81.

---

[1] Wounded at Stono Ferry, South Carolina, June 30, 1779 — *Almon's Remembrancer*, vol. 8, page 302.

[2] A Frenchman who refused to fight against his countrymen and was discharged in 1781.

*Ensigns.*

Wernicke, 1778.
Liebrecht Fleck, 1778.
[1] Kleinschmidt, 1778.
Schroeder, 1778, '79.
Georg Boeske [or Broetke], 1778, '79.
Werner, 1778, '79, '81.
Joseph Heinrich Wiederhold, 1779.
Wilhelm Boecking, 1779, '81.
Friedrich Georg Mathæus, 1781.
Goebell, 1781.
Gombrecht, 1781.
Schmidt, 1782, '83.                    July 31, '78.
Hatzfeldt, 1783.                       Mar. 6, '82.
Schultze, 1783.                        Mar. 10, '82.

*Adjutant.*

Liebrecht Fleck, 1779.

*Quarter-Masters.*

Fitz, 1778, '79.
Bokeloh, 1783.

*Surgeons.*

Holtzschuh, 1778, '79.
Girrard, 1783.

REGIMENT TRUMBACH, 1778.

REGIMENT BOSE, 1779, 1783.

*Lieutenant-General.*

Carl von Bose, 1782, '83.              Mar. 8, '81.

---

[1] Deserted on account of his debts, Aug. 11, 1778 — *Von Kraft's Journal, Collections of the New York Historical Society*, 1882, page 59.
His portrait was fixed to the gallows as a deserter, Oct. 1, 1781.—*Ibid*, page 151.

### Colonels.
[1] Carl Ernst von Bischhausen, 1778–80.
Baron H. von Muenchausen, 1783.   May 29, '78.

### Lieutenant-Colonels.
Baron H. von Muenchausen, 1778–82.   Jan. 21, '76.
Chris. du Puy [or Buy], 1782, '83.   Nov. 4, '80.

### Majors.
Chris. du Buy [or Puy], 1778–81.
[2] von O'Reilly, 1782, '83.   Nov. 3, '80.
[2] Friedrich Heinrich Schur, 1782, '83.   Nov. 6, '80.

### Captains.
Friedrich Heinrich Schur, 1778, '79, '81.
[3] Alexander Wilmousky, 1778, '79, '81.
Moritz von Stein, 1778, '79, '81.
[3] Johann Eigenbrod, 1778, '79, '81–83.   Feb. 24, '76.
[4] Rall, 1779, '81.
Wilhelm von Leliva, 1782, '83.   Nov. 1, '80.
Johann Schwaner, 1782, '83.   ——, '80; Sep. 5, '81.
Philipp Butte, 1782, '83.   ——, '80; Sep. 6, '81.

### Lieutenants.
Wilhelm von Leliva, 1778.
Spener, 1778, '79.
Henel, 1779.

### First Lieutenants.
[2] Philipp Butte, 1779, '81.
[2,4] Johann Schwaner, 1781.

---

[1] To be Brigadier General, Oct. 11, 1780.—*Robertson's Orderly Book*.
   Wounded at the battle of Guilford, March 15, 1781.—*Almon's Remembrancer*, volume 12, page 25.

[2] Surrendered at Yorktown.—*Eelking*, volume II, page 252.

[3] Wounded at the Battle of Guilford "and since dead."—*Almon's Remembrancer*, volume 12, page 25.

[4] Wounded at the Battle of Guilford.—*Rivington's Gazette*, August 11, 1781.
   Killed at Yorktown.—*Gaines' Gazette*, November 26, 1781.

*In the American Revolution.* 325

¹ Georg Christoph Hoepfner, 1778, '79, '81–83.
 Aug. 1, '79.
² Johann Josias Geyso, 1778, '79, '81–83.  Aug. 2, '79.
Ludwig Wilhelm Henel, 1782, '83.  Aug. 3, '79.

*Second Lieutenants.*
Ludwig Wilhelm Henel, 1778.
³ Hartmann, 1778, '79, '82.  Mar. 4, '74.
¹ Joseph Wilhelm Netzner, 1778, '79, '81–83.
 Mar. 5, '74.
Johann Frederick Kuntzet [or Kuntzook], 1783.
 Nov. 10, '77.
¹ Carl William von Burghoff, 1779, '81–83.
 Nov. 11, '77.
Nikolaus Kuntsch, 1779, '82.  { Nov. 20, '77.
 { Nov. 10, '77.
Nikolaus von Runk, 1783.  Sept. 5, '81.
Adolph von Roden, 1783.  Sept. 6, '81.
Wilhelm Brauns, 1783.  Mar. 9, '82.
⁴ Johann Philipp von Krafft, 1782.  Sept. 15, '82.

*Ensigns.*
Johann Friedrich von Kuntzook [or Kuntzet], 1778.
Carl William von Burghoff, 1778.
von Horn, 1778.
Ernst von Trott, 1778, '79, '81.
¹ Nikolaus Runk, 1778, '79, '81, '82.  June 9, '77.
¹ Adolph von Roden, 1779, '82.  Oct. 19, '77.
¹ Wilhelm Brauns, 1779, '81, '82.  Feb. 26, '78.

---

 1 Surrendered at Yorktown.—*Eelking* 2, page 252.
 2 Wounded at the Battle of Guilford, March 15, 1781.—*Almon's Remembrancer*, volume 12, page 25.
 3 Died in New York. Oct. 21. 1782.—Von Krafft's Journal, *New York Historical Societiy's Collections,* 1882, page 170.
 4 His journal, with a memoir prefixed. will be found in *New York Historical Society's Collections, 1882,* and the date of his commission appears on p. 181.

[1] Spangenberg, 1781, '82.                Aug. 1, '78.
Biskamp, 1782, '83.                     Mar. 7, '81.
Johann Philipp von Krafft, 1783.        Sept. 5, '81.
de Rantzow, 1783.                       Feb. 10, '82.
Meugersen, 1783.                        Mar. 9, '82.
Meisner, 1783.                          Mar. 10, '82.

*Adjutants.*

Henel, 1779.
Adolph von Roden, 1781, '82.

*Quarter-Master.*

Conrad Strube, 1778, '79, '81–83.

*Surgeons.*

Muller, 1778.
[2] W. Wurffelman, 1779, '81–83.

---

REGIMENT HUYNE, 1778–1781.

REGIMENT VON BENNING, 1782, 1783.

*Major-General.*

von Huyne, 1778.

*Colonels.*

Friedrich von Benning, 1782, '83.       May 23, '78.

*Lieutenant-Colonels.*

Ludwig Franz Kurtz, 1778–82.            Sept. 17, '78.
Johann Philip Hillebrand, 1780–83.      Nov. 13, '78.
Melchior Martini, 1782, '83.            Nov. 7, '80.

---

[1] Wounded at Yorktown.—*Gaines' New York Gazette*, Nov. 26, 1781. Surrendered at Yorktown —*Eelking*, vol. II, p. 252.

[2] Surrendered at Yorktown.—*Eelking*, vol. II, p 252.

[3] Died in New York, July 25, 1780, in his 60th year.—*Gaines' New York Gazette*, July 31, 1780.

*Majors.*
Johann Philip Hillebrand, 1778, '79.
Melchior Martini, 1778–81.

*Captains.*
¹ von Schallern, 1778.
² Wegener, 1778.
Heinrich Sonneborn, 1778, '79, '81, '82.   May 14, '76.
Reinhard Heilmann, 1778, '79, '81–83.   Mar. 15, '76.
Dietrich Reinhardt, 1778, '79, '81–83.   { June 23, '72.
                                          { June 23, '77.
Claudius Stueck, 1781–83.   Dec. 13, '78.
Johann Hoecker, 1781–83.   Dec. 15, '78.

*Lieutenant.*
³ Justi [1776].

*First Lieutenants.*
Claudius Stueck, 1778, '79.
Johann Hoecker, 1778, '79.
Jerome Roepenack, 1778, '79, '81–83.   Dec. 13, '78.
Franz Adam Kuhl, 1778, '79, '81–83.   Dec. 14, '78.
Johann Knipp [or Krupp], 1782, '83.   Feb. 16, '81.
Friedrich Starckloff, 1782, '83.   Feb. 17, '81.
von Waldschmidt, 1782, '83.   Mar. 1, '81.

*Second Lieutenants.*
Wendt, 1778, '79.
Ludwig Grau, 1779.
Johann Knipp [or Krupp], 1778, '79, '81.
Friedrich Starckloff, 1779.
Conrad Hillebrand, 1781–83.   Dec. 13, '78.

---

¹ Killed in Rhode Island, Aug. 29, 1778.—*Almon's Remembrancer*, vol. VII, p. 35.

² Wounded in Rhode Island, Aug. 29, 1778.—*Almon's Remembrancer*, vol. VII, p. 35.

³ Killed at Fort Washington, Nov. 16, 1776.—*Gaines' New York Gazette*, March 17, 1777.

Otto Roland Schenck, 1781–83.     Dec. 14, '78.
Bernhardt Eugen Eckhard, 1782, '83.     Mar. 7, '81.
Johann Martini, 1782, '83.     Mar. 8, '81.

*Ensigns.*

[1] Wendt [1776].
Kersting, 1778.
Duncker, 1778.
Wiscker, 1778.
Ludwig Grau, 1778.
Conrad Hillebrand, 1778, '79.
Otto Roland Schenck, 1779.
Bernhardt Eugen Eckhard, 1779, '81.
Johann Martini, 1779, '81.
Johann Christoph Hartung, 1781–83.     Nov. 15, '78.
Daniel Georg Reinhardt, 1781–83.     Dec. 13, '78.
Friedrich Goeschell, 1782, '83.     Mar. 7, '81.
Just Wenderoth, 1782, '83.     Mar. 8, '81.

*Chaplain.*

Kummel, 1778, '79, '81–83.

*Adjutants.*

Friedrich Starckloff, 1778, '79, '81, '83.
Johann Christoph Hartung, 1782.

*Quarter-Master.*

Kleinschmidt, 1778, '79, '81–83.

*Judge-Advocates.*

Steuber, 1778, '79, '83.
Kleinsteuber, 1781, '82.

*Surgeon.*

Johann Witte, 1778, '79, '81–83.

---

[1] Wounded at Fort Washington, Nov. 16, 1776. *Gaines' New York Gazette*, March 17, 1777.

*In the American Revolution.*

REGIMENT BUENAU, 1778–1783.

*Colonels.*

Rudolph von Buenau, 1778–83.  { Feb. 21, '75.
                                Feb. 25, '75.
Johann Adam Schaeffer, 1783.   Nov. 6, '80.

*Lieutenant-Colonel.*

Johann Adam Schaeffer, 1778, '79, '81, '82.
                                             Nov. 6, '80.

*Majors.*

Mathias, 1778.
Heinrich Bocking, 1779–81.
Friedrich Platte, 1779–83.    Feb. 3, '78.
Ludwig Bocking, 1782.
Heinrich Christian Hessenmuller, 1782, '83.
                                             Nov. 7, '80.

*Captains.*

Studenroth, 1778.
Ferrand, 1778, '79.
Johann Christian Goebel, 1778, '79, '81–83.
                                             Mar. 8, '76.
Philipp Virnhuber, 1778, '79, '81–83.   Mar. 9, '76.
[1] August Christ Noltenius, 1778, '79, '81–83.
                                             Mar. 17, '76.
Johann Bartholomew Becker, 1782, '83.   Dec. 16, '78.
Fritsch, 1782.                           Dec. 17, '78.
Johann Christoph Feldner, 1782, '83.    Dec. 18, '78.
Balthasar Mertz, 1782, '83.             Nov. 20, '78.

*Lieutenants.*

Bornemann, 1778, '79.
von Harstall, 1778, '79.

---

[1] Wounded at Rhode Island, Aug 29, 1778 —*Almon's Remembrancer*, vol. VII, p. 35.

### First Lieutenants.

Johann Bartholomew Becker, 1778, '79, '81.
Johann Christoph Feldner, 1779, '81.
Werner, 1781.
Christoph Otto Frohn, 1782, '83.   Mar. 7, '81.

### Second Lieutenants.

Christoph Otto Frohn, 1778, '79, '81.
Heinrich Bauer, 1778, '79, '81–83.   { Feb. 22, '76.
                                      { Feb. 22, '77.
Wolff de Guetenberg, 1778, '79, '81–83.  Feb. 25, '76.
Kleinsteuber, 1779, '81, '82.   Feb. 3, '78.
Georg Lyncker, 1782, '83.   Nov. 1, '78; Nov. 1, '80.
Cam. Friedrich Gombert, 1783.   July 15, '79.
Reinhardt Friedrich Schaeffer, 1782, '83.   Mar. 7, '81.
Brauns, 1782, '83.   Mar. 8, '81.
Carl Hillebrand, 1783.   Nov. 4, '81.

### Ensigns.

Kleinsteuber, 1778.
Cam. Friedrich Gombert, 1778, '79.
Bode, 1778, '79.
Georg Lyncker, 1778, '79, '81.
Reinhardt Friedrich Schaeffer, 1778, '79, '81.
Carl Hillebrand, 1779, '81, '82.   Feb. 3, '78.
Gotton Grebe, 1781–83.   Dec. 22, '78.
Georg [or Peter Wilhelm] Quentell, 1782, '83.
                                    May 14, '80.
Peter Muench, 1782, '83.   Nov. 2, '80.
Friedrich Wilhelm Kuester, 1782, '83.   Nov. 8, '80.
M. K. Seelig, 1782, '83.   Mar. 7, '81.

### Adjutants.

Johann Christoph Feldner, 1778, '79.
Cam. Friedrich Gombert, 1781–83.   Apr. 15, '79.

*Quarter-Masters.*

Meisterling, 1778.
Strahle, 1779, '81, '82.                          Mar. 1, '78.

*Surgeon.*

Beck, 1778, '79, '81, '82.                        Feb. 1, '76.

---

ARTILLERY, 1778–1783.

*Lieutenant-Colonel.*

Hans Heinrich Eitel, 1778–83.                     Dec. 25, '77.

*Major.*

Pauli, 1778, '79.

*Captains.*

[1] Georg Krug, 1778, '79, '81–83.                Jan. 26, '76.
Johann Schleenstein, 1778, '79, '81–83.   { Feb. 3, '78.
                                          { Feb. 13, '69.
[2] Werner, 1779.

*Lieutenants.*

Werner, 1778.
Deitzel, 1779.

*First Lieutenant.*

Johann Georg Kaiser, 1778, '79, '81–83.           Feb. 3, '78.

*Second Lieutenants.*

Fischer, 1778, '79, '81.
Philipp Scheimer, 1778, '79, '81–83.   { Mar. 12, '76.
                                       { Mar. 13, '76.

---

[1] *See Bancroft's United States, Centennial Edition*, vol. v, p 398.
[2] A few days since died after a lingering il'ness, Captain Werner, of the Hessian Artillery and Maj r of Brigade to General Knyphausen, a Gentleman of eminence in his profession and universally beloved by a very extensive acquaintance.—*Gaines' New York Gazette*, August 6, 1781.

Casimer Gerke, 1778, '79, '81–83.  Mar. 15, '76.
Christoph Schmidt, 1778, '79, '81–83.  Mar. 16, '76.
Johann Schaeffer, 1778, '79, '81–83.  Mar. 18, '76.
Johann Engelhard, 1778, '79, '81–83.  Mar. 19, '76.
Schwartzenberg, 1778, '79, '81, '82.  Mar. 27, '76.
¹ Carl August de Gironcourt [de Vomecourt], 1779, '82, '83.  Apr. 1, '76.
Carl Justus Korngiebell, 1778, '79, '81–83.
Feb. 22, '77.

*Adjutants.*

Dietzel, 1778.
Carl Justus Korngiebell, 1782.

*Quarter-Master.*

Wiederhold, 1778, '79, '81, '82.

---

CHASSEURS, 1778–1780.

MOUNTED AND DISMOUNTED YAGERS, 1779, '81–83.

*Colonel.*

Ludwig J. Adolph von Wurmb, 1783.  Jan. 3, '78.

*Lieutenant-Colonels.*

Ludwig J. Adolph von Wurmb, 1778–82. Jan. 25, '76.
Ernst Carl von Bruschenck [Pruschenck], 1781–83.
Nov. 15, '79.

*Majors.*

Ernst Carl von Bruschenck, 1778–80.
Philipp von Wurmb, 1779–83.  May 4, '77.

---

¹ Married on Sunday evening last [Aug. 10, 1783] Baron de Gironcourt, Lieutenant of Artillery, and Deputy Quarter Master General to the Hessian Troops to Miss Elizabeth Corne, daughter of Captain Peter Corné, of this city.—*Gaines' New York Gazette,* August 18, 1783.

*Captains.*

von Wreeden, 1778, '79.
Lorrey, 1778, '79.
[1] von Rau, 1778, '79, '81.
[2] Johann Ewald, 1778, '79, '81–83.     Mar. 6, '74.
[3] Hon. George Hanger, 1779, '81–83.   { Jan. 18, '78.
                                              { June 18, '78.
Moritz von Donop, 1779, '81–83.        Feb. 3, '78.
Johann Heinrichs, 1779, '81–83.         Feb. 4, '78.
Friedrich Adolph von Wangenheim, 1781–83.
                                                 Dec. 13, '78.
von Bodungen, 1781.
von Hagen, 1783.                             Nov. 9, '81.

*Captain-Lieutenant.*

Romrodt, 1782.                                July 5, '76.

*Lieutenants.*

von Donop, 1778.
[4] Mertz, 1778.
[5] Montluisant, 1778.
von Bodungen, 1778, '79.
Friedrich Adolph von Wangenheim, 1778, '79.

*First Lieutenants.*

[6] von Rau [1776].
Johann Heinrichs, 1778.
von Muise, 1778, '79, '81.

---

[1] Killed at Kingsbridge, New York, 1781.

[2] Surrendered at Yorktown.—*Eelking*, vol. 2, p. 252.

[3] Afterwards fourth and last Baron Coleraine.

[4] Wounded and taken prisoner, September 30, 1778.—Von Krafft's Journal, *New York Historical Society's Collection*, 1882, p. 62.

[5] A Frenchman, who entered the Army only to get to America, was discharged, tried to join the American Army was seized and sent to England.

[6] Wounded at the passage of the Bronx, October 28, 1776.—*Gaines' New York Gazette*, March 17, 1777.
Wounded July 2, 1781.—Von Krafft's Journal, *New York Historical Society's Collection*, 1882, p. 142.

Wilhelm von Hagen, 1778, '79, '81, '82.  Feb. 3, '78.
Carl E. von Hagen, 1778, '79, '81, '82.  Feb. 4, '78.
Friedrich Kellerhaus, 1778, '79, '82, '83.  Jan. 8, '79.
Heinrich Wolff, 1778, '79, '81–83.  Feb. 9, '79.
Ernst von Winzengerode, 1781–83.  Mar. 8, '79.
Johann Schaeffer, 1782, '83.  Mar. 21, '80.
¹ Wilhelm [or Alexander] Bickell, 1783.  Nov. 7, '81.

*Second Lieutenants.*

Johann Schaeffer, 1778, '79, '81.
Wilhelm [or Alexander] Bickell, 1779, '81, '82.
   Dec. 24, '77.
Maximillian Cornelius, 1779, '81–83.  Feb. 26, '78.
Conrad Flies, 1779, '81–83.  Feb. 27, '78.
¹ Friedrich Francis Bohlen, 1781–83.  Mar. 8, '79.
Engel Besger, 1782, '83.  Apr. 16, '80.
Wilhelm [or Ludwig] von Gerresheim, 1782, '83.
   May 1, '80.
Friedrich Ochse, 1782, '83.  Sept. 7, '81.
Baur, 1783.  Feb. 10, '82.

*Adjutants.*

Johann Schaeffer, 1778.
Friedrich Kellerhaus, 1779, '81.
Ernst von Winzingerode, 1782.
Friedrich Ochse, 1783.

*Quarter-Master.*

Beckmann, 1778, '79, '81–83.

*Judge-Advocate.*

Wiscker, 1778, '79, '81–83.

*Surgeon.*

August Hencke, 1778, '79, '81–83.

---

¹ Surrendered at Yorktown.—*Eelking*, volume 2, p. 252.

¹FIRST REGIMENT OF BRANDENBURG ANSPACH,
1778, 1779.

REGIMENT VOIT, 1781, 1782.

FIRST BATTALION ANSPACH, 1783.

*Colonels.*

von Eybe, 1778, '79.
²*Fr. August Valentin Voit von Salsburg, 1781–83.*
            Jan. 28, '77.

*Lieutenant-Colonel.*

² Christ. Ludwig von Reitzenstein, 1781–83.
            Aug. 18, '78.

*Majors.*

Christ. Ludwig von Reitzenstein, 1778, '79, '81.
² Friedrich Philipp von Seitz, 1781–83. Aug. 18, '78.

*Captains.*

von Waldenfels, 1778, '79.
² Christ. Philipp von Ellrodt, 1778, '79, '81–83.
            Dec. 27, '74.
² Heinrich Carl Friedrich von Stein [*zum Reitzenstein*], 1778, '79, '81–83. Feb. 9, '77.
*Heinrich Christoph von Metzsch.* July 9, '78.

*Captain Lieutenants.*

*Christian Theodor Sigismund* von Molitor, 1778, '79.
²Carl Christoph Ernst Tritschler, 1781–83.
            Aug. 18, '78.
²August Christoph Friedrich von Koenig, 1781–83.
            Mar. 2, '79.
*Wilhelm Friedrich von Kruse* [*1782, '83*]. *Mar. 1, '82.*

---

¹ Names in italics are taken from *Geisler*, p. 578.
² Surrendered at Yorktown.—*Eelking*, volume 2, p. 252.

*First Lieutenants.*
von Stoeder, 1778, '79
Chletsich, 1778, '79
Carl Christoph Ernst von Tritschler, 1778, '79.
August Christoph Friedrich von Koenig, 1778, '79
von der Heydell, 1778, '79.
¹Friedrich Wilhelm von Reitzenstein, 1778, '79,'81–83.
            July 28, '75.
Carl Friedrich von Schoenfeldt, 1778–83. July 27, '76.
¹Friedrich von Keller, 1781–83.   Feb 6, '78.
¹Wilhelm Fr. Marschall von Bierbenstein, 1781–83.
            July 9, '78.
¹*Albrecht Ernst Ludwig Treschel von Teufstetten,*
 *1781–83.*        Mar. 2, '79.
¹Wilhelm von Diemar, 1781–83. Mar. 2, '79.
*Johann Ernst Prechtel.*
*Georg Friedrich Philipp Guttenberg.*

*Second Lieutenants.*
Friedrich von Keller, 1778, '79.
Wilhelm Fr. Marschall von Bierbenstein, 1778, '79.
Albrecht Ernst Ludwig Treschel von Teufstetten,
 1778, '79.
von Chlardefeldt, 1778, '79.
Wilhelm von Diemar, 1778, '79.
¹Friedrich von Foetor, 1781–83.   June 1, '77.
¹Johann Ernst Prechtel, 1778, '79, '81–83 Sept. 28, '77.
¹Georg Friedrich Philipp Guttenberg, 1778, '79,'81–83
            Sept. 28, '77.
¹Johann Christian von Drexel, 1781–83. Oct 3, '78.
¹*Johann Gottfried* Minameyer, 1781–83. Oct 3, '78.
¹*Christian Gottfried* Baumann, 1781–83. Oct. 3, '78.
¹*Johann Christoph* Doehlemann, 1781–83. Oct. 3, '78.
Johann Friedrich Foerster, 1781–83.  Dec. 20, '78.

---
¹ Surrendered at Yorktown —*Eelking*, volume 2, p. 252.

*In the American Revolution.*

¹Johann von Fabrice, 1781–83.  May 1, '79.
Deahna, 1782.  July 26, '79.
¹*Georg Simon Halbmeyer, 1781, '82.*  Oct. 29, '79.
¹*Georg Matthias Beyer, 1782.*  Aug. 6, '81.

*Adjutants.*

Friedrich von Foeter, 1781.
Johann [or Christ] Gott Minameyer, 1782.

*Chaplain.*

¹Johann Christoph Wagner, 1781–83.  Feb. *1*, '77.

*Judge-Advocate.*

¹*Johann Carl Conrad* Rummel, 1781–83.

*Surgeon.*

¹Friedrich Jacob Rapp, 1781–83.  Feb. 1, '77.

*Quarter-Master General.*

¹Carl Wilhelm Fr. Meyer, 1781–83.

*Commissary.*

Johann Christoph Hermann, 1781–83.

*Artillery Officer.*

Friedrich Hoffmann, 1783.  May 22, '69.

---

¹ Surrendered at Yorktown.—*Eelking*, volume 2, p. 252.

[1]SECOND REGIMENT OF BRANDENBURG ANSPACH.

REGIMENT VON VOIT, 1778, 1779.

REGIMENT SEYBOTHEN, 1781, 1782.

SECOND BATTALION ANSPACH, 1783.

Colonels.

August Valentin Voit von Saltzburg, 1778, '79.
[2]*Franz Johann Heinrich Wilhelm Christian* von Seybothen, 1781–83.     Feb. 6, '78.

Majors.

[2]*Franz Johann Heinrich Wilhelm Christian* von Seybothen, 1778, '79.
[2]*Ernst Friedrich Carl* von Beust, 1781–83.

Feb. 6, '78.

Captains.

Ernst Friedrich Carl von Beust, 1778, '79.
von Seitz, 1778, '79.
[2,3] Friedrich Ludwig von Eyl, 1778, '79, '81–83.

June 22, '69.
[2]*Christian Theodor Sigismund* von Molitor, 1781–83.

July 1, '77, July 17, '77.
[2]Georg Heinrich von Quesnoy, 1781–83. Oct. 24, '77.

Captain Lieutenants.

Georg Heinrich von Quesnoy, 1778, '79.
*Heinrich Christoph Friedrich von Metzsch, 1781–83.*

July 9, '78.
*Johann Christoph Seidel.*

---

[1] Names in italics are taken from *Geisler*, p. 579.
[2] Surrendered at Yorktown.—*Eelking*, volume 2, p. 252.
[3] Wounded at Forts Clinton and Montgomery, October 6, 1779.—*Pennsylvania Ledger*, March 11, 1778.

*First Lieutenants.*

von Schwart, 1778, '79.
von Woellwarth, 1778, '79.
¹ Wilhelm Friedrich von Kruse, 1778, '79, '81–83.
                                                        June 26, '75.
¹ Johann Christoph Seidel, 1778, '79, '81–83.
                                                        Feb. 1, '77.
Philipp Otho von Beust, 1778, '79, '81–83. Feb. 2, '77.
¹ Carl Friedrich von Adelheim, 1778, '79, '81–83.
                                                      Feb. 13, '77.
¹ Friedrich Ernst von Reitzenstein, 1778, '79, '81–83.
                                                    Oct. 24, '77.
Maximilian von Streit, 1781–83.     Feb. 6, '78.
Carl Alexander von Weiterschausen, 1781–83.
                                                    July 9, '78.
*Georg Gustav Lebrecht von Tunderfeldt.*
*Heinrich Wenhardt.*
*Johann Anton Carl von Altenstein.*

*Second Lieutenants.*

¹ Maximilian von Streit, 1778, '79.
¹ Carl Alexander von Weiterschausen, 1778, '79.
von Weigner, 1778, '79.
² von Diemar, 1778, '79.
Christoph von Molitor, 1778, '79.
von Strahlendorf, 1778, '79.
¹ Georg Gustav Lebrecht von Tunderfeldt, 1778, '79,
   '81–83.                                     Feb. 5, '77.
¹ Johann Anton Carl von Altenstein, 1778, '79, '81–83.
                                                    Feb. 6, '77.
¹ Heinrich Weinhardt, 1778, '79, '81–83. Feb. 9, '77.
Heinrich S. Nagler, 1781–83.     Oct. 8, '77.

---

[1] Surrendered at Yorktown.—*Eelking*, vol. II, p. 252.
[2] Ernst von Diemar to be Major of the Fort at Brooklyn, January 8, 1783. *Gaines' New Yoro Gazette*, January 20, 1783.

¹Johann Andreas Gottlob von Ciriarsi [or Cyriatzy],
    1778, '79, '81–83.                   Oct. 31, '77.
¹Johann Hermann Lindemeyer, 1781–83. Mar. 14, '78.
Carl Godfried Schuchard, 1781–83.     July 24, '78.
¹Johann Gottfried Hirsch, 1781–83.    Dec. 19, '78.
¹Carl Christoph Graebner, 1781–83.    Mar. 2, '79.
¹Johann Heinrich von Matolay, 1781–83.
                         Apr. 1, '79, Apr. 12, '79.
¹Johann Heinrich Popp, 1782.    { Sept. 15, '81.
                                { Oct. 17, '81.

*Adjutants.*

Herrnbauer, 1778, '79.
Johann Christoph Seidel, 1781–83.

*Judge-Advocate.*

Christoph Laurenz Pflug, 1782.        Feb. 1, '77.

*Chaplain.*

Johann Georg Philipp Erb, 1781–83.    Jan. 11, '78.

*Quarter-Master.*

¹Johann Georg Chris. Daig, 1778, '79, '81–83.
                                      Feb. 1, '77.

*Surgeon.*

¹Johann Heinrich [or Friedrich Wilhelm] Schneller,
    1781–83.                          Dec. 10, '79.

---

ARTILLERY.

*Captain.*
Nikolaus Friedrich Hoffmann, 1782, '83. Aug. 1, '81.

*First Lieutenant.*
Nikolaus Friedrich Hoffmann, 1781.    Dec. 1, '80.

---

¹ Surrendered at Yorktown.—*Eelking*, volume 2, p. 252.

[1]ANSPACH JAGERS, 1781–1783.

*Colonel.*
*Christoph Ludwig Rudolph Freiherr von Reitzenstein*
[1783]. Dec. 2, '82.

*Lieutenant-Colonel.*
*Christoph Ludwig Rudolph Freiherr* von Reitzenstein,
1782. Aug. 18, '78.

*Captains.*
*Christoph Fr. Joseph von* Waldenfels, 1781–83.
Feb. 1, '77; Feb. 9, '77.
*Friedrich Wilhelm* von Roeder, 1781, '82. Feb. 6, '78.
*Carl Christian Ernst Tretschler von Falkenstein.*
Mar. 1, '82.
*August Christian Friedrich von Koenitz.* Mar. 1, '82.
*Ernst Wilhelm Friedrich Adolph von Wurmb.*
Mar. 1, '82.

*Captain Lieutenants.*
*Friedrich Wilhelm, Freiherr von Reitzenstein.*
Mar. 1, '82.
*Carl Friedrich Rudolph von Schoenfeldt.* Mar. 1, '82.

*Lieutenant.*
de Forstner [1777].

*First Lieutenants.*
*Moritz Wilhelm von der* Heydte, 1781–83. Feb. 3, '77.
*Friedrich Ernst, Freiherr von Reitzenstein.*
*Oct. 24,* '77.
Just von Diemar, 1781–83. Mar. 2, '79.

---

[1] New York, July 16.—Yesterday embarked for Bremerlehe, in Germany, the Anspach Jagers.—*Gaines' New York Gazette,* July 21, 1783.

Names in italics are taken from *Geisler,* p. 581.

[2] Wounded at the Battle of Germantown, September 11, 1777.—*Pennsylvania Ledger,* March 4, 1778.

### Second Lieutenants.

| | |
|---|---|
| von Reitzenstein, 1781, '82. | { Oct. 20, '77.<br>{ Oct. 27, '77. |
| *Christian* Friedrich Bartholomai, 1781–83. | |
| | Oct. 27, '77. |
| Jacob Ernst Kling, 1781–83. | Mar. 1, '79. |
| *Just Hermann Drahua.* | July 26, '79. |
| *Ehrenfried Hansz Friedrich Ferdinand Busch.* | |
| | Apr. 1, '80. |
| [1] *Joseph* Bach, 1781, '82.   *June 9, '80;* | July 9, '80. |
| Wilhelm de Hiller, 1782, '83. | Jan. 1, '81. |
| *Ferdinand von Killer.* | Feb. 1, '81. |
| *Friedrich Adolph Karl von Eyb.* | Apr. 5, '81. |
| *Julius von Massenbach.* | June 18, '81. |
| *Franz Graf von Bubna und Lititz.* | Nov. 1, '81. |
| *Albertus Magnus Frank.* | Mar. 2, '82. |
| *August Wilhelm Neithardt von Gneisenau.* | |
| | Mar. 3, '82. |
| *Christian Kaspar Morg.* | Mar. 4, '82. |
| Christoph Georg Philipp Otto, 1783. | Mar. 28, '82. |

### Adjutant.

| | |
|---|---|
| *Christoph Georg Philipp Otto.* | Mar. 1, '82. |

### Judge-Advocate.

| | |
|---|---|
| *Johann Paul* Frisch, 1782. | Feb. 1, '81. |

### Quarter-Master.

*Johann Leonhardt Hauselt* [or Hausett], 1782.

### Surgeon.

Friedrich Siegmund Arnold, 1782.

### Chaplain.

| | |
|---|---|
| *Georg Christoph Elias Erb.* | Mar. 1, '82. |

---

[1] Surrendered at Yorktown.—*Eelking*, volume 2, p. 252.

*Staff Physician for the three Brandenburg, Anspach and Bayreuth Regiments.*
David Schoepf.                                    Feb. *11*, '77.

---

YAGER CORPS, 1778, 1779.

*Colonel.*
[1] Carl Emil Kurt von Donop.

*Captains.*
[2] Trautvitter.
von Cramon, 1778, '79.
[3] Heppe.

*First Lieutenant.*
von Feilitsch, 1778, '79.

*Second Lieutenants.*
[4] Ebenauer, 1778, '79.
[5] von Donop.

*Artillery Lieutenant.*
Hoffman, 1778, '79.

*Adjutant.*
Staab, 1778, '79.

*Chaplain.*
Wagner, 1778, '79.

*Judge-Advocate.*
Stummel, 1778, '79.

---

[1] Killed at Red Bank.
[2] Mortally wounded at Battle of Brandywine.—*Pennsylvania Ledger*, March 4, 1778.
[3] Mortally wounded at Gloucester, September 25, 1777.
[4] Killed at Springfield, New Jersey, June 8, 1780.—*Eelking*, volume 2, p. 91.
[5] Died in New York in 1777.

*Quarter-Master.*
Model, 1778, '79.
*Surgeon.*
Stapp, 1778, '79.

NOTE.—See note at end of the Regiment Mirbach.

---

REGIMENT DONOP, 1779-1783.
*Lieutenant-General.*
Wilhelm Heinrich August Donop, 1782, '83.
                                        Oct. 24, '72.
*Colonels.*
David von Gosen, 1779, '80.
Erasmus Ernst Hinte, 1783.    { Jan. 24, '76.
                                        { June 2, '78.
Carl Philipp Heymell, 1782, '83.   May 22, '78.
*Lieutenant-Colonel.*
Erasmus Ernst Hinte, 1779-82.
*Majors.*
Christ. Moritz von Kutzleben, 1779, '82, '83.
                                        Feb. 24, '77.
Carl von Wurmb, 1779-83.     Apr. 5, '77.
*Captains.*
Jean Matthew Gissot, 1779, '81-83.   { May 29, '69.
                                        { May 22, '79.
Just Verater, 1779, '81-83.     Feb. 21, '75.
Dietrich von Donop, 1779, '81, '82.  { Feb. 22, '75.
                                        { Feb. 22, '76.
Friedrich Wm. Geissler, 1779-83.   Apr. 27, '77.
Philipp Heinrich Murhard, 1779-83.  Dec. 25, '77.
Christoph Friedrich von Donop, 1783.

*First Lieutenants.*
Emanuel R. Hausmann, 1782, '83.   Nov. 23, '76.
Johann Philipp Reiss, 1782, '83.   June 28, '77.

*Second Lieutenants.*
[1] Wilhelm Carl von Donop, 1779, '81.
Johann Ernst von Freyenhagen, 1779, '81.
Heinrich von Bardeleben, 1779–83.   Sept. 4, '74.
Heinrich Ludwig von Nagele, 1779, '81–83.
　　　　　　　　　　Mar. 5, '74; May 5, '74.
Wilhelm von Lepell, 1779–83.   Feb. 1, '76.
Carl August von Freyenhagen, 1779, '81–83.
　　　　　　　　　　　　　　Feb. 3, '76.
Jerome von Lossberg, 1782, '83.   Nov. 23, '76.
Carl Fried. von Nagele, 1779, '81–83.  { Mar. 4, '77.
　　　　　　　　　　　　　　　　　　{ May 4, '77.
Eytell William von Trott, 1779, '81–83.   Feb. 3, '78.
W. J. von Freyenhagen, 1782.   Feb. 4, '78.
Friedrich Ferd. Murhard, 1783.   May 30, '82.

*Ensigns.*
Carl von Knoblauch, 1779, '81.
Friedrich Ferd. Murhard, 1779, '81, '82.   Nov. 16, '76.
Georg von Lehrbach, 1779, '81–83.   June 9, '77.
Lon. [*sic*] C. A. von Hausen, 1782, '83.   Mar. 7, '81.
Johann Henckel, 1782, '83.   Mar. 9, '81.
Boeking, 1783.   Mar. 30, '82.

*Chaplain.*
Koester, 1779, '81–83.   Jan. 29, '76.

*Adjutant.*
Wilhelm von Lepell, 1779, '81–83.   Feb. 1, '76.

*Quarter-Master.*
Georg Zinn, 1779–82.   Feb. 1, '69.

---

[1] Appointed Chamberlain to the Duke of Mecklenberg-Schwerin, 1780.—Von Krafft's Journal, *New York Historical Society's Collection*, 1782, p. 125.

*Judge-Advocate.*
Ernst Heymele, 1779–82.   Feb. 2, '76.
*Surgeons.*
Jacob Stieglitz, 1779–81.   Feb. 1, '74.
Ludwig Stieglitz, 1782.

---

[1] REGIMENT WALDECK, 1782, 1783.
*Colonel.*
[2] *von Hanxleden.*
*Lieutenant-Colonels.*
[3] Albrecht von Horn, 1782, '83.   Apr. 14, '79.
*von Dalwigk.*
*Majors.*
Albrecht von Horn, 1781.
[4] Friedrich Pentzel, 1782, '83.   Apr. 14, '79.
*Captains.*
von Staakerg, 1782.   Apr. 19, '76.
Georg von Haacke, 1783.   Apr. 19, '76.
Christ. Alberti, 1782.   Sept. 20, '77.
*Alexander von Baumbach.*
August *Alberti.*

---

[1] Two Captains, Three Lieutenants and Three Surgeon's Mates taken prisoner at Baton Rouge, September, 1779. One Captain taken prisoner on the Lakes, Louisiana.—*Almon's Remembrancer*, volume 9, p. 364.
 Names in italics are from *Geisler*, p. 583.

[2] Killed at Frenchtown, on the Mississippi, January 7, 1781.—*Eelking*, volume 2, p. 148.

[3] New York, July 16.—Yesterday embarked for Bremerleh, in Germany, the 3rd Regiment of Waldeck, commanded by Lieut. Col. Horn.—*Gaines' New York Gazette*, July 21, 1783.

[4] Taken prisoner at Pensacola, together with one Lieutenant, one Ensign, one Surgeon's Mate of same regiment, May 11, 1781.—*Almon's Remembrancer*, volume 11, p. 280.

*Captain Lieutenants.*

[1] Alexander von Baumbach, 1782, '83.  { Mar. 16, '76.
{ Apr. 16, '76.
August Alberti, 1782, '83.   Mar. 5, '77.
[2] Heinrich Heldring, 1782, '83.   Apr. 25, '80.

*Lieutenants.*

[3] *Leonhardi* [1779].
*Knipshild.*
[4] *Stierlein.*

*First Lieutenants.*

Wilhelm Keppel, 1782, '83.   Mar. 7, '76.
Friedrich von Wilmousky, 1782, '83.   Mar. 8, '76.
Carl Struberg, 1782, '83.   Mar. 5, '77.
Andreas Brumhard, 1782, '83.   Apr. 14, '79.

*Second Lieutenants.*

*Roelting.*
[5] *von Gosen.*
[6] *Alberti.*
Carl Strohmann, 1782.   Apr. 25, '80.
Carl Hohmann, *Sr.*, 1783.

*Ensigns.*

[7] *von Axleven.*
*von Horn.*

---

[1] Wounded at Frenchtown, on the Mississippi, January 7, 1781.—*Eelking*, volume 2, p. 148.

[2] Taken prisoner at Pensacola.—*Almon's Remembrancer*, volume 12, p. 281.

[3] Killed at Fort Manchac, September, 1779.—*The Political Magazine*, 1780, p. 342.

[4] Killed at Frenchtown, on the Mississippi, January 7, 1781.—*Eelking*, volume 2, p. 148.

[5] Died in New Orleans, July 20, 1781.—*Eelking*, volume 2, p. 152.

[6] Died in New Orleans, July 21, 1781.—*Eelking*, volume 2, p. 152.

[7] Left the Regiment, November 18, 1779.—*Geisler*, p. 584.

[1] Nolting [1779].
Ludwig Schmidt, 1782, '83.     Apr. 14, '79.
Carl Muller, *Sr.*, 1782, '83.     Apr. 15, '79.
Hohmann, *Jr.*
[2] Ursall.
Muller, *Jr.*
Philipp Wirths, 1783.     Apr. 25, '82.
Bernhardt Schreiber, 1783.     Aug. 25, '82.

### Chaplain.

Philipp Waldeck, 1782, '83.     Apr. 24, '76.

### Adjutants.

Stierlein.
Heinrich Jacob Knipchild, 1782, '83.     Apr. 25, '80.

### Quarter-Master.

Earl Wiegand, 1782, '83.     Mar. 2, '76.

### Auditor.

Philip Marc, 1782, '83.     Mar. 2, '76.

### Surgeons.

Christ. Mattern, 1782, '83.     Apr. 20, '76.

---

[1] Killed at Baton Rouge, September, 1779.—*Almon's Remembrancer*, volume 9, p. 365.

[2] Killed at the siege of Pensacola.—*Gaines' New York Gazette*, July 9, 1781.

[1]FREE BATTALION OF HESSE HANAU, 1782, 1783.

*Lieutenant-Colonel.*

Michael von Janecke, 1782, '83.　　　Jan. 4, '81.

*Major.*

Carl August Scheel, 1783.　　　Jan. 5, '82.

*Captains.*

Just Friedrich von Franck, 1782, '83.　Jan. 3, '81.
Carl Dittmar Spangenberg, 1782, '83.　Jan. 4, '81.
Christ. Ludwig, Graf von Leiningen, 1782, '83.
　　　　　　　　　　　　　　　　　Jan. 13, '81.
Christ. Ludwig von Schelm, 1782, '83.　Jan. 15, '81.

*Captain-Lieutenant.*

Thylo von Westerhagen, 1782, '83.　Jan. 21, '81.

*First Lieutenants.*

Godfried Heinrich von Kerner, 1782, '83.
　　　　　　　　　　　　　　　　　Jan. 14, '81.
Johann Georg Kock, 1782, '83.　　　Jan. 15, '81.
Carl Philipp Eytelwein, 1782, '83.　　Jan. 16, '81.
Conrad Bernhardt Zipff, 1782.　　　Mar. 18, '81.

*Second Lieutenants.*

Christian Hoelcken, 1782, '83.　　　Jan. 14, '81.
Philipp Schaeffer, 1782, '83.　　　　Jan. 15, '81.
Friedrich Goerdewk, 1782, '83.　　　Jan. 18, '81.
Jerome Conradi, 1782, '83.　　　　　Jan. 31, '81.
Johann Godfried von Stockel, 1782, '83.　Mar. 19, '81.
Friedrich Just Genner, 1782.　　　　Mar. 24, '81.

---

[1] New York, July 16.—Yesterday embarked for Bremerlehe, in Germany.
—*Gaines' New York Gazette*, July 21, 1783.

### Ensigns.

von Huth, 1782. Jan. 4, '81.
Friedrich von Mayerfeld, 1782, '83. Jan. 6, '81.
von Benckendorf, 1782. Mar. 8, '81.
Nicholaus Schweinebraden, 1783. Jan. 19, '82.
Wilhelm von Seiff, 1783. Jan. 20, '82.

### Adjutant.

Godfried Heinrich von Kerner, 1782.

### Quarter-Master.

von der Velden, 1782.

### Surgeon.

Mentzel, 1782.

---

## [1] ANHALT ZERBST, 1783.

### Majors.

[2] von Luttichau, 1783. Jan. 1, '80.
Wiedersheim, 1783.

### First Lieutenant.

von Bibra, 1783. Feb. 20, '81.

### Second Lieutenants.

Rustig, 1783. June 10, '79.
von Schomberg, 1783. July 19, '79.
von Klapprotto, 1783. Jan. 23, '80.
von Pollnitz, 1783. Feb. 18, '81.
Imhoff, 1783. Feb. 21, '81.
von Oppen, 1783. Feb. 22, '81.

---

[1] New York, July 16.—Yesterday embarked for Bremerlehe, in Germany.—*Gaines' New York Gazette*, July 21, 1783.

[2] "Died since printing."—Correction to *Army List* of 1783.

## RAHL'S REGIMENT.

*Captain.*
[1] Walter.

*Lieutenants.*
[2] Kunen.
[3] Mulhausen.

*Ensign.*
[2] Wernick.

---

[1] Killed at Fort Washington, November 16, 1776.—*Gaines' New York Gazette*, March 17, 1777.

[2] Wounded at Fort Washington. November 16, 1776.—*Gaines' New York Gazette*, March 17, 1777.

[3] Wounded at the passage of the Bronx, October 28, 1776.—*Gaines' New York Gazette*, March 17, 1777.

# I. INDEX OF NAMES.

Adams, 40.
Agnew, 114.
Alberti, Lieutenant, 225.
Alberti, Captain, 48, 220.
v. Altenbockum, Captain, 66, 76.
André, Major, 154.
Arbuthnot, Admiral, 171, 196.
Armand, 159.
Armstrong, General, 110.
Arnold, General, 90, 135, 201.
Bach, Lieutenant, 131.
Backer, Chaplain, 238.
Bär, 94.
v. Barner, Lt.-Col., 148, 240, 248.
Baum, Captain, 12, 69, 277.
Baum, Lieut.-Col., 87, 130, 271.
v. Baumbach, Lieut., 113, 222.
Bauermeister, Major, 254.
v. Benning, Colonel, 76, 198.
v. Bentheim, Lieut., 124, 258.
v. Beust, Major, 215.
Bickel, Lieutenant, 113, 161, 205.
Bill, Lieutenant, 11, 71, 277.
v. Biesenroth, Major-Gen., 70, 197.
v. Bischoffshausen, Major-Geu., 197, 269.
v. Block, Colonel, 38, 110, 269.
v. Bockum, Capt., 137.
v. Bojatzky, Colonel, 119.
v. Borbeck, Colonel, 51, 175, 269.
v. Bork, Colonel, 185, 192, 269.
v. Borning, Captain, 51.
v. Bose, General, 162, 172, 198, 269.
Braun, General, 88.
Braunsdorf, Chaplain, 238.
Brandenburg, 220.
Brethauer, Lieut.-Colonel, 66, 258.
Bremer, Colonel, 162.
Breymann, Colonel, 87, 126, 131.
Brisbon, Commodore, 163.

Brunhardt, Lieutenant, 223.
v. Bunau, Colonel, 269.
Burmeister, Captain, 11.
Burgoyne, General, 89, 125, 137, 235.
Butler, 242.
Byron, Admiral, 161.
Cadwalader, General, 77.
Campbell, Major-General, 105.
Carleton, Gen., 25, 125, 161, 232, 235.
Carleton, Major, 240.
St. Clair, General, 127.
v. Cleve, Major, 13, 244.
Clinton, J., General, 123.
Clinton, G., General, 123, 226.
Clinton, Sir H., General, 25, 154.
Collier, Admiral, 174.
Cornwallis, Lord, General, 29, 104, 184, 211.
Cooper, 256.
Corves, Lieutenant, 240.
Corvan, Ensign, 187.
v. Dahlstierna, Captain, 146.
van Dassel, 73.
v. Dechow, Major, 61, 76, 257.
v. Diemer, Captain, 151, 274.
v. Diemar, Lieutenant, 195.
v. Dieskau, Major, 168.
v. Dincklage, Major, 11, 107, 115, 198, 232.
Döhla, 14, 101, 190, 213, 266.
v. Donop, General, 269.
v. Donop, Captain, 34, 75, 161.
v. Donop, Colonel, 105, 116, 270.
v. Dörnberg, 256.
Dupuy, Lieutenant, 113.
Du Puy, Major, 193, 197, 201.
Duplessis, Captain, 119.
Ebenauer, Lieutenant, 193.
v. Eckert, Captain, 102, 123.
v. Ehrenkrook, Lt.-Col., 126, 233, 25

Eigeubrod, Captain, 201.
v. Eitel, Colonel, 270.
Elbing, Lieut.-Col., 189.
Emmerich, Colonel, 73, 159, 227.
v. Ende, Lieut.-Col., 198.
d'Estaing, Admiral, 163, 175, 241.
Ewald, Captain, 45, 53, 75, 104, 158, 176, 201, 209, 265.
Ewing, General, 77.
v. Eyb, Colonel, 102.
v. Eyb, Captain, 123.
de Fasquel, 266.
Faucit, W., Col , 16, 88, 153, 258.
Fichtelberger, 170.
Fliess, Lieutenant, 266, 288.
Flockshaar, Sergeant, 12.
v. Forstner, Lieutenant, 113.
Foy, Lieutenant, 96.
Franklin, 40.
Fraser, 127.
Frazer, 91.
v. Fredersdorf, Captain, 134, 146.
Gage, General, 26.
Galvez, Don B., 221.
v. Gall, Colonel, 89, 126, 133, 148.
Gates, General, 213.
Gebhardt, 13.
v. Geisan, Captain, 128.
v. Gerlach, Captain, 128, 138.
Germain, Lord, 19, 107, 271.
v. Geyling, Ensign, 146.
Geyso, Lieutenant, 201.
v. Gleissenberg, Captain, 132, 146.
v. Gneisenau, 256.
Gogel, Captain, 238.
v. Goren, Lieutenant, 225.
v. Gosen, Major-General, 197, 269.
Grasse, Admiral, 233.
v. Grammont, Captain, 106.
Granby, 33.
Grant, General, 32, 59, 64, 75, 114.
Grant, Colonel, 34.
Grau, Captain, 192.
Greene, Gen., 28, 71, 165, 199, 213.
Green, Christopher, Colonel, 117.
Grenke, Lieutenant, 27.
Grey, 114.
v. Griesheim, Captain, 52.
Griffin, Colonel, 77.
v. Grothausen, Lieutenant, 59, 70.
v. Huchenberg, Major-General, 193, 198, 269.
Hacken, Captain, 48.

v. Hacke, Captain, 227.
Häberlin, Ensign, 241.
Haldimand, General, 239.
v. Hambach, Captain, 240.
Hand, Colonel, 31.
v. Hnstein, Major, 68, 188, 258.
v. Hanxleben, Colonel, 47, 220.
v. Hatzfeld, Colonel, 231.
Haugher, Captain, 267.
v. Hayden, Lieutenant, 214.
Heath, General, 144.
v. Heeringen, Colonel, 11, 30,41, 258.
v. Heister, Lt.-Gen., 23, 48, 270, 273.
Heinrichs, Captain, 266.
Henel, Lieuteuant, 12, 256.
Henkelmann, Lieutenant, 12.
Henndorf, Ensign, 187.
Heymel, Lieutenant, 119.
v. Heymel, Lieut.-Colonel, 186, 198.
Hildebrand, Lieutenant, 141.
Hille, Lieutenant, 119.
v. Hille, 248.
Hofmann, Captain, 218.
Hohendorf, Count, 275.
v. Hohenstein, Captain, 51.
Holper, 102.
Hopkins, Major, 148.
v. Horn, Colonel, 48, 110.
v. Horn, Major, 220, 222, 269.
Hotham, Admiral, 25, 219.
Howe, Lord R., Admiral, 26.
Howe, G., Gen., 26, 57, 82, 105, 271.
Hugget, Captain, 243.
v. Huyne, General, 57, 183, 267.
Jaritz, Lieutenant, 238.
John, Colonel, 35.
Johnson, Major, 240.
Kapp, F., 276.
Keppenau, Captain, 237.
Kimm, Lieutenant, 76.
Kleinschmidt, Lieutenant, 25.
v. Knoblauch, Major-General, 198.
v. Knyphausen, Lieut.-General, 51, 158, 189, 232, 270.
v. Kochenhausen, Lieut.-Col., 106.
Köhler, 51, 122.
Köhler, 162.
Köhler, Lieut.-Colonel, 197, 270.
Kohli, Chaplain, 94.
v. Kospoth, Gen., 162, 183, 259, 269.
v. Kreutzburg, Lieut.-Colonel, 101, 133, 236, 243, 267.
Kurtz, Colonel, 162, 269.

Lafayette, General, 157, 165, 203.
v. Langen, 256.
Lange, Lieutenant-Colonel, 258.
de Lauzun, Duc, 210.
Lee, General, 50, 81.
St. Leger, Colonel, 92.
v. Lengerke, Colonel, 117.
Leonhardt, Lieutenant, 221.
Leslie, General, 40, 199.
Lindenberger, Lieutenant, 81.
v. Linsingen, Lieutenant, 40, 113.
v. Linsingen, Colonel, 117, 269.
Lincoln, General, 175, 184, 218.
v. d. Lippe, Captain, 25.
Littehau, Lieutenant, 238.
v. Loos, Colonel, 106, 185, 192.
v. Lorey, Captain, 40, 173.
v. Lossberg, General, 35, 167, 193, 198, 233.
Lotheisen, 11, 113, 260.
v. Löwenstein, Lieut.-Colonel, 188.
Lucke, Major, 247.
Magraw, Colonel, 51.
Mahlburger, Captain, 13, 154.
v. Maiborne, Major, 251.
v. d. Malsburg, Captain, 11, 44, 164, 198.
Martin, Captain, 12, 63, 277.
Massereau, 145.
Matbäus, Major, 12, 62, 277.
Mathias, Major, 258.
Maxwell, General, 110.
v. Medern, 51.
Melzheimer, Chaplain, 13.
v. Mengen, Lieut.-Colonel, 148, 251.
Mertz, Lieutenant, 161.
de Messey, 266.
v. Minnigerode, Colonel, 38, 106, 177, 269.
v. Mirbach, General, 32, 197, 270.
Mirabeau, 276.
v. Möhring, Lieutenant, 238.
Möller, Lieutenant, 188.
v. Molitor, Lieutenant, 168.
v. Molitor, Captain, 168.
Montgomery, 96.
Montluisant, 266.
Morgan, General, 199.
Mühlenberg, General, 214.
v. Münchhausen, Captain, 11, 50.
Muravius, Lieutenant, 167.
Naumann, Chaplain, 238.
Noltenius, Captain, 167.

Noltin, Ensign, 221.
North, Lord, 265.
v. Ochs, General, 18, 113, 122, 157.
Ochs, A. L., Lieutenant, 266.
v. Offenbach, Lieutenant, 119.
Oliva, Chaplain, 187.
Pahmer, Lieutenant, 238.
Pakendorff, Dr., 238.
v. Papet, Major, 14, 38, 240.
Parker, Admiral, 24, 161.
Patterson, General, 196.
Pauli, Captain, 12, 277.
Pauly, Major, 34.
v. Pausch, Captain, 93.
Pentzel, Major, 48, 222.
Percy, Lord, 30, 58.
Peters, Colonel, 131.
Pfister, Major, 255, 265.
Phillips, General, 89.
Pigot, General, 163.
v. Piquet, Major, 237.
v. Plessen, Captain, 240.
Powell, 96.
Prätorius, Lieut.-Colonel, 87, 240.
Prescot, General, 81, 168.
v. Prüschenk, Major, 101, 196, 227, 265.
Pulaski, 157.
Putnam, General, 33, 77.
Quesnoy, Captain, 260.
v. Rall, Colonel, 32, 51, 70, 258, 269, 276.
Rathmann, Ensign, 188.
Rau, Captain, 174, 206, 227.
v. Rauchhaupt, General, 225.
v. Rauschenplatt, Colonel, 237.
v. Ranzau, Captain, 13.
Raynal, Abbé, 276.
Recknagel, Caspar, 13.
Reineking, Lieutenant, 253.
v. Reitzenstein, Major, 169.
Reuber, Corporal, 13, 64, 82.
v. Rhetz, Colonel, 126.
v. Riedesel zu Eysenbach, Maj.-Gen., 13, 49, 87, 126, 226, 247, 263, 271.
v. Riedesel, Madame, 140.
v. Riess, Colonel, 12, 257.
Riese, Captain, 76.
Riemann, Lieutenant, 119.
de Rochambeau, Duc, 249.
v. Röder, Captain, 195.
Rodney, Admiral, 233.
Rogers, Lieut.-Colonel, 44.

Romstädt, Captain, 100.
Rosenberg, Captain, 240.
Rübenkönig, Sergeant, 228.
Ruff, Captain, 240.
Rüffer, Lieutenant, 12, 36.
Saarbrück-Zweibrücken, Prince, 212.
Sackville, Lord, 19.
v. Schäffer, Lieut.-Colonel, 12, 198.
Schäffer, Lieutenant, 227.
Schäffer, Captain, 266.
v. Schallern, Captain, 167, 174.
v. Schaumburg, Count, 275.
v. Scheffer, Lieut.-Col., 64, 257, 276.
Scheiter, Lieut.-Col., 88.
Scheither, Corporal, 14.
v. Schick, Lieut.-Col., 106, 119.
v. Schill, Captain, 244.
v. Schlagenteuffel, Capt., 132, 240.
v. Schlammersdorf, Colonel, 225.
v. Schlieffen, 19.
v. Schlieffen, General, 257, 273.
Schmidt, 51.
v. Schmidt, Major-Gen., 197, 270.
v. Schöll, Captain, 245.
Schöpf, Dr., 169, 184.
Schottelius, Captain, 128.
Schreiber, Colonel, 269.
Schreyvogel, Lieut.-Col., 107.
v. Schuchhardt, Lieutenant, 207.
v. Schüler, Colonel, 197.
v. Schüler, v. Senden, Gen., 13, 130.
Schuler, 13.
Schwabe, Lieutenant, 76.
Schwaner, Lieutenant, 201.
v. Schwarzburg-Sondershausen, Prince, 238.
Scott, Colonel, 42.
v. Seitz, Captain, 122, 169.
v. Seitz, Lieutenant, 161.
Seitz, Major, 193.
v. Seyboth, Colonel, 213, 261.
Sippel, Sergeant, 205.
Spangenberg, Lieutenant, 132.
v. Specht, Colonel, 13, 126.
v. Specht, Captain, 134.
v. Speth, Lieut.-Col., 87, 91, 139, 146, 241.
v. Stamford, Captain, 117.
Stark, Colonel, 131.
Steding, Captain, 63, 188.
Sternickel, Lieutenant, 71.
v. Steuben, General, 158, 202.
Steuernagel, 14, 220.

Stirling, General, 32, 105, 179.
v. Stirn, Major-General, 29, 270.
Stirn, 114.
Stöden, Captain, 239.
Strubberg, Lieutenant, 225.
Skene, Major, 131.
Suffolk, Lord, 19.
Sullivan, General, 77, 165.
v. Tannenburg, Captain, 190.
Tarleton, Colonel, 198.
Taylor, Captain, 188.
Thomä, Captain, 240.
Trautvetter, Captain, 113.
v. Trott, Lieutenant, 201.
v. Trümbach, Lieutenant, 113.
Tryon, General, 174, 260.
Tunderfeld, Captain, 13.
Udell, General, 33.
v. Uechtritz, 110.
Valentin, General, 255.
Vaughan, General, 173.
Vierermal, Lieutenant, 238.
Villet, Colonel, 252.
v. Voight, Colonel, 101.
Wagner, Chaplain, 260.
Wagner, Captain, 119, 167.
Wahl, 65.
Waldeck, Chaplain, 14, 122, 222.
Waldeck, Ensign, 188.
Waldschmidt, Ensign, 187.
v. Wangenheim, Colonel, 117, 266.
Washington, 71, 213.
Wayne, General, 111, 174, 213.
Weedon, Colonel, 79.
Weiss, Captain, 239.
v. Weissenfels, Colonel, 142.
v. Weitersheim, Major, 225, 257.
v. Westernhagen, Captain, 114.
Wiederhold, Capt., 61, 79, 186, 193.
v. Wilmowsky, Captain, 201.
v. Wintersheim, Captain, 238.
v. Winzingerode, Lieutenant, 177.
Wolwarth, 155.
Woodhull, 33.
v. Wreden, Captain, 40, 110, 265.
v. Wurmb, Colonel, 40, 110, 114, 192, 227, 265.
v. Wurmb, Lieutenant, 119, 188.
v. Wurmb, Major-Gen., 197, 265.
v. York, 256.
v. Zengen, Ensign, 188.
v. Zielberg, Captain, 240.
Zoll, Lieutenant, 37, 76, 187.

# II. INDEX OF PLACES.

Albany, 50, 92, 129, 242, 252.
Amboy, 103.
Anhalt-Zerbst, 18, 153.
Ansbach Bayreuth, 18, 98.
Ansbach, 101, 153.
Ashley river, 179.
Assanpink, the, 60, 77.
l'Assomption, 246.

Baltimore, 81.
Bayreuth, 101.
Bedford, 28, 177.
Bergen Point, 52.
Besancourt, 248.
Berthier, 236, 246, 251.
Bethlehem, 150.
Black Point, 163.
Bloomingdale, 38, 197.
Bordentown, 54, 59.
Boston, 26, 143.
Bound Brook, 104.
Brandywine, the, 110.
Bremen, 24, 48.
Brenton's Neck, 163.
Brooklyn, 28, 226, 234.
Brooklyn Heights, 28.
Bronx River, 44.
Brunswick, 18, 53, 88, 262.
Burlington, 54, 60.
Bushwick, 37, 42.

Cambridge, 143.
Canada, 27, 89, 125, 185, 235, 251, 271.
Cape Charles, 109, 229.
Carleton Island, 223.
Carolina, 24, 219.
Cassel, 20, 153, 231, 260.
Catawba, the, 199.

Chadd's Ford, 110.
Chambly, 92.
Champlain Parish, 240.
Charleston, 162, 175, 199, 233.
Charlottesville, 149.
Chateaugay, 248.
Chatham, 260.
Chesapeake Bay, 81, 109, 207, 229.
Chester, 111.
Chestnut Hill, 121.
Church Bridge, 179.
Cliffs, the, 223.
Conanicut, 158.
Connecticut, 43.
Connecticut, the, 249.
Cooper River, 180.
Cork, 241.
Cowpens, 199.
Crown Point, 92, 126.
Cumberland Head, 126.

Darmstadt, 266.
Delaware, the, 53, 156, 272.
Delaware Bay, 186.
Dilworth, 110.
Dobbs' Ferry, 160, 227.
Dover, 260.
Draw Creek, 60.
Dumfries, 81.

East Chester, 44, 172.
East River, 28, 36, 54, 195.
East River (Seconset), 163.
Edge Hill, 121.
Elbe, the, 88.
Elizabeth, 53, 104, 122, 193.
Elk, 109.

Fairfield, 174.
Falmouth, 82.
Fishkill, 148.
Flatbush, 28.
Fleur de Hundred, 202.
Florida, 18, 251.
Flushing, 37.
Fogland Ferry, 164.
Fort St. Anna, 129.
Fort Carillon, 127.
Fort Chambly, 95.
Fort Clinton, 123, 172.
Fort Dalrymple, 42.
Fort Edward, 129, 133.
Fort St. George, 54.
Fort George, 129, 222.
Fort Iudependence, 50, 127, 160.
Fort Johnstone, 178.
Fort St. John, 178.
Fort Knyphausen, 52.
Fort Lee, 50.
Fort Mercer, 117.
Fort Mifflin, 116.
Fort Miller, 131.
Fort Montgomery, 123, 172.
Fort Moultrie, 181.
Fort Niagara, 242, 252.
Fort Stanwix, 92, 130, 141.
Fort Ticonderoga, 127.
Fort Waldeck, 222.
Fort Washington, 44, 50, 60.
Frederick, 214
Fredericksburg, 82, 214.
Frederick Springs, 150.
French Village, 223.
Frogs Neck, 43.

Georgia, 151, 220. 234.
Germantown, 114, 155.
Gibraltar, 16.
Gloucester, 206.
Gowan's Bay, 28.
Gowan's Pass, 39.
Gravesend, 29.
Great Island, 96.
Greenwich, 197.
Gulf of St. Lawrence, 247.

Hackensack, 190.
Haddonfield, 158.
Halifax, 26. 161, 231, 241, 250.
Hamilton's Ferry, 178.
Hampton, 214.

Hanau, 225, 239.
Harlem, 38.
Hartford, 249.
Havannah, 90.
Hellgate, 37.
Hesse-Cassel, 18, 98.
Hesse-Hanau, 18.
Hillsborough, 199.
Holland, 274.
Holstein, 266.
Horen's Hook, 39, 63.
Hudson, the, 30, 52, 92, 101, 171, 190.

Isle Orleans, 246.
Isle aux Noix, 93, 243.

Jamaica, 219.
James Island, 178.
James River, 206.
Jericho, 197.
Jersey, 52.
John's Island, 178,
Johnson's Ferry, 62.

King's Bridge, 38, 123, 159, 171, 190.
Kips Bay, 38.
Konigshagen, 210.

Lake Champlain, 126, 244.
Lake Erie, 248.
Lake George, 139.
Lake St. Peter, 240.
Lancaster, 81, 149, 216.
La Prairie, 93, 244.
Little Egg Harbour, 187.
London, 239.
Long Island, 27, 79, 158, 189, 230
Louisiana, 221.                [261.

Maidenhead, 64.
Manhattan Island, 37.
Marmaroneck, 44.
Maryland, 211.
Massachusetts, 253.
Masquinonge, 240.
Mecklenburg, 98.
Millerstown, 82.
Minden, 19.
Mississippi, the, 220.
Mobile. 219.
Mohawk the, 92, 133.
Morris' Heights 39.
Morristown, 189.

*Index.*

Mount Holly, 75.
Monmouth County, 78.
Montreal, 91, 236, 241, 246.
Mud Island, 116.

Narrows, the, 28.
Narragansett Bay, 163.
Neck, the, 121.
Newark, 110.
New Brunswick, 59.
Newbury, 149.
New Castle, 120.
New England, 240.
Newfoundland, 253.
New Frankfort, 82.
New Hampshire, 128.
New Haven, 174.
New Jersey, 57, 189, 192, 272.
New Orleans, 225.
Newport, 57, 156, 169, 249.
New Rochelle, 44.
Newtown, 37, 78.
New York, 28, 54, 92, 159, 174, 184, 225, 232, 247.
Norfolk, 174.
North Carolina, 199.
Norwalk, 174.
Nova Scotia, 259.

Orange, 52.
Oriskany, 133.
Osnabrück, 19.
Oswego, 92, 248.

Paulus' Hook, 174.
Peekskill, 149.
Pells' Neck, 49.
Pennsylvania, 211.
Pennington Hill, 60.
Penobscot, 252.
Pensacola, 218.
Perdido, the, 222.
Pfaltz, the, 73.
Philadelphia, 80, 105, 155, 188, 234, [253.
Plymouth, 89, 177, 260.
Portsmouth, 24, 48, 88, 174, 202, 247,
Point au Fer, 95, 248.    [260.
Point du Lac, 240.
Point Levi, 250.
Point Judith, 163.
Potomac, 81.
Princeton, 53, 60, 64, 184.
Providence, 57, 164.

Prudence Island, 57.
Purisburg, 179.

Quebec, 24, 89, 192, 236, 241, 262.

Randolph Creek, 179.
Rappahannock, the, 82.
Raritan Landing, 104.
Reading, 188.
Red Bank. 116.
Redwood Hill, 166.
Reedy Island, 117.
Rhode Island, 57, 159, 227.
Richmond, 201.
Richelieu, the, 97.
Rivière la Colle, 95, 251.
Rivière du Loup, 240.
Russia, 153.

Sachse-Gotha, 98.
Sachuest Beach, 163.
Salisbury, 148.
Sandy Hook, 24, 159, 176, 186.
Savannah, 93, 162.
Savannah River, 175.
Schuylkill, the, 121, 155.
Shelter Island, 58.
Simon's Island, 177.
Skeneshorough, 129.
Skippack Creek, 114.
Sorel, 95, 236, 251.
South Carolina, 27, 175, 184.
Springfield, 193, 249.
Suffolk, 174, 206.
Sugar Hill, 128.
Sullivan's Island, 180.
Stade 94, 239.
Staten Island, 26, 184, 195, 229.
Staunton, 82.
Stillwater, 129.
Stony Point, 123, 172.
Stono Ferry, 162, 178.
Stowentown, 82.
Stuyvesant's Cove, 38.
Switzerland, 153.
St. Anna, 246.
St. Antoine, 251.
St. Charles, 251.
St Culbert, 240.
St. Dennis, 251.
St. François, 251.
St. Francis, 243.
St. Hyacinthe, 240.

St. Ives, 177.
St. John, 244.
St. Johns, 93.
St. Lawrence, the, 97, 243.
St. Sulpice, 251.
St. Valier, 246.

Tammany Hill, 165.
Tarrytown, 160.
Terrebonne, 236.
Three Rivers, 89.
Ticonderoga, 92.
Trenton, 53, 58, 186, 272.
Trois Rivieres, 97, 236, 252.
Turtle Bay, 38.
Tybee Island, 176.

Utrecht, 30.

Valentine's Hill, 44.
Valley Forge, 123.
Vanrenil, 240.
Vergères, 92, 248.
Vermont, 248.
Verplanck's Point, 172.

Versailles, 234.
Virginia, 149, 174, 186, 211, 227.

Waldau, 100.
Waldeck, 18, 47.
Wallabout Bay, 30.
Wangeroge, 225.
Weissenfels, 339.
Weser, 225.
Westchester County, 43, 190.
Whitemarsh, 121, 155.
White Plains, 44, 60, 159.
Wilmington, 114, 120.
Williamsburg, 204.
Windmill Hill, 163.
Winchester, 181, 214.
Winter Hill, 143.
Wolfenbüttel, 82.
Würtemberg, 98.

Yorktown, 206.
York River, 206.

Zerbst, 238.

www.ingramcontent.com/pod-product-compliance
Lightning Source LLC
Chambersburg PA
CBHW051803230426
43672CB00012B/2618